CAMBRIDGE STUDIES
IN ENGLISH LEGAL HISTORY

Edited by
J. H. BAKER
Fellow of St Catharine's College, Cambridge

SIR HENRY MAINE

A STUDY IN VICTORIAN JURISPRUDENCE

Sir Henry Maine died in 1888 and since then his ideas have been used by lawyers, historians, sociologists and many others. This is the first book to concentrate upon what he said about the law itself, and, as such, it explores the pioneering work Maine did in explaining law not by reference to abstract analysis but by placing it firmly in its social and historical context. Instead of concentrating on concepts such as sovereignty he looked at the realities of law as it was practised by professionals and experienced by laymen. The result was a controversial achievement stressing the reforming duties of jurists and citizens at times of social change.

This is neither a conventional biography nor an abstract analysis of Maine's thought, but a demonstration of the contemporary context and significance of his views. Although primarily a study of one man's ideas, it throws important new light on a number of controversial issues of the mid-Victorian period, not least the rise of the modern notion of English legal history.

SIR HENRY MAINE

A STUDY IN VICTORIAN JURISPRUDENCE

R. C. J. COCKS

CAMBRIDGE UNIVERSITY PRESS

CAMBRIDGE
NEW YORK NEW ROCHELLE
MELBOURNE SYDNEY

PUBLISHED BY THE PRESS SYNDICATE OF THE UNIVERSITY OF CAMBRIDGE
The Pitt Building, Trumpington Street, Cambridge, United Kingdom

CAMBRIDGE UNIVERSITY PRESS
The Edinburgh Building, Cambridge CB2 2RU, UK
40 West 20th Street, New York NY 10011–4211, USA
477 Williamstown Road, Port Melbourne, VIC 3207, Australia
Ruiz de Alarcón 13, 28014 Madrid, Spain
Dock House, The Waterfront, Cape Town 8001, South Africa

http://www.cambridge.org

First published 1988
First paperback edition 2004

A catalogue record for this book is available from the British Library

Library of Congress Cataloguing in Publication data
Cocks, Raymond.
Sir Henry Maine: a study in Victorian jurisprudence,
R. C. J. Cocks.
p. cm. – (Cambridge studies in English legal history)
Includes index.
ISBN 0 521 35343 2 hardback
1. Maine, Henry Sumner, Sir, 1882–1888. 2. Law – Great Britain –
History and criticism. 3. Jurisprudence – History. I. Title.
II. Series.
KD631.M28C63 1988
349.41–dc19
[344.1] 88-10228 CIP

ISBN 0 521 35343 2 hardback
ISBN 0 521 52496 2 paperback

CONTENTS

ACKNOWLEDGMENTS

Drafts of this book have been read by Professor William Twining, Professor William Cornish and Professor Peter Stein and I am most grateful for all their comments upon the typescripts. I am also thankful for the work and advice of the editor of this series, Dr J. H. Baker.

Maine's thought is a synthesis of very diverse elements, and in the course of writing the book I have consulted many individuals on many topics. I am particularly indebted to Geoffrey Best, John Burrow, John Cairns, Geoffrey Chapman, Pramit Chaudhuri, Richard Clutterbuck, Richard Coates, Stefan Collini, Kim Economides, Melvyn Elliott, Geoffrey Hand, Daire Hogan, Michael Ireland, Theo Mars, Keith Middlemas, Geoffrey MacCormack, Hilary Prescott, Bruce Renton, Gerry Rubin, Vera Sachs, Adrian Smith, Geoffrey Samuel, David Sugarman, Norman Vance, Stephen Yeo, and Alistair Young. I should also add that Cherry Horwill and the staff of the Inter-Library Loan department at the University of Sussex have been both determined and successful in their searches for materials relating to Maine's ideas.

Fellow lawyers teaching at the university have encouraged me in the research for this book at a difficult time when academic leave has been out of the question and administrative duties have been heavy. Also a number of good typists have assisted me and in this connection I must mention the efforts of Helen Warner, Mary Golby and Angie Glenn. My family have been helpful. Merry and Katey have tolerated the intolerable once again; and this time two children have expressed their own very clear views on what their father should be doing instead.

INTRODUCTION

MAINE'S IDEAS

In 1861 Maine published a book which he hoped would do much to improve the condition of English jurisprudence. In *Ancient Law, its Connection with the Early History of Society and its Relation to Modern Ideas* he wished to describe very old types of law, to explain these types by reference to their social and intellectual context, and to consider the relationship between them and modern forms of legal analysis. In the words of the brief preface to the first edition: 'the direct object of the following pages is to indicate some of the earliest ideas of mankind as they are reflected in ancient law, and to point out the relation of these ideas to modern thought'.

Within a few years of its publication it was clear that he had written a popular book. In the view of a modern commentator discussing the development of law in the nineteenth century, Sir Henry Maine 'wrote the only legal best seller of that, or perhaps any other century'.[1] The popularity is easy to explain. The book is so well written that it has an appeal to readers of any generation; and to Victorians it had the added attraction of containing references to numerous topics which were fashionable at the time. For example, it explored matters such as the moral issues relating to the financial collapse of large banks; the importance of comparative studies of different societies in any attempt to discover the responsibilities of imperial government in India; and the possible relevance to British politics of continental ideas about liberty.[2] Throughout, topics such as these were related to controversial themes and it was particularly noticeable that almost everything he said could be given a place in the Victorian debate about

[1] A. W. B. Simpson, 'Contract: The Twitching Corpse', *Oxford Journal of Legal Studies*, vol. 1 (1981), p. 265 at p. 268.

[2] These and numerous other topics of concern to his Victorian contemporaries are considered in chapter 3 below.

progress. Like his contemporaries, he sought constantly to assess whether or not certain practices encouraged or impeded the development of societies. On a level of great generality it was even possible for his readers to compare his observations on the evolutionary progress of social groups with, say, Darwin's analysis of organic change, or Herbert Spencer's attempt to reveal the laws of transformation for the universe.

Maine's interest in these ideas requires a two-fold response from the legal mind of the late twentieth century. Firstly, it is necessary to resist the temptation to detach his jurisprudential arguments from his Victorian concerns because, as we will see, the latter did much to influence his approach to law. Secondly, and more important, any attempt to isolate Maine's jurisprudential thought is likely to draw attention away from one of his chief beliefs about legal analysis; he believed that in seeking to understand law the best results could be achieved by making constant references to non-legal topics. Ultimately, law had to be accounted for and criticised in non-legal terms. After all, a man who wrote about progress had at some stage to write about legal change and was then confronted by the fact that law did not create itself and was not changed by itself.

Writers on Maine's jurisprudence have often responded to his interest in the context of law by contrasting his ideas with those of the utilitarian jurists who preceded him, Bentham and Austin.[3] It is sometimes said that the latter two jurists provided an explanation of law which was almost wholly abstract. Their names have been linked with the notion that law may be explained entirely in terms of concepts such as 'sovereignty' and 'command' rather than by reference to social practices and historical events. Viewed in the former way, law has the same qualities in all places at all times, and therefore may be explained in terms which are independent of any particular place in which it functions.

For Maine such a view was incorrect; law was the product of time and place, and the theories of Bentham and Austin were themselves products of particular 'limited' historical circumstances; the emphasis upon 'sovereignty' and 'command' arose out of the need to explain aspects of the social, political and legal structure of industrial societies in the west. It followed that such terms were inappropriate for the analysis of, say, the ancient laws of India. The correct study of law

[3] The reception of his ideas in the context of English jurisprudence is considered in chapter 6 below, pp. 183–95.

began with the observation of its place in any particular society; and such a starting point revealed that it was impossible to describe law by using the same terms for all legal phenomena in all areas.

In itself, this common view of Maine as a critic of 'merely' abstract theories of law is well-founded. When he wrote *Ancient Law* he believed that his critical remarks about the utilitarian jurists constituted one of the improvements which he could bring to English jurisprudence.[4] However, in isolation such comments give Maine's writing a negative quality which is unrepresentative of his work as a whole. There is an additional, positive aspect to his analysis which is best introduced by looking to his account of what other Victorian jurists called 'the natural history of law'.[5] Maine set out to reveal the phases of evolutionary legal development. He believed in an initial stage in which the unregulated personal commands of someone in authority are thought to be of divine inspiration. 'They are simply adjudications on insulated states of fact, and do not necessarily follow each other in any orderly sequence.'[6] In the course of time the individuals who issued such commands were replaced by groups such as aristocracies who knew the law and administered it. Unlike their predecessors they 'do not appear to have pretended to direct inspiration for each sentence'.[7] The law 'known exclusively to a privileged minority, whether a caste, an aristocracy, priestly tribe, or a sacerdotal college, is true unwritten law'.[8] After this 'period of Customary law we come to another sharply defined epoch in the history of jurisprudence. We arrive at the era of Codes, those ancient codes of which the Twelve Tables of Rome were the most famous specimen . . . laws engraven on tablets and published to the people take the place of usages deposited with the recollection of a privileged oligarchy.'[9] The chief cause of the change was easily identified: 'though democratic sentiment may have added to their popularity, the codes were certainly in the main a direct result of the invention of writing'.[10]

4 He considers the matter in forceful terms in chapter 1 of *Ancient Law* (London, 1905) pp. 7–8. On p. 7 he wrote that 'it is curious that, the farther we penetrate into the primitive history of thought, the farther we find ourselves from a conception of law which at all resembles a compound of the elements which Bentham determined'.

5 For example, Sir Frederick Pollock, in 'Sir Henry Maine as a Jurist', *Edinburgh Review*, vol. 177 (July 1893), p. 104, and in *Introduction and Notes to Sir Henry Maine's 'Ancient Law'* (London, 1906), p. viii.

6 *Ancient Law*, p. 9 and, at p. 5, ' . . . they cannot be supposed to be connected by any thread of principle; they are separate, isolated judgments'.

7 *Ibid.*, p. 12, chapter 1.

8 *Ibid.*, p. 13, chapter 1.

9 *Ibid.*, p. 14, chapter 1.

10 *Ibid.*, p. 15, chapter 1.

Most societies never moved, as it were, beyond this stage. 'When primitive law has once been embodied in a Code, there is an end to what may be called its spontaneous development. Henceforward the changes effected in it, if effected at all, are effected deliberately and from without.'[11] However, if change did happen, the stages of subsequent progressive alterations could be identified by pointing to the agencies by which law was brought into harmony with novel social conditions. Maine wrote: 'These instrumentalities seem to me to be three in number, Legal Fictions, Equity and Legislation. Their historical order is that in which I have placed them . . . I know of no instance in which the order of their appearance has been changed or inverted.'[12] In the words of a modern writer, the 'thesis implied a natural progress from making changes while pretending not to (fictions), through making exceptions in particular cases (equity), to direct change by virtue of authority or power'.[13] The content of the law in progressive societies also changed. In one of his most famous observations, Maine stated that there was a transition from status to contract. Status rights, such as those which could be claimed by a woman by reason of her being a woman, gave way to contractual rights arising out of negotiations between individuals.[14]

However, any account of Maine's jurisprudence which attempts to respond to the positive aspects of his writing has to contain more than a description of evolutionary change in law. In the course of the present book it will be argued that these descriptive accounts of historical change need to be integrated into a broader argument concerned with the social responsibilities of lawyers and other citizens. In particular, it will be argued that Maine tried to explore the responsibilities people had in respect of law reform and social improvement. Admittedly, this has already been considered to some extent by other writers such as Dias and Harris who have observed, in substance, that Maine was no antiquarian devoted to the past for its

[11] *Ibid.*, p. 21, chapter 1. [12] *Ibid.*, p. 25, chapter 2.

[13] J. H. Baker, *An Introduction to English Legal History* (London, 1979), p. 170. This aspect of Maine's work has received comparatively little attention in modern times.

[14] For example: 'Starting, as from one terminus of history, from a condition of society in which all the relations of Persons are summed up in the relations of Family, we seem to have steadily moved towards a phase of social order in which all these relations arise from the free agreement of Individuals.' (*Ancient Law*, p. 169, chapter 5.) But Maine described the change in different ways in other places, and there is a problem in deciding which is most appropriate: see, generally, chapter 6, pp. 169–80 below, and G. MacCormack, 'Status: Problems of Definition and Use', *Cambridge Law Journal* (1984), pp. 361–76.

own sake.[15] It is implicit, too, in the commentaries which stress Maine's hopes as to the possible change in law from rights based upon status to those based upon contract; he had a personal enthusiasm for the change. But the present study seeks to go beyond such observations and show that Maine related these and many other recommendations to a wider theory. We will see that for him, when law was understood in terms of the social developments which he described, certain facts about legal change became much clearer than they had been. There might be intricate disputes about the best way of defining the phases of legal change (was an age of Equity always succeeded by an age of Statute, and so on?) but it was safe to predict that usually social conditions changed law rather than that law changed social conditions. Because of the propensity for law to 'grow' out of harmony with social interests, the jurist had a duty to do what he could to ensure that law and social interests did not draw apart and this, in turn, meant that he had to explain how laws could be changed. Usually the jurist had to concentrate on removing elements which were obscure to the layman because these obscurities concealed the gap between the law and real social interests. If the obscurities were defended by practising lawyers it was the task of the jurist to expose what the lawyers were doing and to suggest alternatives. The best response took the form of the scientific analysis of law which (as we will see) involved in part the attempt to discover principles which could be stated in simple terms and incorporated in a code. Such a form of law could be understood by all informed citizens and could be criticised and revised in the light of public debate concerned with ensuring that law responded to social events. In this way the law served the interest of society rather than that of a few legal experts.

If this had already been said by Bentham (and others) then the difference in Maine's case lay in his explicit confidence in the capacity for a cultured elite to produce law which responded appropriately to social changes by having regard to the facts of the legal past. When social conditions in combination with a suitable response from this elite enabled law to move from status to contract Maine was pleased, but this was, as it were, a bonus. His usual concern was with preventing law from becoming unrelated to society. Law varied greatly with place and time but, subject to a few qualifications, in progressive

15 R. W. M. Dias, *Jurisprudence* (London, 1985), p. 388: Maine 'often contended that the confused state of English law was due to its pre-eminently judge-made character'; J. W. Harris, *Legal Philosophies* (London, 1980), p. 223.

societies at least the jurist had the same task in all places at all times. Above all, he had to reveal which laws were most appropriate for any given social situation; and in order to do this he had to have a knowledge of history. This would enable him both to understand change and to reveal the inadequacies of those lawyers who resisted desirable reforms or (more rarely) sought immediate measures which were too radical. For example, the jurist could criticise utilitarian or natural law theorists when the latter justified their arguments by reference to grandiose definitions of law which had little relationship to social facts. In the course of time, everything about law changed, and lawyers were never justified in opposing change by referring to their preconceived ideas. This was particularly so in progressive societies:

> with respect to them it may be laid down that social necessities and social opinion are always more or less in advance of Law. We may come indefinitely near to the closing of the gap between them, but it has a perpetual tendency to reopen. Law is stable; the societies we are speaking of are progressive. The greater or less happiness of a people depends on the degree of promptitude with which the gulf is narrowed.[16]

Lawyers had the humble task of responding to social events by rethinking their ideas about law; and when they did this they were obliged to adopt arguments which could be understood and appreciated by informed citizens as well as fellow lawyers. By itself the legal mind could never create good law. It had to be guided by people with experience outside the world of law. It was as if, for Maine, when new law was being created the lawyer had the task of a midwife rather than a parent.

But even an attempt to integrate his evolutionary information into his broader interpretation of what made for good law fails to provide a complete outline of the essential and more positive parts of Maine's jurisprudence. It does not take account of the fact that the constant application of historical analysis to a great range of contrasting examples and theories has a significant cumulative effect. Unfortunately, it is hard to define.

Another Victorian jurist, Sir Frederick Pollock, saw that Maine's work presented special problems in this respect. In terms which were self-consciously vague he argued that

[16] *Ancient Law*, p. 24, chapter 2.

Maine's work is not architectural but organic. His ideas are not presented in the form of finished propositions that can be maintained and controverted in the manner of a thesis. Rather they appear to grow before our eyes, and they have never done growing. The roots are the same, the flowers and fruit are various. We are constantly brought home again after digressions and excursions, often in quite unexpected ways. Therefore Maine's books cannot be arranged in a linear series as chapters of an *opus magnum*. It would be idle to prescribe a fixed order for reading them, as if they were a history or a code. Those who expect to find instruction ready made in them will hardly be satisfied; those who seek not compendious formulas to be learnt by rote or set down in notebooks, but thoughts to be assimilated for the guidance and education of the historic faculty, will seldom indeed be disappointed. In this we see no more than the proper and almost necessary attribute of a master whose business is to give us examples of method, not to inform us of facts.[17]

This lack of interest in 'compendious formulas' on Maine's part makes a succinct description of his jurisprudence almost impossible and requires that any brief account is expressed in a manner which is unrepresentative of his style. However, if the *content* of his jurisprudence could be described in a few words it might be done by referring, firstly, to his evolutionary account of law with its emphasis upon the context of legal systems and, secondly, to his analysis of how good legal reforms could be obtained. If the *approach* he adopted was to be put in a few words it would have to be described as consisting in the presentation of information about the past in such a way as to change and improve legal thought. An awareness of the salient facts of legal history ensured that lawyers and non-lawyers knew that there was nothing permanent in law, and at the same time it provided them with the best guide for the management of legal change.

There is nothing contentious in pointing out above that Maine was concerned with explaining the historical development of law, and with using his historical information to reveal inadequacies in the work of utilitarian theorists or writers on natural law. However, what has been said about other matters does require justification. It will be necessary to describe in some detail the prescriptive elements in Maine's writing, and to relate them to his general analysis of the duties of people involved in legal and social reform; and, of course, it is also necessary to explore the full range of the uses to which he put history in the course of developing his arguments. In doing these things it will become clear that a study of such topics require a reduction in the

[17] Pollock, 'Sir Henry Maine as a Jurist', p. 102.

emphasis which commentators with other objectives have previously given to certain elements in his work. In particular, much less attention will be given to his writing on Roman Law and Patriarchal Societies; both these aspects of his thought merit separate study in their own right but there are limits to the extent to which they can be used as guides to his jurisprudence. In contrast, much more attention will be given to subjects such as his writing on the science of law, the legal profession and legal education. In the course of doing this, the context in which he placed law will not be explained (as it sometimes has been) almost entirely by reference to the facts of ancient history. Instead, in accordance with his expressed intentions, the references to earlier events will be linked to his writing on later issues and, in considering this, the importance of his commitment to Victorian debates will become apparent. This change in perspective will make it possible to reassess the quality of his writing on law.

The justification for producing the present study is simply that Maine has often been regarded as an important jurist but there has never before been a book exclusively concerned with his jurisprudence. No doubt the explanation for this lies in the sort of problem observed by Pollock; there is a diffuse aspect to Maine's ideas which makes it difficult to write about any single element in his works, such as law, without constant qualifications to statements of general principle and numerous references to other subjects. However, the attempt to respond to this in the chapters which follow is made easier by three modern studies which have done much to clarify various themes in Maine's writing as a whole. Peter Stein has provided an analysis of Maine's place in the development of ideas about 'legal evolution', and has alerted us to the latter's links with thinkers not usually thought of in the context of English jurisprudence.[18] John Burrow has located Maine's role in nineteenth-century theories of social evolution and, in doing so, has revealed the extent to which the latter was much more than a jurist.[19] George Feaver, in his study *From Status to Contract* has written a very useful life of Maine which explores many of his interests and relates them in detail to his background and experiences.[20] The present study provides its own interpretation of Maine's jurisprudence, but without Feaver's work it would have been much more difficult to place Maine's legal thought in the context of his

[18] P. Stein, *Legal Evolution: The Story of an Idea* (Cambridge, 1980).
[19] J. W. Burrow, *Evolution and Society* (Cambridge, 1966).
[20] G. Feaver, *From Status to Contract* (London, 1969).

whole life; Feaver's *From Status to Contract* provides valuable support for more specialised studies of Maine's writing, whether they relate to law or anthropology or history or any of the other topics which concerned him.

MAINE'S LIFE

Maine's father was a doctor and this in itself gave his son a background quite unlike that of other Victorian jurists.[21] Pollock was born into a family which had already provided famous lawyers; Fitzjames Stephen's father was involved in the problems of government and law reform; Dicey's family was committed to public debate about political and constitutional matters.[22] When Maine was a young child in the 1820s it would have required an extraordinary act of imagination to suggest that his later thoughts would turn to the problems of English jurisprudence. In a sense he was an 'outsider' from the start.

Little is known of Maine's early years. His parents separated when he was young and his family circumstances were not happy. He was a delicate child, prone to illness, and this may have encouraged an introspective frame of mind and an interest in poetry. After early years at Henley-on-Thames he was sent to Christ's Hospital School where he was recognised as a promising pupil with an enthusiasm for literature. In 1840 he went to Cambridge as an Exhibitioner of Pembroke College and made an impression as a young classicist of unusual ability. He carried off numerous prizes and was the best classical scholar of his year. In 1844 he accepted a tutorship at Trinity Hall and began a sustained study of ancient laws and legal systems. Such was Maine's reputation at the university that as early as 1847, at the age of twenty-five, he was appointed to the Regius Professorship of Civil Law.

In retrospect, what followed has the appearance of untroubled achievement. Within a few years he had become a Reader at the Inns of Court in London and was providing courses for intending barristers. He also developed a strong interest in journalism; he wrote for

21 The aspects of Maine's career which are mentioned in this section are considered in more detail in Feaver, *From Status to Contract*.

22 Fitzjames Stephen's life and background have recently received attention in J. A. Colaiaco, *James Fitzjames Stephen and the Crisis of Victorian Thought* (London, 1983); Dicey has also been the subject of a helpful study in R. A. Cosgrove's biography, *The Rule of Law: Albert Venn Dicey, Victorian Jurist* (London, 1980). Pollock awaits his biographer.

the *Morning Chronicle* and, after its establishment in 1855, for the *Saturday Review*. The latter in particular involved Maine in writing about legal matters such as the reform of the Inns of Court and political issues of general interest such as the abolition of the East India Company. In 1862, after the publication of *Ancient Law*, he went to India where, as legal member of the Governor-General's Council, he played a part in the development of new statutory laws for the subcontinent. By the end of the 1860s he had returned and become the Corpus Professor of Jurisprudence at the University of Oxford. He gave some remarkable courses of lectures to his students and after these were published they enhanced what was, by now, an international reputation as a jurist concerned not only with Roman Law but also with 'primitive law' and modern law in all of their respective forms. Maine's *Village Communities*, and *Early History of Institutions*[23] were produced at this time.

In 1878 he accepted an invitation to become the master of Trinity Hall, Cambridge, and in the following years he was notable chiefly for *Early Law and Custom*; a controversial political study called *Popular Government*; and his appointment as Whewell Professor of International Law.[24] However, throughout these later years, he also continued his journalism and even carried heavy administrative duties at the India Office in London where his advice was much respected. In 1887 his health deteriorated seriously and in 1888, at the age of sixty-six, he died. Soon afterwards his friends were allowed to set up a memorial to him in Westminster Abbey.

After his death the same friends were sometimes to speak of his personality in slightly mixed terms. They sympathised with him for the fact that his health was usually poor. They took pleasure in the extent to which he was a brilliant conversationalist, succinct and illuminating. No one ever doubted his loyalty as a friend, and after he married in 1847 his family circumstances seem to have become much happier although, obviously, much of the praise for this should be directed towards Jane, his wife. But throughout his adult life there was a reserve in Maine's manner which had an unpleasant aspect. In the words of Sir Leslie Stephen: 'To casual observers he might appear

[23] *Village Communities* (London, 1871); *Lectures on the Early History of Institutions* (London, 1875).

[24] *Dissertations on Early Law and Custom* (London, 1883); *Popular Government* (London, 1885). There was also a posthumous work, *International Law: The Whewell Lectures* (London, 1888), edited for publication by Frederick Pollock and Frederic Harrison.

as somewhat cold and sarcastic, but closer friends recognised both the sweetness of his temper and the tenderness of his nature.'[25] He often engendered admiration rather than endearment.

Also, on closer analysis, the picture of uniform success in public life is misleading. As we will see, it conceals a strong sense of frustration towards the ideas of many of his fellow Victorians. In his twenties he believed that Cambridge was failing to provide a valuable form of legal education for its students; and when he went to London and gained some knowledge of legal work he soon developed a hostile attitude towards the Bar and its practices. During his years in Calcutta he had the consolation of knowing that *Ancient Law* had been very well received, but again there was much which left him dissatisfied. He gained little pleasure from attention to the minute details of law reform, and was frequently saddened by the inability of both European and Indian lawyers to recognise the need for very general changes in their respective approaches to legal problems. He always had difficulties in relating his adventurous ideas about law to the realities of life on the subcontinent.

When he returned in 1869 to the professorship at Oxford any hopes he still retained for changes in legal education were soon to vanish. A joint degree in law and history came to an end, and a degree in English law already showed signs of concentrating on the interpretation of certain statutes and cases rather than on issues associated with the development of law and the possibilities of reform. By the time of his (unexpected) election as master of Trinity Hall in Cambridge the practical irrelevance of much that he had written about law was becoming more and more obvious. The greater part of his writing after *Ancient Law* hardly related to the content of the new law degrees. He had achieved public eminence without seeing the substance of any of the educational reforms which he had tried to obtain.

These difficulties were compounded throughout his life by political problems. He wrote numerous articles on political topics and all of them were committed to a radical, reforming conservatism. He was openly elitist and distrusted all extensions of the franchise. But he believed just as strongly in the abolition of any anachronisms which perpetuated inefficient practices and encouraged popular resentment. Since Maine included most legal institutions and the greater part of the common law in the latter category his ideas were, once again, likely to produce the sort of resentment which could cause him severe

[25] *The Dictionary of National Biography* (London, 1903).

difficulties. Yet developments in legal and political thought made him almost intransigent in his later years. In response to what he saw as the very damaging introduction of the vote for all adult males there was (as he saw it) an equally damaging attempt to glorify the past. By the 1880s the common law was becoming more popular in public debate than it had been for half a century. Instead of an interest in radical measures which could preserve 'property' in a new age there was respect for inappropriate traditions. It was no wonder that he 'often appeared to be rather a spectator than an actor in affairs';[26] few events engaged his enthusiasm.

All of these educational and political problems were joined by many others in the course of Maine's life, and one of the purposes of the present study is to show how they provide a better guide to his jurisprudential work than the apparent account of one success followed by another. Maine's work is of value today, but it has to be explained by reference to the nature of Victorian legal thought and the specific opportunities which confronted him.

[26] *Ibid.*

1

THE EARLY THOUGHTS ABOUT LAW

SOURCES AND THEMES

Maine's jurisprudence was characterised by reasoning which began with the analysis of non-legal phenomena and arrived, ultimately, at conclusions about law. For example, observations on the political role of 'public opinion' in social change were used to explore the best methods of legal reform. Thoughts about the history of language were the means to dispute theories which claimed that law could be understood independently of social phenomena. Anthropological observations on societies, both past and present, were used in the course of arguments designed to reveal the inadequacies of theories of natural law. To take a more specific example, the argument that progressive legal change required a movement from status to contract was never presented by Maine as if it was a necessary truth about law. Instead the nature of the change was revealed by numerous historical investigations; in *Ancient Law* Maine only presents the argument about status and contract at the end of his fifth chapter.

There is an almost bewildering variety of topics in his work. It seems that he was prepared to discuss any subject. He wrote about ancient customs, modern politics, scientific theories, the development of languages, statute law, poetry, philosophy, literature, whether women are more conservative than men, the extent to which law changes society and society changes law, Roman agriculture, Greek civilisation, the caste systems of India, the failings of Bentham, the achievements of Bentham, the consequences of imposing British law on societies governed by custom, the merits of American social values and many, many other matters.

The impression of variety is increased when the reader asks how these numerous subjects are linked together. It is soon clear that Maine employed contrasting, sometimes even mutually inconsistent arguments in the course of discussing his diverse facts. In places he was engaged in using the information for polemical purposes; in places he was clearly claiming scientific status for his views; in places he justified the use of his material in terms of 'common sense'; in places he claimed to be writing about jurisprudence and in other, unpredictable places he claimed the opposite.

Initial impressions of diversity were made even stronger by Maine's obvious dislike for writing a sustained comparison between his own views and those of preceding jurists. The reader of Hart's *Concept of Law* is introduced to new ideas by the reassuring route of arguments which contrast Hart's ideas with well-known elements in Austin's jurisprudence. Such landmarks make for easier navigation at the start of a journey leading eventually into the unknown, but the reader of Maine's books is given no comparable assistance.

Here, we will directly confront the diversity of content which characterised his work, and inevitably this will involve successive references to topics which at first seem to bear little or no relation to each other. To the modern mind they often *are* unrelated. It will look as if he was choosing at random from a great variety of Victorian ideas about non-legal and legal subjects. The first two chapters of the present book therefore require an act of faith on the part of the reader. They should be read on the assumption that in the actual writing of *Ancient Law* (considered in chapter 3) Maine succeeded in producing a remarkable synthesis of ideas.

VICTORIAN LEGAL SCIENCE

Many Victorian lawyers thought that scientific analysis could be used to resolve major legal problems. In the period 1840 to 1870 writers on law were almost obsessed with scientific analysis although, unfortunately, they defined it in the vaguest terms. For example, when, in the 1840s, Parliament decided to enquire into the state of legal education, Brougham and other legal reformers, such as Maine himself, were at one in commending the scientific study of law. This involved more than theories relating to legislative change. It required a proper study of history and politics, and a proper respect for the 'lessons' provided by laws of countries other than Britain. Above all, it implied a regard for those who looked beyond the letter of the law and discovered principles which enabled the law properly to be categorised and criticised. As Professor Stein has shown, these days were characterised by much thought about legal training which cannot be understood without an appreciation of the belief in legal science.[1]

The law books of the mid-nineteenth century reflected this concern. The hope that science would enable lawyers once and for all to solve all legal problems was expressed tediously and at extraordinary length in James Caulfield Heron's work on the history of jurisprudence.[2] His book was published two years before *Ancient Law* and its 800 pages of analysis reflect an inextinguishable confidence in the value of scientific method when applied to the history, analysis and practice of law. He had a good knowledge of the problems which concerned the lawyers of the day, and some of his ideas were strikingly like those which Maine was to consider in *Ancient Law*; for example, Heron wrote about social change in terms which were very similar to Maine's use of 'status' and 'contract'.

No legal topic could escape scientific treatment. The increasing interest in the 'proper' analysis of the law of evidence was very noticeable. This was the era in which Best and Stephen produced their respective works on the subject, and reviewers were quick to point out that this part of the law was particularly well-adapted to scientific study because it involved a discussion of human nature.[3] By

[1] Stein, *Legal Evolution* at, in particular, pp. 78–9 (the Committee on Legal Education) and p. 80 (George Long's explanation that the object of the new scientific legal education was to give the student a view of the whole of the law, instead of merely certain fragments of it).

[2] J. C. Heron, *Introduction to the History of Jurisprudence* (London, 1860). Heron produced other significant works and his ideas merit further study: he has been totally obscured by Maine's achievements.

[3] W. M. Best, *A Treatise on the Principles of the Law of Evidence, with Rules for the Examination of Witnesses* (London, 1849). For the place of this work in the development of thought about the law of evidence see Professor Twining's 'The Rationalist Tradition of Evidence Scholarship' in Louis Waller and Enid Campbell (eds.), *Well and Truly Tried* (Melbourne, 1982). He points out that 'Best managed to integrate theoretical and historical analysis with principled exposition in a way which has since only been bettered by Wigmore and which has not been repeated in England in this century.' He also emphasises the extent to which Best was a well-informed but critical scholar of Benthamite theory. For Fitzjames Stephen's work see *A Digest of the Law of Evidence* (London, 1876). Twining relates this to Stephen's earlier studies and points out that he was in certain respects strongly critical of Bentham's ideas and saw considerable merits in the substance – if not the form – of contemporary English Law. Predictably, Stephen was concerned with 'natural divisions': Twining points out that in the introduction Stephen wrote that 'an object . . . has been to separate the subject of evidence from other branches of the law with which it has commonly been mixed up; to reduce it into a compact systematic form, distributed according to the natural division of the subject matter . . .' For a review of 'evidence scholarship' at the time see *Solicitor's Journal*, vol. 4 (1860), p. 727. We are in need of much more research into the nineteenth-century reviews of legal works for the obvious reason

the 1870s Sheldon Amos had produced a popular work called *The Science of Law* which was based upon his earlier and more specialised *A Systematic View of the Science of Jurisprudence*.[4] Such titles were in accordance with well-established fashions, and he wrote confidently of 'the preparatory acquaintance with scientific methods of thought (which) I have held myself entitled to anticipate in my readers'. This, he continued, had enabled him 'to dilate with more minuteness than I could elsewhere on the essential relations of Law to Morality, on the one hand, and to the general constitution of society and of the state, on the other'.[5]

An equally strong, if at times rather confused, concern for science could be clearly seen in the works of one of the men who taught alongside Maine in London. Herbert Broom is now remembered for his work on the 'maxims' of the law, but during his life he was more remarkable for his efforts to pursue new methods of legal education for barristers. In the 1870s he published editions of the lectures which he had delivered to intending barristers since 1852, and much of their content consisted of what a modern lawyer might regard as straightforward common law. However, in contrast to the content, the presentation attempted to be fully scientific. The title to the work was *The Philosophy of Law* and at the start he distinguished his book from the problems of everyday practice. 'Legal science' he wrote, 'concerns itself with first principles, and secondly, procedure.' This commitment to science led him to observe that 'Law being a science the use of technical words in discussing it can scarcely be avoided . . .'; and this form of reasoning enabled him to present his lectures as 'the result of much thought devoted to the adapting of legal knowledge to the ordinary concerns of life'.[6]

that the reviewers crisply reveal the topics and methods of analysis which were then regarded as important and which greatly influenced all legal authors. It might be possible to show that many of the Victorian legal classics are now being significantly misinterpreted. We have lost this part of their context.

[4] Sheldon Amos, *The Science of Law* (London, 1874) and *A Systematic View of the Science of Jurisprudence* (London, 1872). The earlier work is rather 'legalistic' and based on lectures for students. As Amos saw it, Maine had demonstrated that when law had reached the stage at which a science of law was possible it could become a 'true' science because 'it is concerned with certain sequences of facts which, within the limits of recorded experience, are invariably the same for all times and places'. The forces of Amos' views on this topic seem to have made an impression upon Holdsworth: see *A History of English Law* (A. L. Goodhart and H. G. Hanbury, eds.) vol. 17 (London, 1965), p. 357.

[5] Amos, *The Science of Law*, p. vi. For contemporary concern with legal science in Parliament see *Hansard*, vol. 209, series 3, column 1221.

[6] Herbert Broom, *The Philosophy of Law* (London, 1876), pp. 1–5.

Many recent studies of nineteenth-century law have revealed just how impossible it is to regard the latter as some autonomous development concerned with wholly technical issues. Even the changes in the common law are now recognised as having links with developments in social, philosophical, economic and political thought. The picture of Victorian legal change which is emerging is very complicated in its details, but all writers on the subject agree that there was an attempt to discover principles, and that this search for principles was often regarded as being a form of scientific inquiry. Science was seen as the best instrument both for understanding the law and for developing appropriate reforms.[7]

The popularity of scientific legal reasoning was such that it was put to a great variety of uses. For some, science simply referred to a desire to categorise the different parts of the law and thereby to render it easier to learn. For others, such as Heron, it seems science pointed to a much more serious effort to relate law to some external criterion such as 'good nature' and thereby to present a programme for reform and codification. Whereas in Broom's case it was seen as the means to link law with the ordinary concerns of life. Such contradictions seem clearer in retrospect than they did to contemporaries who saw the multiple roles of science in legal writing as a confirmation of its value rather than as a source of difficulty.

MAINE AND LEGAL SCIENCE

Maine was not worried by any inconsistencies in the use of science by lawyers. From the early pages of *Ancient Law* he made it obvious that he had the greatest confidence in scientific methods, and that he would use them in any number of ways. This interest cannot be

[7] See, in particular, P. S. Atiyah, *The Rise and Fall of Freedom of Contract* (Clarendon Press, 1979); A. W. B. Simpson, 'Innovation in Nineteenth-Century Contract Law', *Law Quarterly Review*, vol. 91 (1975), p. 247; and R. Stevens, *Law and Politics: The House of Lords as a Judicial Body 1800–1976* (London, 1979). Holdsworth's account of nineteenth-century writing may be found chiefly in *A History of English Law*, vol. 15, particularly pp. 275–376. The extent to which his apparently descriptive analysis is in fact controversial is revealed by his persistent lack of attention to the speculative and scientific achievements of the early and mid-Victorian lawyers. Instead he emphasised the achievements of the later writers who offered a more secure place for the common law in their view of the legal world. His strange attempt to put Maine forward as a man who had *not* tried to attack the common law was very much in tune with this approach: see, for example, pp. 361–8. Robson saw the failings of such an interpretation of Maine's work: see W. A. Robson, 'Sir Henry Maine Today', in A. L. Goodhart *et al.*, *Modern Theories of Law* (Oxford, 1933), pp. 160–79.

explained in terms of the influence of a single person such as Brougham or a single book such as, say, Heron's jurisprudential study. Maine simply had great enthusiasm for a widespread fashion of thought.

At the start of *Ancient Law* he was particularly concerned with *justifying* the sources of information upon which he placed most reliance. The Preface accounts for, and justifies, the use of Roman Law whilst stressing that the book is certainly not to be seen as a treatise on Roman Jurisprudence. The second paragraph of the book explains, with regard to 'the early phenomena of law' that 'until philology has effected a complete analysis of the Sanskrit literature, our best sources of knowledge are undoubtedly the Greek Homeric poems, considered of course not as a history of actual occurrences, but as a description, not wholly idealised, of a state of society known to the writer'.

The shift of focus away from speculation as to what actually existed to a careful interpretation of past ideas as *indirect* evidence of what *probably* existed is typical. Maine employed exactly the same device with the common law: the ideals and supposed methods of the old common law may not always have been reflected in what common lawyers in fact did, but the ideals and supposed methods are important as rough guides to reality because they had a great influence. Whenever there was doubt about ancient evidence – and there usually was – we are told, rather self-consciously, that we may rely upon the probable influence of an idea.

The source of information having been justified, Maine is in a position to go on to attack those of his fellow analysts who have so signally failed to observe scientific standards. By the end of the second paragraph of *Ancient Law*, he has used science as an instrument of attack upon almost all the lawyers of the past.

If by any means we can determine the early forms of jural conceptions, they will be invaluable to us. These rudimentary ideas are to the jurist what the primary crusts of the earth are to the geologist. They contain, potentially, all the forms in which law has subsequently exhibited itself. The haste or the prejudice which has generally refused them all but the most superficial examination, must bear the blame of the unsatisfactory condition in which we find the science of jurisprudence. The inquiries of the jurist are in truth prosecuted much as inquiry into physics and physiology was prosecuted before observation had taken the place of assumption. Theories, plausible and comprehensive, but absolutely unverified, such as the Law of Nature or the Social Compact, enjoy a universal preference over sober research into the primitive history of society and law; and they obscure the truth not only by diverting attention from the only quarter in which it can be found, but by that most real and most important influence which, when once entertained and believed in, they are enabled to exercise on the later stages of jurisprudence.

It is apparent, then, that Maine puts himself forward as the diligent servant of 'sober research'. Any other approach may offer emotional satisfaction, but it can have no pretensions to being scientific. Given the strength of this early commitment it is not surprising that the same concern with 'modern' scientific standards persists throughout *Ancient Law*. For example, at the start of chapter 5 Maine observes rather disdainfully that

the necessity of submitting the subject of jurisprudence to scientific treatment has never been entirely lost sight of in modern times, and the essays which the consciousness of this necessity has produced have proceeded from minds of very various calibre, but there is not much presumption, I think, in asserting that what has hitherto stood in the place of a science has for the most part been a set of guesses . . .

Science provided Maine with his justification for writing about topics which, in some cases, had been the subject of analysis for over two thousand years. It was science which enabled him to claim to his own satisfaction that his methods and ideas were significant; and it was science which enabled him to relate his jurisprudential ideas to the dominant fashion in legal writing. His scientific analysis was very thorough within its own terms, but the initial assumption that legal subjects were susceptible of scientific analysis was crudely and confidently asserted.

PHILOLOGY, INDIA AND ROMAN LAW

Maine's interest in science and law was closely linked with his personal reinterpretation of a number of major areas of thought which had not previously been related in any detailed way to English jurisprudence. For modern minds the strangest of these interests was philology. In the form which was most attractive to Maine, that of comparative philology, this may be defined as 'the comparison of languages (through comparison of items within them) that are, or are assumed to be, genetically related, with the object of establishing such relationships and reconstructing original forms, from which derivation may be made'.[8] The languages of, say, India and Europe could be compared with a view to discovering whether or not they might both have evolved from a single ancient language. A scientific study of modern and ancient languages could produce evidence of numerous historical changes: like geology, the Victorian studies of philology were concerned with the reconstruction of states of no longer directly observable phenomena by means of classification into stages. They provided, as it were, a way of reconstructing the past; and since this necessarily involved the study of words, and words were the best guide to ancient laws, it was peculiarly suited to jurisprudence.

John Burrow, writing in 1966, was the first to stress the full importance of philology in Maine's thought and to explore the possibility that Maine was thinking about the themes of *Ancient Law* twenty years before the book was published.[9] In other words, it may be that Maine began to develop theoretical ideas about the use of language in understanding historical change when he was a classicist and was not greatly interested in ancient laws or ancient Indian customs or, indeed, any other of the particular bodies of knowledge with which his work has subsequently been explained by a succession of critics.

Some of the early Victorian philologists seem almost to have provided Maine with a model for the arguments of *Ancient Law*. For example, the remarkable scholar and eccentric, J. M. Kemble, was very interested in philology during the 1830s and through his strong (and frequently acrimonious) relationship with people at Cambridge it is more than likely that Maine (who subsequently quoted him) knew very well of his investigations.[10] He was surely attracted by Kemble's enthusiasm for plundering the past in such a way as to feed present controversies and there are places in Kemble's works where the author writes very much in the manner of *Ancient Law*. In his study of *The Saxons of England* (1849) he remarked on 'traditions borrowed from the most heterogeneous sources, compacted rudely with little ingenuity, and in which the smallest possible amount of historical truth is involved in a great deal of fable. Yet the truth which such traditions

[8] J. F. Ellis, 'General Linguistics and Comparative Philology', *Lingua* (1957–8), vol. 7 no. 2: quoted in Burrow, *Evolution and Society*, p. 152.

[9] *Ibid.*, pp. 149–53.

[10] Today, the increasing interest in Kemble is apparent in Stein, *Legal Evolution* and J. Burrow, *A Liberal Descent: Victorian Historians and the English Past* (Cambridge, 1981). For an intellectual world which Maine and Kemble had in common see, P. Allen, *The Cambridge Apostles: The Early Years* (Cambridge, 1978).

do nevertheless contain, yields to the alchemy of our days a golden harvest.' In considering the Anglo-Saxons themselves Kemble pointed out that 'the intimate relations of mythology, law and social institutions, which later ages are too apt scornfully to despise, or superstitiously to imitate, are for them living springs of action: they are believed in, not played with . . . '[11] The style is less elegant than Maine's, but the similarity to *Ancient Law* is striking. In particular, there is a belief in the importance of ideas as instruments of social analysis in the proper application of a modern 'alchemy' or science. In this view, the systematic study of jurisprudence properly consists in the scientific study of languages, both past and present: a purely abstract jurisprudence can never accommodate the information which languages provide about law.

This interest in the history of languages as a possible guide to the development of law had already been considered in general terms by an English lawyer whose works would certainly have been known to Maine, and they make it easier to understand what the latter was trying to do in relating philology to jurisprudence. Sir William Jones (1746–1794) was a jurist and an orientalist with a great enthusiasm for Indian law, both Islamic and Hindu, and he combined his interest with a strong grasp of English common law which he developed as a barrister in London and, later, as a judge of the High Court at Calcutta.[12] In 1781 he published *The Law of Bailments* which was recognised by the mid-nineteenth century as a classic.[13] In it, the 'unregulated chaos' of the common law was reduced to order, related to principle, explained in terms of utility and expressed in a clear and coherent form. It was as if a craft confined to a few experienced lawyers had been converted into a science accessible to any educated mind.

But a reading of Jones had even more to offer Maine.[14] Jones was an outstanding linguist with great proficiency in twelve languages, one of which was Sanskrit, and he put this knowledge to work in the production of readable translations which in many cases provided a guide to

[11] J. M. Kemble, *The Saxons in England: A History of the English Commonwealth Till the Period of the Norman Conquest* (London, 1848), vol. 1, p. 35.

[12] For a bibliography of books by Jones and some of the other works related to his concerns see S. N. Mukerjee, *Sir William Jones: A Study in Eighteenth-Century British Attitudes to India* (Cambridge, 1968), pp. 181–94.

[13] Sir William Jones, *An Essay on the Law of Bailments* (London, 1848). See Simpson, 'Innovation in Nineteenth-Century Contract Law', pp. 250–3.

[14] Burrow tantalisingly refers to both Jones and Maine but does not suggest that many of the latter's ideas may be explained by reference to the works of Jones.

ancient laws. Jones is also noted amongst philologists for his interest in the history of languages, and for his concern with the affinities of many languages, which now appear to be, in most respects, quite different from each other. Through a process of comparison, Jones was led to link languages together in much the same way that Maine was to adopt in later years.

If Maine ever felt a personal liking for the character and outlook of Sir William Jones he had good reason for doing so. From a very early age – long before he was old enough to practise at the Bar – Jones amused legal acquaintances 'by reasoning with them on old cases, which were supposed to be confined to the learned in the profession'. He developed a liking for comparing the respective merits of Roman and English law and the latter filled him with an almost literary enthusiasm. 'I have just begun', he wrote,

> to contemplate the stately edifice of the laws of England, 'The gather'd wisdom of a thousand years' – if you will allow me to parody a line of Pope. I do not see why the study of the law is called dry and unpleasant; and I very much suspect that it seems so to those only who could think any study unpleasant which required great application of the mind, and exertion of the memory.[15]

Sentiments such as these find the clearest echo in the thoughts of Maine and highlight his major concerns. They reflected many of the important things he believed about law: that its study should be scientific and yet historical; that it should be understood in precise terms but never divorced from literature; that it should involve the comparison of laws and legal systems and that, more often than not, it should lead to criticism rather than complacency. For both men, law was to be understood as a species of intellectual adventure; it demanded mental engagement of the broadest and most challenging kind.

Maine's initial interest in India and its laws did not arise out of visits to Indian villages; his first experience of the subcontinent came after he had written *Ancient Law*. Instead, it seems his interest was the product of curiosity about the history of languages and that it was through this perspective that he was to see the developments of Indian and other laws. Today he is sometimes regarded as a defective anthropologist in his writing on India. In fact, when he was writing *Ancient Law*, he was much more interested in the history of languages than in observing village customs and the like.

[15] Quoted in Lord Teignmouth, *Sir William Jones, with a Life of the Author* (London, 1807), vol. 1, pp. 45–6, 172–3, 245, 344.

A similar judgment might be made of his use of Roman law. Despite his frequent reference to the latter in *Ancient Law* it would be wrong to think of the book as having been concerned with Roman law for its own sake. The thought that his work might be interpreted in this way worried Maine and in the Preface to the first edition of *Ancient Law* he wrote that it had 'not been his intention to write a treatise on Roman jurisprudence, and he had as much as possible avoided all discussions which might give that appearance to his work'. Instead, examples from Roman law were used to illustrate points arising from his attempt to explore other topics such as the past development of languages. *Ancient Law* was in no sense the work of a conventional student of Roman law.

In this respect, the parallel with information about India is close. Just as in later years Maine was taken to have tried to produce a defective form of anthropology (which never in fact existed) and to have failed in the attempt, so, also, he was later taken to have provided an analysis of Roman law which contained numerous errors and amounted to an unconvincing treatise. This rather amused some of Maine's friends who knew very well that he has never been the strongest of 'Roman lawyers' and had himself been careful to make no claims for his prowess in this field.[16]

[16] In later books Maine gave even less attention to Roman law, and his contemporaries became increasingly blunt about the deficiencies of his knowledge in this area. For a typical, and critical, judgment of a friend see A. G. Gardiner, *The Life of Sir William Harcourt* (London, 1923), vol. 1, p. 39 (quoting Sir Leslie Stephen in support) and pp. 86–7. Frederick Harrison was delighted to have been taught Roman law by Maine but even he admitted: 'Henry Sumner Maine, whose private pupil I was in 1857, when he was giving his lectures on *Ancient Law*, was rather historian than lawyer, and more social philosopher than jurist', *Autobiographical Memoirs* (London, 1911), vol. 2, p. 76 and see vol. 1 at p. 152. Pollock was often cautious and defensive in his remarks about Maine's interpretation of Roman law: see *Law Quarterly Review* vol. 21 (1905), p. 165 and vol. 22 (1906), p. 73. It is therefore no surprise that books written on Roman law at the turn of the century were, in places, notably hostile. For an example see W. A. Hunter, *A Systematic and Historical Exposition of Roman Law in the Order of a Code* (London, 1898), pp. 536–9. In his introductory guide for students Hunter almost completely ignored Maine: *Introduction to Roman Law* (London, 1897).

In the twentieth century, writers on Roman law seem to have used Maine in a polite and often incidental fashion. W. W. Buckland was prepared to use him for occasional, illustrative purposes: *A Textbook of Roman Law from Augustus to Justinian* (3rd ed., revised by P. Stein, Cambridge, 1966); and the same can be said, of, say, B. Nicholas, *An Introduction to Roman Law* (Oxford, 1962, and reissued), for example p. 106, fn. 2. As one might expect there are some sympathetic references in those studies of Roman law which also looked beyond Roman law: e.g. F. H. Lawson, *A Common Lawyer looks at the Civil Law* (Greenwood, 1955) but there is less enthusiasm in W. W. Buckland and A. McNair, *Roman Law and Common*

HISTORICAL JURISPRUDENCE

All studies of Maine's legal thought have explained it in part by reference to German historical jurisprudence. In modern works it is common to find mention of the extent to which German jurists such as Savigny achieved international eminence in the years before Maine wrote *Ancient Law*, and the same works often go on to assert with great confidence that Maine responded with enthusiasm to this school of thought. After all, as some of these authorities have pointed out, Maine himself referred to Savigny as 'the great German jurist'.[17]

In a well-known article in the *Law Quarterly Review* Kantorowicz brought together the chief concerns of German historical jurisprudence.[18] He emphasised that it had to be contrasted with both natural law theory and any analysis of law which concentrated upon the capacity of a legislator to create good law by considering abstract criteria rather than the historical realities of society. The content of a nation's law is necessarily determined by the nation's peculiar character; law has no separate existence and should be seen as part of the whole life of the country. To begin with, all law is largely the common custom of the people, but later, with the development of civilisation, law becomes a distinct function and is implemented by a profession.

Law: A Comparison in Outline (2nd ed. revised by F. H. Lawson, Cambridge, 1965) (consider for example p. 191). Moderate praise is mixed with criticism in H. F. Jolowicz, *Roman Foundations of Modern Law* (Oxford, 1961), (see pp. 55, 63 and 66). One might have expected favourable remarks in historical studies but there seems to be little interest in Maine in H. F. Jolowicz and B. Nicholas, *Historical Introduction to the Study of Roman Law* (Cambridge, 1972); however, see p. 127, fn. 8. There are more references to Vinogradoff than Maine in R. W. Lee's *Historical Conspectus of Roman Law* (2nd revised impression, London, 1956). The full irrelevance of Maine in this context can be seen by looking at W. Kunkel, *An Introduction to Roman Legal and Constitutional History* (trans. J. M. Kelly), (Oxford, 1966), Bibliographical Appendix pp. 179–210.

Perhaps it would require a *very* strong revival of interest in the problems of legal change and the relationship between law and society before there could be a restoration of significant interest in what Maine said about Roman law. For a possible development, see P. Stein, *Regulae Juris: From Juristic Rules to Legal Maxims* (Edinburgh, 1966), pp. 3–6. (I am grateful to Vera Sachs for her help in considering the reception of Maine's ideas about Roman law.)

[17] *Ancient Law*, p. 254, chapter 8.

[18] H. U. Kantorowicz, 'Savigny and the Historical School of Law', *Law Quarterly Review*, vol. 53 (1937), pp. 326–43. Of course, numerous additional sources could be mentioned such as Stein, *Legal Evolution*, chapter 3. I am most grateful to Professor Stein for his advice on matters relating to German historical jurisprudence.

Even at this stage the law remains an expression of the national community, and the jurist is charged with the task of representing the people and their ways in the creation of law. The law 'arises from silent, anonymous forces, which are not directed by arbitrary and conscious intention, but operate in the way of customary law'. Imposed legislation is an aberration, for nations in their prime have no need of it.

This form of legal analysis was presented at its most forceful in the work of Savigny, and it is best understood when it is contrasted with the views of his opponents, such as Thibaut. The latter sought to codify the law of the German states and looked for inspiration to the French civil code based upon Roman law. It is easy, therefore, to see how in public debate it was possible to oppose two radically different views of legal analysis. The one appealed to the received history of a people and responded to their distinctive values, and the other appealed to those laws which are justified in terms of careful reasoning and methodical analysis based upon assumptions supposed to be applicable to any society.

Unfortunately, comparing Maine's jurisprudence with these ideas with a view to determining the extent to which they influenced his thought is likely to produce confused results. Obviously, there are some similarities: like the German theorists in question, he was convinced of the defects of abstract analysis and the need to replace it with thorough historical studies; and these studies should be based upon the analysis of legal change in terms of evolutionary growth. Within this framework both Maine and the German writers stressed common topics such as the relationship of law and language with both elements evolving over time and without direct human intervention. However, the contrasts are just as obvious. For example, the distinction between an historical explanation and justification for law on the one hand, and schemes of legislative reform and codification on the other, was in total conflict with Maine's views of history and legal reform. For Maine, detailed historical study revealed the need for modern codification and this, by itself, constituted one of the chief themes of *Ancient Law*. Admittedly, Savigny also believed that codes were appropriate in certain circumstances but for Maine they were almost a precondition of progress.

These inconsistencies are reflected in the modern responses to the problem of Maine's possible use of German thought. For example, Pollock's hesitation was obvious when he observed that Maine 'began his work in the mighty and still present shadow of Savigny'.[19] It is very difficult to know what precisely was meant by this, and it is only a little more helpful to turn to Vinogradoff's more detailed reference to Maine as

> the English disciple of Savigny who often dwells on the idea that the greater part of the social and intellectual structure of a nation is bequeathed to it by former generations, that unconscious tradition is perhaps the most potent agent in historical life, that the margin of change is increasingly small and progressive nations quite exceptional.[20]

The problem raised by this remark is that Maine himself never acknowledged any form of substantial indebtedness to Savigny and was always suspicious of observations which contained even a hint that law could be related in some way to national character. Perhaps Vinogradoff's remarks conform not so much to what Maine had written as to what Vinogradoff wished Maine had written. Recently, Professor Stein considered the problem in more convincing terms which avoid Pollock's vague words and Vinogradoff's enthusiasm. In Stein's view, Maine was

> concerned with the history of legal institutions in the manner of Savigny, whose influence on him is clear. Just as Savigny combatted the view that law consists of the statutes of the legislator guided by natural law, so Maine rejected the view that it was the command of a legislator motivated by utilitarian principles.

Also,

> Maine no doubt felt that he was more scientific and less romantic than Savigny, but they shared a similar preoccupation with 'progressive' (Maine) and 'nobler' (Savigny) nations, of which Romans were the model; they agreed on the importance of the Roman juristic method for an understanding of the mechanisms of legal change, and they were at one in their emphasis on the continuity of national traditions.[21]

However, in contrast to all of these remarks, Sir Carleton Allen made the robust assertion that there is not in fact a lot of evidence that Maine actually knew much of Savigny's work, still less that it influenced him in any significant way. Along with Kantorowicz he believed that Maine made more use of the 'younger' school of historical jurists associated with the work of Rudolf von Ihering.[22] But, un-

[19] Sir Frederick Pollock, *Oxford Lectures* (Oxford, 1890), p. 153. Burrow rightly refers to Pollock's 'elastic phraseology': *Evolution and Society*, p. 143.

[20] Sir Paul Vinogradoff, 'The Teaching of Sir Henry Maine', *Law Quarterly Review*, vol. 20 (1904), p. 119.

[21] Stein, *Legal Evolution*, pp. 89–90.

[22] See Allen's introduction to *Ancient Law* (Oxford, 1954), p. xiii.

fortunately, as John Burrow has emphasised, this view raises problems as to the way in which Maine's ideas developed. Ihering's work, which is supposed to have influenced Maine, appeared in 1858 and if we were to argue that it did have a great influence upon him we would have to conclude that Maine's ideas developed very quickly indeed between 1858 and the publication of *Ancient Law* in 1861, and we would almost have to ignore the possible significance of an early interest in subjects such as philology.[23]

These contrasting views of Maine's critics do at least suggest that his reaction to German historical jurisprudence was neither very positive, nor very negative. He did not reject it in clear terms but, equally, he did not follow the example of a contemporary Victorian barrister, Nathaniel Lindley, and engage in enthusiastic translation.[24] His reaction was more equivocal and might be compared with that of John Austin whose response was mixed and often difficult to identify.[25]

In Maine's case, the influence of German ideas may well have been reduced by reason of the fact that he could derive information from purely English sources. Maine probably knew of other nineteenth-century English writers who had already considered the explanation of law, including ancient law, in historical terms. It is true that he never mentions them, but why should he do so when he barely mentioned Savigny himself? For example, George Spence was an author of standing on Chancery matters, but in the years before 1826 he had turned his attention to the whole historical development of the law. In 1826 he published his *Inquiry into the Origin of the Laws and Political Institutions of Modern Europe, Particularly those of England*.[26] Like Austin, a lot of his thoughts had been prompted by a consideration of foreign laws based on traditions which many took to

[23] Burrow, *Evolution and Society*, pp. 142–3.

[24] See N. Lindley, *Introduction to the Study of Jurisprudence* (London, 1855). Admittedly, the source in question was Thibaut. Nathaniel Lindley (1828–1921), the first Baron Lindley, Master of the Rolls (1897–1900), and a Lord of Appeal in Ordinary (1900–1905), is remembered chiefly today for being the last survivor of the order of serjeants-at-law and author of *A Treatise on the Law of Partnership* (London, 1860) which became known as 'Lindley on Partnership'.

[25] For the place of German ideas in Austin's thought see A. B. Schwartz, 'John Austin and the Jurisprudence of his Time', *Politica* (1934–5), pp. 177–99; and Janet Ross, *Three Generations of Englishwomen* (London, 1893), pp. 67–9. In the course of his visit to Germany Austin 'was impressed by the early Pandectists, one of the most prominent of whom was Savigny's adversary, Thibaut' – see Stein, *Legal Evolution*, p. 71. It is very difficult to be precise about Austin's reaction to Savigny: see W. L. Morison, *John Austin* (London, 1982), p. 61.

[26] (London, 1826).

be very different from those of the common law. In Spence's case the prompting came from an analysis of the Napoleonic Code. He 'was induced in consequence to look attentively into the Civil Law of the Romans, where he found that a great proportion of the doctrines of the common law of England, even many of those which are purely artificial, were to be found in the Institutes, the Pandects, the Code, and the Novels'.[27] In the words of an enthusiastic reviewer, this led on to an attempt 'to study the civil and criminal code of the Romans with some minuteness, and to compare it with the political and judicial institutions of modern Europe, and of our own country in particular'.[28]

These are striking remarks. It was not just that the writer was discussing Roman law: he was doing so and finding links between ancient and modern systems very much in the manner of Maine. Like the more famous author of *Ancient Law*, Spence was concerned with – to adapt the subtitle of *Ancient Law* itself – the beginnings of the legal world and 'its Relation to Modern Ideas'. It also is worth noting that Spence was very much aware of Savigny's work: he had not read the German theorist's ideas when he was writing his own book, but, subsequently, he turned to Savigny and he was the first to say that by comparison his own efforts were slender. In saying this Spence was more than a little modest since his book ran to hundreds of pages and no one could dispute that it was the product of sustained analysis. Plainly, it is important that Spence at least felt that he and Savigny were engaged in the same sort of enterprise: thirty-five years before Maine's *Ancient Law*, there was the clearest acknowledgement in print of the need to understand modern English law in terms of the sort of approach which was also adopted by the German school of historical jurisprudence: but the approach was *not* founded upon the influence of the Germans and cannot be explained in 'Germanic' terms.

There is nothing fanciful in seeing similarities between this sort of legal writing and that of Maine. In both there is, as it were, an incidental interest in Roman law which is viewed in such a way as to reveal its possible relevance to modern conditions; it is used for the purpose of illustrations in the course of explaining human progress. In both the approach is inextricably bound up with the attempt to consider what it was that had produced change in civilised societies.

[27] *Ibid.*, Prefatory Introduction.

[28] *Law Magazine and Review* (1830), vol. 4, p. 110.

Probably, we will never conclusively know if Maine read Spence, but we can say that Spence's eminence in the world of Chancery matters must have kept his name in the everyday conversation of lawyers and it is difficult to imagine that his book was rapidly forgotten.

However, in Maine's case any attempt to search for a major English or German influence upon the manner in which he used historical information is likely to be unrewarding. Enough has been said in the preceding sections to suggest that he was unlikely to identify his own ideas with any particular school of thought. He was more interested in producing a synthesis of ideas from diverse sources. In other words, his response to the historical arguments of other people was likely to have developed gradually as he brought together his thoughts on languages, the common law and so on.

Some of the ideas which appear in *Ancient Law* may, then, have been in his mind by the late 1840s and have been subject to further development in the course of the lectures he gave in London during the next decade.[29] Fortunately, an outline of these lectures was published in the periodical press from the time of their commencement. On 5 November 1853 the *Law Times* announced that the Reader in Jurisprudence and Civil Law would give six lectures on the following subjects:

On General or Scientific Jurisprudence – On some of the primary technical terms of Legal Science – On the relation of Law to Moral Philosophy – on the Ius Gentium of the Roman Jurists, and on some modern theories of Natural law – on the Sources of the Roman Civil Law and the Composition of the Corpus Juris – On the Relation of the Roman Civil Law to General Jurisprudence – On the Order and Connection of the Departments of Law, and on the Systems of Classification adopted by certain Modern Jurists.

Whatever else this points to, it clearly reveals an enthusiasm for a

[29] Feaver, in *From Status to Contract*, reveals the strength of Maine's early interest in history (see, in particular, chapter 2). There is dispute over precisely when the various drafts of *Ancient Law* were prepared. See Feaver, p. 41 and Burrow, *Evolution and Society*, p. 140. There is relevant evidence in *Ancient Law*; in the course of discussing the influence of morality on crime in chapter 9 Maine remarks that 'At the moment at which I write, the newest chapter in the English criminal law is one which attempts to prescribe punishment for the frauds of trustees.' This refers to 20 and 21 Vict., c. 54, which became law in August 1857 (see the observations of P. Stein in *Legal Evolution*, p. 88, fn. 24). Whatever the precise date of preparation it seems clear that as early as the 1840s Maine was interested in the historical analysis of ancient laws and that the references in the *Law Times* point to the preparation of relevant written material. People subsequently spoke of *Ancient Law* as having been based upon his lectures in London: see for example Harrison, *Autobiographic Memoirs*, vol. 1, p. 152. For evidence of the enduring reputation of Maine's lectures see *Law Times*, vol. 109 (1900), p. 371.

great variety of sources. The start seems to be both scientific and utilitarian: the terms almost might have been taken from John Austin's *Introduction to the Province of Jurisprudence*. The subsequent reference to 'Legal Science' must have been reassuring to other English legal writers and to reformers of the day such as Brougham and Bethell. Even the reference to law and moral philosophy in an early lecture constitutes a strongly Austinian approach to public lectures on jurisprudence.

However, it is plain that after this Maine moved to a different emphasis. It looks as if at this stage there is more concern with Roman Law than was shown by Austin. If this was in fact the case it is hardly surprising since it was upon this subject that Maine had been lecturing since 1847 at Cambridge. But at the same time it is clear that his audience was not faced with a merely descriptive approach to the study of Roman Law; instead it was integrated into the study of more general forms of jurisprudence.

It is possible to go into a little more detail at this point. The first series of public lectures was given in the Michaelmas Term of 1853 and already, by 21 December, a new series of lectures had been announced for the next term and these appear to have taken over where the others ended. Maine began with a reference to the last topic of the first series: he would consider 'the Order and Connection of the Departments of Law, and the Systems of Classification adopted by certain Modern Jurists'. But after this there is a sudden change: the next topic would be:

> On Status – on the Definition and Forms of Status – On some Peculiarities in the Condition of Early Societies, and the durable effects which they have produced on Ancient and Modern Jurisprudence – on the Theory of Social Progress originated by G. B. Vico, and on the evidence for and against it afforded by the history of the Roman Law of persons – On the connection of the Roman Law of Persons with the Political Organisation of the Roman State, and on the Historical Character of the Distinction between Private and Public Law – On the Power of the Father, and on the Tutelage of women and Pupils – On the Agencies by which the Roman Law of Persons progressively was modified, on the Praetorian Equity, and the principles descended from it to Jurisprudence.

This prospectus of December 1853 seems to have significant elements of *Ancient Law* within its sweeping phrases. It may be that 'Status' here did not have exactly the same meaning which it was given in the later book, but plainly there is some approximate connection between the two uses of the word. The analysis of status is linked to what seems to have been a philological concern with the 'durable' elements of early societies and this, in turn, is linked to an interest in theories of progress or rather 'Social Progress'. The subsequent references to Roman Law, particularly the remarks about progressive modification, seem to involve an attempt to relate the problems of status and social transformation to a body of law itself.

In fact, further possible links with his future work may be found in the remaining sections of his lectures. There is a notable concern with International Law, although perhaps this was only to be expected at a time when International Law and jurisprudence were closely related in legal writing. More significant is the final section concerned with 'Obligation and Contract'. This was concerned with:

> The Roman Theory of Obligation, and on the mode in which it has been interpreted by Pothier and others – On the Necessary Elements of Contract, and on the Manner in which they are discriminated by the Roman Jurists – On Pollicitations and Pacts – On the Classification of Contracts.

These outlines touch on the concerns of *Ancient Law* at various points, but they are more important for the extent to which they reveal the attempt on Maine's part to bring together a wide range of historical materials and to analyse them in various ways. In part the materials are considered in, as it were, their own right; in part they are related to various notions of progressive change; and in part they are subject to systems of legal and (in the Victorian sense) scientific classification. They suggest a mind open both to a wide variety of subjects and to different ways of looking at them. Also the fact that he sustained his interest in these topics for a considerable length of time suggests that he was determined to develop his own distinct ideas, and that when he wrote *Ancient Law* he would not produce something which could be explained by reference to a pre-existing school of historical jurisprudence.[30] His interests were too broad.

30 There is a significant lack of references to Maine in D. Sugarman's recent discussion of the Germanic influences upon Victorian English Law: see 'The Making of a Textbook Tradition' in W. Twining (ed.), *Legal Theory and Common Law* (Oxford, 1986), p. 45. But for a clear reference to 'The tendency of German juridical opinion' see p. 53 where reference is made to *Dissertations on Early Law and Custom* (1901 edition), pp. 360–1. There is no reference to Maine in C. E. McClelland, *The German Historians and England* (Cambridge, 1971). For studies of German influence see Burrow, *A Liberal Descent*, C. H. S. Fifoot, *Judge and Jurist in the Reign of Victoria* (London, 1959) and references in G. R. Rubin and D. Sugarman (eds.), *Law, Economy and Society* (London, 1984), Introduction, fn. 289. In considering the diversity of sources which Maine may have had in mind when he began to think of historical jurisprudence, it is worth remembering that W. Friedmann mentions

MAINE, SCIENCE AND HISTORY

In *Ancient Law* Maine makes references to an 'Historical Method'. For example, in attacking French political theorists who sought to sustain their views by reference to 'the hypothesis of a state of nature', Maine asserted that such an hypothesis was 'still the great antagonist of the Historical Method; and whenever (religious objections apart) any mind is seen to resist or condemn that mode of investigation, it will generally be found under the influence of a prejudice or vicious bias traceable to a conscious or unconscious reliance on a non-historical, natural condition of society or the individual'.[31]

The 'Historical Method' clearly involves a rejection of reasoning which claims to be based on historical events but which in fact is not. Unfortunately, it is much more difficult to go beyond this bland point and show, say, that the 'Historical Method' can be used to reveal certain truths about social change and modern society. To give another example, in considering testamentary law Maine criticises various theories on the ground that they fail properly to respond to the historical facts which, here as elsewhere, can reveal the potential complexity of legal arrangements.

> It is not difficult to point out the extreme difference of the conclusions forced on us by the historical treatment of the subject, from those to which we are conducted when, without the help of history, we merely strive to analyse our *prima facie* impressions. I suppose there is nobody who, starting from the popular or even the legal conception of a Will, would not imagine that certain qualities are necessarily attached to it. He would say, for example, that a Will necessarily takes effect *at death only* – that it is secret, not known as a matter of course to persons taking interests under its provisions – that it is *revocable*, *i.e.* always capable of being superseded by a new act of testation. Yet I shall be able to show that there was a time when none of these characteristics belonged to a Will.[32]

Maine's delight in using history to reveal the weakness of *prima facie*, non-historical reasoning is obvious and may be found on page after page of *Ancient Law*. But, again, it is difficult to see how such an approach can reveal more than the deficiencies of modern ideas which make wrong assumptions about the past. For instance, such a theory

Edmund Burke in the context of 'Historical Evolution as a Guide to Legal Thought': 'Before the German jurists who form the nucleus of the historical school, Edmund Burke had formulated its principle political and philosophical beliefs': *Legal Theory* (London, 1967), chapter 18 and p. 210.

31 *Ancient Law*, p. 91, chapter 4.

32 *Ibid.*, p. 174, chapter 6.

has no clear predictive power: Maine does not seem to be suggesting that his inquiry into the past will reveal laws which will enable him to make accurate predictions as to the course of future social events.

However, in many parts of *Ancient Law* it is clear that Maine was frustrated by this restricted role for history in jurisprudence; it is as if he wished to be more than an historically-minded court jester who embarrassed famous theorists by awkward references to past experience. Once again he had reason for persistent curiosity about the possible relationship between jurisprudence and science. In considering 'primitive society and ancient law' he was sufficiently concerned about the issue to explain his views on the 'proper mode of inquiry'. 'There is', he wrote,

> such widespread dissatisfaction with existing theories of jurisprudence, and so general a conviction that they do not really solve the question they pretend to dispose of, as to justify the suspicion that some line of inquiry, necessary to a perfect result has been incompletely followed or altogether omitted by their authors. And indeed there is one remarkable omission with which all these speculations are chargeable, except perhaps those of Montesquieu. They take no account of what law has actually been at epochs remote from the particular period at which they made their appearance. Their originators carefully observed the institutions of their own age and civilisations with which they had some degree of intellectual sympathy, but, when they turned their attention to archaic states of society which exhibited much superficial difference from their own, they uniformly ceased to observe and began guessing. The mistake which they committed is therefore analogous to the error of one who, in investigating the laws of the material universe, should commence by contemplating the existing physical world as a whole, instead of beginning with the particles which are its simplest ingredients. One does not certainly see why such a scientific solecism should be more defensible in jurisprudence than in any other region of thought. It would seem antecedently that we ought to commence with the simplest social forms in a state as near as possible to their rudimentary condition. In other words, if we followed the course usual in such inquiries, we should penetrate as far up as we could in the history of primitive societies.[33]

There are other, similar statements in *Ancient Law* and they imply the following. Firstly, in failing properly to consider history, numerous theories have been guilty of a remarkable omission. Secondly, this omission has *not* deprived jurisprudence of the imaginative or even intuitive insights which some associate with historical understanding; instead, it has, as it were, deprived jurisprudence of relevant *facts* – the facts of the legal past are ascertainable and are relevant to the legal

[33] *Ibid.*, pp. 118–19, chapter 5.

present. In other words, the omission is not an understanding of the past but the facts of the past. Third, it follows that scientific jurisprudence can provide a more complete account of law than previous theories of legal philosophy, and that it does so by providing an accurate 'integration' of information from the past and the present. At this stage at least Maine is not asking for some special jurisprudential insight based upon an imaginative understanding of the place of the past in man's thinking; he simply wants the past to be used as a new source of relevant, scientifically interpreted facts.

This is associated with an interest on Maine's part in the laws of social and legal development: for example, he spoke of the need to ascertain 'the germs out of which has assuredly been unfolded every form of moral restraint which controls our actions and shapes our conduct at the present moment'.[34] It is even possible within the terms of such reasoning to identify past errors which have impeded progress: for instance, 'unhappily there is a law of development which ever threatens to operate upon unwritten usage';[35] and of fictions Maine could write that 'to revile them as merely fraudulent is to betray ignorance of their peculiar office in the historical development of law'.[36]

It is particularly significant that he had an interest in the 'Comparative Method.' This was totally unlike modern studies of 'Comparative Law' in that it was seen as being a scientific theory which could explain changes in the actual content of ancient and modern law. In Maine's words: 'As societies do not advance concurrently, but at different rates of progress, there have been epochs at which men trained to habits of methodical observation have really been in a position to watch and describe the infancy of mankind.'[37] Such men are in a

[34] *Ibid.*, p. 120, chapter 5. [35] *Ibid.*, p. 19, chapter 1.

[36] *Ibid.*, p. 27, chapter 2.

[37] *Ibid.*, p. 120, chapter 5. It is hardly surprising that the comparative lawyers of the twentieth century seem to have expressed little interest in the works of Maine. David and Brierley describe him as a founder of the modern comparative study of law (see R. David and J. E. C. Brierley, *Major Legal Systems in the World Today* (London, 1978), p. 4). But the emphasis is upon his standing as a founder rather than a modern authority, and the precise links between his books and subsequent developments are not explored. Gutteridge could be severely critical, as when he criticised Maine for having failed to comprehend the proper significance of his own books, such as *Village Communities*, for the comparative study of law (H. C. Gutteridge, *Comparative Law* (Cambridge, 1949), pp. 3 and 63). Many studies with comparative themes have pointed to incidental failings on Maine's part (for example, A. Allott, *The Limits of Law* (London, 1980) p. 169). A general, and balanced view has been put forward in colourful terms by Derrett in his capacity as editor and contributor to J. Duncan

position to see the possible relationship between the development of societies in different parts of the world; for example, they might observe similarities in the stages of legal development in places as far apart as Ireland and India. As a matter of observation, it might be possible to conclude that:

> with these differences . . . that in the East aristocracies became religious, in the West civil or political, the proposition that a historical era of aristocracies succeeded a historical era of heroic kings may be considered as true, if not of all mankind, at all events of all branches of the Indo-European family of nations.[38]

From reasoning such as this it followed that scientific jurisprudence could, amongst many other things, explain the development of modern western law by reference to the present condition of certain Asian societies.

There were further reasons for Maine's strong interest in the Comparative Method. It was closely linked to contemporary philological studies, and it had obvious potential as an instrument for relating the legal past to the legal present with such firmness that any future attempt to separate history and jurisprudence would look strange and unjustified. At least one reviewer of *Ancient Law* sensed the importance of the method and regarded it as the central achievement of the book.[39]

M. Derrett, *An Introduction to Legal Systems* (London, 1968). He points out, firstly, that 'perhaps the best-known introduction to comparative jurisprudence is the range of works of Sir Henry Maine, especially his celebrated *Ancient Law* . . .' However, secondly, he remarks that 'it is high time that while we admit his status as a pioneer, and admire his mellifluous style, we substitute for his bland suggestions information such as is demanded both by more recent discoveries and by the concerns of our own day'.

The explanation for these contrasting responses is surely simple. We have seen that Maine's use of the comparative method was highly specialised and inseparably linked to certain mid-Victorian fashions of thought relating to developments in philology, scientific theorising, etc. As such the content of his analysis bears little or no resemblance to the studies of later comparative lawyers. There is not the slightest practical need for a modern comparative lawyer to know of the Victorian comparative method: for a vivid description of the method see S. Collini, D. Winch and J. Burrow, *That Noble Science of Politics: A Study in Nineteenth-Century Intellectual History* (Cambridge, 1983), chapter 7. Viewed in this light it is understandable that Sir Henry Maine left no successor intimately concerned with analytical and comparative studies of Indian law: in this respect 'England was a dry well' (see J. D. M. Derrett, *Juridical Ethnology: The Life and Work of Giuseppe Mazzarella* (Stuttgart, 1960), p. 29.

38 *Ancient Law*, p. 11, chapter 1.

39 See the *Saturday Review*, 16 February 1861, p. 677.

However, there are strict limits to the extent to which this clear and colourful theory can be said to have provided Maine with the ideal application of science to legal phenomena. If Maine had unequivocal faith in its application he would, surely, have referred to it with some frequency in *Ancient Law*. He would have used it to resolve the historical disputes which he considered; and he would have used it systematically as a weapon against those who used unhistorical arguments based on, say, the law of nature. Instead, in *Ancient Law* there is a very open quality about the use which Maine makes of the Comparative Method; it is remarked upon in an almost incidental fashion and it is not pursued with any great consistency. It was as if he could hardly believe in his good fortune at having discovered a particular law of scientific jurisprudence which could be given specific application. Or perhaps, as is more likely, he thought it might be convincingly refuted and he did not wish its failure to prejudice the creation of a general scientific jurisprudence. In later years the Comparative Method was to assume much greater importance in his thought; but by then (for reasons which are explored in chapter 4) Maine was far less concerned with its potential for jurisprudence.

Shortly after the publication of *Ancient Law* it became clear that he was still very interested in the potential for a science of history, whether or not it was related to particular laws such as those associated with the Comparative Method. In *An Address to the University of Calcutta*, he stated bluntly that:

> It is now affirmed, and was felt long before it was affirmed, that the truth of history, if it exists, cannot differ from any other form of truth. If it be truth at all, it must be scientific truth. There can be no essential difference between the truths of the Astronomer, of the Physiologist, and of the historian. The great principle which underlies all our knowledge of the physical world, that Nature is ever consistent with herself, must also be true of human nature and of human society which is made up of human nature. It is not indeed meant that there are no truths except of the external world, but that all truth, of whatever character, must conform to the same conditions, so that if indeed history be true, it must teach that which every other science teaches, continuous sequence, inflexible order, and eternal law.[40]

Nobody could suggest that Maine had carried out such a project in *Ancient Law*. He had not discovered the scientific laws of jurisprudence; he had not even claimed to have made such a discovery. But his observation to an audience in Calcutta is not in any way inconsistent

[40] The lecture is reprinted in certain editions of *Village Communities*, for example 4th ed. (London, 1881), p. 255, see pp. 265–6.

with the arguments of *Ancient Law* and it serves as a powerful reminder of the ultimate objectives which Maine had in mind for jurisprudence. It alerts us to the fact that a scientific interpretation of history guided him to many of his chief concerns. It hints at the experimental nature of *Ancient Law*; it suggests that the arguments of *Ancient Law* have, as it were, an open-ended quality which sought to redirect jurisprudence for future study rather than to provide final answers to jurisprudential problems. In retrospect a concern with scientific history looks strange; but to Maine it was of decisive importance.

Two other commentators have explored his commitment to science. Burrow has seen it as an additional element in Maine's jurisprudence, a supplement to his historical concerns rather than, as I have argued above, the instrument for a general synthesis.[41] Vinogradoff may have exaggerated Maine's links with the German school of historical jurisprudence but his final judgment on his scientific method was forceful and persuasive. 'Maine', he wrote,

> brings into the field of inquiry a new element, the element of *science* in the English sense of the word, that is of exact knowledge based on observation and aiming at the foundation of laws. The fact is that Maine did not only stand under the influence of the preceding generation, which had given an extraordinary impulse to historical research, but also under the sign of his own time with its craving for a scientific treatment of the problems of social life.

For Vinogradoff, the concern with science was central to an understanding of Maine. In considering the latter's teaching he isolated four chief commitments:

1. The study of law is not merely a preparation for professional duties and an introduction to the art of handling professional problems. It may also be treated as a scientific subject.
2. The methods of scientific investigation may be applied to the study of law: the method of deductive analysis on the basis of abstractions from the present state of legal ideas and rules, and the method of inductive generalisation on the basis of historical and ethnographical observations.
3. In the domain of inductive jurisprudence, law appears as one of the expressions of history and history is taken in the wide sense of all knowledge as to the social evolution of mankind.
4. In so much as every science ought to be directed to the discovery of laws, that is general principles governing particular cases, the historical method of jurisprudence is necessarily a comparative one.[42]

[41] Burrow, *Evolution and Society*, chapter 5, section 2.
[42] Vinogradoff, 'The Teaching of Sir Henry Maine', pp. 119–22.

These four points of Vinogradoff's provide a concentrated description of Maine's multiple scientific commitments. There is a bit of everything. There is the general interest in science. There is the concern with applying scientific methods to social study. There is deductive analysis, based, ultimately, on observation of the present. There is inductive reasoning based upon evidence of the past. There is an analysis of history within a framework concerned with the entirety of social development. There is the potential to provide a synthesis of many themes and contrasting sources of information.

2

LAWYERS AND MAINE'S JURISPRUDENCE

BEING A LAWYER

Modern jurisprudence is largely unconcerned with the problems which are of greatest importance to practitioners. For instance, in many countries the practising lawyers of the mid-twentieth century have been concerned with the question: if the law is to be effectively and fairly administered is it necessary to have a politically powerful and independent organisation of professional lawyers? Admittedly, academics have asked this question in some contexts; it is seen as being of obvious significance for a critical analysis of legal professions and the provision of legal services. But academics have not seen it as being primarily a jurisprudential issue which may be decided by, say, discovering some necessary quality of law or integrating historical facts about legal practice into legal philosophy.

For someone such as Maine, this modern approach would seem strange and inappropriate. In so far as jurisprudence was concerned with the study of ideas about law it was an odd view of the subject which excluded from consideration the ideas which were regarded as important by those who actually practised law. Maine himself wished very much to know the answer to questions such as: how did being a lawyer change the way in which a man thought about the law? What was it in progressive societies which could set off a reaction in legal thought which produced a preponderant role firstly for fictions, secondly for equity and thirdly for statutes? If processes such as this could be understood and the true nature of law explained by reference to such events, then what were the duties of a lawyer? What was his proper role in an era of legal or social change? How should he use old laws when they no longer served their original purpose? A concern with the duties of a lawyer provided a focal point for the moral, political and social issues which inevitably arose for consideration when law was regarded as something which had to be explained, at least in part, by reference to the ideas of practitioners. Maine was always concerned with the problem of what it was to be a lawyer, and this persistently drove his jurisprudential thought in directions which were different from those taken by nearly all of modern legal theory.

LEGAL PRACTICE

Maine's interest in the Bar probably developed a few years before he joined an Inn of Court in 1847. When he had first given his attention to the study of early law in the 1840s there was every reason to expect his ideas to travel in the direction of legal subjects such as international law and that this, in turn, would encourage him to join the profession. Other people with theoretical interests had taken the same path before him, and such a development was made all the more likely by reason of the fact that becoming a barrister in the middle of the nineteenth century was an easy task for anyone who had some social standing. There were no examinations to be taken save for a few which were introduced in 1852, and even these remained voluntary until 1872. It was true that Maine had to be accepted by the Inn to which he applied and, in accordance with custom, eat some dinners in the company of other would-be lawyers. But acceptance of someone such as him was a matter of form at this time. Given his other interests, it would have been strange if Maine had chosen not to become a barrister.

The profession of the time was different from today's Bar. The role of the Inns of Court, for example, was radically different. Today's Inns, by comparison, are fairly active in the administration of legal education and the general management of the profession; generally, the Inns play a larger part in the everyday life of the profession than they did in the 1840s. In part this is because the Benchers of those early years left a great many of the Bar's problems to be regulated by the Circuits in the provinces; but in part it simply arose out of the fact that those who administered the Inns just did not wish to interfere with everyday professional life.

This was of importance to Maine in his capacity as a young man with a lively mind and an increasing interest in the law. It was hardly likely that such a state of affairs would impress him. It was much more probable that it would lead him to an interest in reform and a suspicion of the more traditional elements of the Bar. A critical view was all the more likely by reason of the fact that what mattered most in practical terms for someone in his position in the late 1840s and early 1850s was the great problem of how, once he had been called, he could go on to establish a practice. This was no easy task at the time for there was a great deal of well-grounded pessimism about a young man's prospects at the Bar.[1] In particular it was feared that the new, local, County Courts would take away much of the work which previously had been done by beginners at the assizes. This entailed much more than a change of venue for barristers, for attornies and solicitors were to be given a right of audience in the new courts: in other words it looked as if, after the creation of these courts in 1846, a lot of work would leave the Bar and fall into the hands of the other half of the profession. Worse still, it was well known that some barristers, for very obvious reasons, had done all they could to prevent this reform from being accepted by Parliament. They had heaped abuse on reformers such as Brougham and raised a great many rather odd arguments which more or less suggested that after the establishment of these new courts English citizens would forever be deprived of justice. When the legislation was finally passed many barristers seem to have felt a sense of humiliation. It was as if they had been called to account for themselves in public and been found wanting.

This squares somewhat strangely with the fact that at the time the number of young men who were becoming barristers underwent a sudden increase. The figures revealed in the *Law List* are very difficult to interpret for these years, and it is impossible to be certain how many of those who were called actually intended to practise, but if complaints in the legal press are a good guide it seems that just when the Bar's work was in decline its membership was expanding.[2] Perhaps the explanation for this lies in the possibility that other professions such as the army and the navy were, for a whole variety of reasons, becoming less popular than they had been.[3]

Against this background of strong competition for decreasing quantities of work Maine had further, special, difficulties peculiar to his own circumstances. He had to choose one of the provincial Circuits

[1] For a general view of the Bar during these years see Raymond Cocks, *Foundations of the Modern Bar* (London, 1983), particularly chapter 4.

[2] For an attempt to interpret the *Law Lists* see D. Duman, 'Pathway to Professionalism: the English Bar in the Eighteenth and Nineteenth Centuries', *Journal of Social History*, Summer 1980, pp. 615–28, *n.b.* fn. 21.

[3] See Horace Twiss, *The Public and Private Life of Lord Chancellor Eldon* (3 vols.) (London, 1844), p. 124.

and attend its Mess. At the time, England and Wales were divided up into seven Circuits which each consisted of the assize towns of various counties that were visited in sequence by one or two judges. The largest Circuit of all was the Northern which included towns such as Lancaster. Smaller ones, sometimes much smaller ones, were to be found elsewhere and Maine as a resident of Cambridge could be expected to join the local Norfolk Circuit which, despite its name, took in most of the East Anglian towns.[4]

In one respect this was a blessing for Maine since the university had strong links with the Circuit Mess which used to dine in the town when the assizes were being held at Cambridge. Serjeant Storks and William Pryme, for example, were established Circuiteers who also were much involved in university affairs. But in another respect the Norfolk Circuit presented Maine with problems. It had a well-established reputation as a place where local 'connections' (in reality local links with attornies) were a prerequisite for anyone wishing to build up a practice and he, it seems, had no such advantages.

Also, the Norfolk Circuit was in a state of change. For example, there were new regulations about how people secured election to the Mess and there were numerous expressions of concern with problems of etiquette. Above all, there were very strong personal feuds on the Circuit and these were reflected in disputes about the Circuit's rules. In 1836 Fitzroy Kelly, the future Lord Chief Baron, had been accused by his fellow Circuiteers of electoral corruption. It looks as if the accusation was justified but the powerful and successful Kelly did not simply depart from his practice in East Anglia. As a result there were long drawn out disputes about who should be excluded from the Mess. It may be that tempers had cooled by the late 1840s but anyone in Maine's position would have had to tread carefully in local circuit affairs.

Another development served to make life at the local assizes less congenial than it had been. Before the dispute in 1836, life on Circuit was dominated by rather literary men; for example, Pryme had been an authority on political economy and a would-be writer of poetry, Crabb Robinson, the noted diarist and early supporter of University College in London, had actually been leader of the Circuit; Charles

[4] For the customs of the Norfolk Circuit during the nineteenth century see Cocks, *Foundations of the Modern Bar*, chapter 1 and generally, and 'The Bar at Assizes: Barristers on Three Nineteenth-Century Circuits', *Kingston Law Review*, vol. 6, Spring 1976, pp. 36–52; and 'Dignity and Emoluments: Thomas Blofeld's Life as a Victorian Barrister', *Kingston Law Review*, vol. 8, no. 1, April 1978, pp. 37–48.

Austin, brother of the jurist and a great debater, had been on the Circuit until the mid-1840s. It seems that this particular tradition of mixing legal work with scholarly conversation was in a state of decay on the Norfolk Circuit by about 1850. Many of the more literary men whose company Maine would have enjoyed had gone.

Despite these obstacles Maine explored the possibility of a practice on the Norfolk Circuit. If he had been merely dabbling, he could have been expected to attend the Mess at Cambridge and perhaps at those assizes which were not too distant, such as Huntingdon and Bury St Edmunds. But instead it is apparent that he wandered as far away as Norwich, and this sort of journey can only be explained in terms of some sort of determination to at least understand the work provided on Circuit.[5]

The results were not promising for Maine. After a number of assizes he seems to have given up the attempt to practise in the provinces and he no longer attended the Mess. But at least he now had experience of the law in action and it is likely that his visits to the courts made a lasting impression. They may well have left him with a certain lack of enthusiasm for the ideas of the everyday Circuiteer. They may have left him suspicious of the virtues of corporate life within the legal professions. Above all, however, they may have encouraged him to think about law as something other than a 'static' system of principles. The everyday problems of practice in the country were of great importance – any analysis of law required an analysis of professional ideas.

It was not long before Maine turned to London as the obvious alternative place to develop a practice. He probably felt that his rather academic manner would be more appreciated in the courts of equity which in most respects had a distinct and separate jurisdiction.[6] Here again, however, it was soon apparent that his decision had been a bad one for his hopes of establishing himself at the equity Bar were to fade rapidly. Almost as soon as he arrived in London he experienced periodic bouts of ill-health and any prospect of sustained work in the courts, or even in chambers, was out of the question. In addition to problems caused by his ill-health, there were difficulties which would have confronted anyone who wished to become an equity practitioner

[5] See the Minutes of the Norfolk Circuit Club, July 1851. For access to these private records, please consult the author.

[6] But see Lord Campbell, *Lives of the Lord Chancellors*, vol. 7 (London, 1850), p. 614 (on the value of a common law apprenticeship for equity practitioners).

at this time. It is possible that the early 1850s were the most difficult span of years in the entire modern history of the Chancery Bar. There seems to have been a marked decline in work – it suffered even more than the common law Bar – and this was accompanied by intense public hostility towards what were regarded as the anachronistic and extortionate requirements of Chancery barristers. In retrospect, it is difficult to grasp just how strong this sentiment was until one recalls the popularity of *Bleak House*, published in 1853.

It is hardly surprising, then, if Maine did in fact soon lose interest in the possibilities of such a practice; and it also follows that here, as with the common law Bar, he developed hostile views towards the traditionalists within the profession. It must have been frustrating to a man such as Maine to see rapid changes in the economic life of the nation which contrasted so vividly with the antiquated workings of the Court of Chancery. In social terms there was no possible good reason for such a dearth of legal work. It was as if some lawyers, in their determination to resist all reforms, were doing even more damage to their own profession than to their clients. Above all, it must have struck Maine that there was something extraordinarily inefficient about the practice of law. He had no reason to develop any affection for English law and the English legal system.

Admittedly, in his earlier writing he did make some favourable observations on the legal profession. In discussing the possible abuse of judicial power he put his disparaging views of the profession to one side and wrote admiringly of the fact that the Lord Chancellor was kept in check 'by the strong constraints of professional opinion, restraints of which the stringency can only be appreciated by those who have personally experienced them'.[7] In a further reference to his own activities and, possibly, to the poor health which he experienced at this time, he observed that 'Nobody, except perhaps a professional lawyer is perhaps in a position completely to understand how much of the intellectual strength of individuals law is capable of absorbing . . .'[8]

However, these sympathetic remarks were exceptional. He usually questioned the Bar and its ways, and he seems to have had a particular dislike of those who were taken to symbolise its virtues. For example, he criticised any mystical respect for Blackstone.[9] In an attack which went to the heart of the common law attitude to legal change, Maine

[7] *Ancient Law*, p. 65, chapter 3.
[8] *Ibid.*, p. 360, chapter 9.
[9] *Ibid.*, p. 152, chapter 5.

asserted that 'amid the many inconsistent theories which prevail concerning the character of English jurisprudence, the most popular, or at all events the one which most affects practice, is certainly a theory which assumes the adjudged cases and precedents exist antecedently to rules, principles, and distinctions'.[10]

It is as if the organiser in him could never come to terms with the oddities of an old profession which offended any person with a strong sense of order and a concern for philosophical justification. Although he does not put it in such terms himself, it is as if he was annoyed at his incapacity to defend the Victorian Bar in a scientific way; it is as if it was, for him, an unscientific institution with a habit of using inappropriate arguments and fictions. In 1856, in his *Essay on Roman Law and Legal Education*, he had spoken with obvious hope of far-reaching change: amongst other things he believed the Bar was soon going to have to come to terms with codified law and (although he did not say this explicitly) it seems that he foresaw a less exalted role for the judiciary.[11] Six years later, when *Ancient Law* was published, it was still easy to find such sentiments in his writing. The problems of professional practice always played a significant role in Maine's jurisprudence.

[10] *Ibid.*, pp. 8–9, chapter 1.

[11] *Cambridge Essays* (1856) reprinted in *Village Communities* (4th ed.) (London, 1881), pp. 330–87. One professional debate of the 1850s may have encouraged Maine to think about the transition from status to contractual relationships. In 1851 Lord Chief Justice Denman had observed that the Bar of the late 1840s had witnessed a great increase in its membership. This, he thought, had some important consequences for the way in which the profession administered itself. In the past, he believed, the Bar could be described as a *forum domesticum*: it was, as it were, an extension of family life in which frequently practitioners knew each other well and maintained standards through informal sanctions such as a concern with reputation. They did not rely upon the strict enforcement of written rules. As the Lord Chief Justice saw it, because the number of barristers had greatly increased the Bar now had to choose between one of two paths. Either it would have to develop a set of written regulations which would be enforced (presumably in a contractual manner) by much more active institutions. Or else it could simply throw away all schemes associated with rules and their enforcement – it could use wholly informal arrangements for maintaining discipline. Denman himself came down in support of the latter approach. He believed that rules always failed; competent barristers always could avoid them or interpret them in such a way as to nullify their purpose. The letter was published in *The Times* on 1 November, 1852, p. 5. For the context of the debate see Cocks, *Foundations of the Modern Bar*, pp. 88–9. Maine himself may have been the author of the critical views on the Inns of Court published on 1 December, 1855 in the *Saturday Review*, p. 76.

LEARNING LAW

In 1854, at the age of thirty-two, Maine informed a number of senior judges sitting upon a Royal Commission that the education of English lawyers should be wholly divorced from practice. He thought that there should be an end to the traditional training of lawyers; the modern world demanded an education which could never be obtained through a practical apprenticeship in the form of pupillage. Even the idea that pupillage was a desirable supplement to a theoretical course had to go. There would be no need for such an unsound, unscientific, form of learning the law; instead, apprenticeship was to be replaced by knowledge learned from books and lectures.[12]

Despite his youthfulness, Maine's ideas were taken seriously. The Royal Commission was concerned with the functions of the Inns of Court and it concluded that radical changes were needed in the way barristers were taught; in particular it recommended the creation of a new legal university.[13] Today, Maine's evidence to the Royal Commission would probably strike judges as being extraordinary and very impertinent but, at the time concerned, there was no mystery about its polite reception. As we have seen, the Bar was in a state of weakness in the mid-1850s, and new ideas of any sort were likely to obtain a respectful hearing.

Also, a well-established debate about legal education had been going on for over a quarter of a century. There had been high hopes for legal study when London University (in the form of University College) was founded in 1826. From the very start, law was to be one of the subjects to be taught; and with the appointment of John Austin there was every reason to suppose that the theoretical analysis of law as an integral part of a lawyer's preparation for his profession would come to the fore. This was what many eminent practitioners such as Earle, Spence, and Brougham hoped would happen.

In the early years of the 1830s their enthusiasm produced some notable successes in the attempt to develop legal education in London.[14] Professor Amos gave a series of lectures which won the

[12] *Report of the Commissioners appointed to enquire into the arrangements in the Inns of Court and the Inn of Chancery for promoting the study of the law and Jurisprudence*, British Parliamentary Papers, vol. 18 (1854–5), p. 101.

[13] *Ibid.*, pp. 360–1.

[14] Fortunately, there are an increasing number of studies concerned with this era of rapid change in legal ideas. See, generally, Morison, *John Austin*; Cocks, *Foundations of the Modern Bar*, chapter 2; and, for University College, London, in particular see J. H. Baker, 'University College and Legal Education', *Current Legal Problems* (1977), no. 30, p. 1.

respect and attendance of many barristers, and Professor Park, of King's College, provided a course of study which was almost as popular. The rather traditional opinions of the latter professor in all matters save legal education itself did something to show that the reform of training for the Bar need not become a merely political issue in which theoretically minded Radicals opposed practically minded Tories. Even some traditionalists now wanted a reputable place for theory.

However, it was not long before all of this came to nothing. Austin's lectures were inaudible. Park died a young man. Amos retained an audience by lecturing on what he advertised as being very practical topics. There was opposition to any sort of compulsory examination for the Bar and the one Inn of Court – the Inner Temple – which attempted to impose some sort of examination at this time soon encountered criticism. Even if there was an interest in new ideas, the early Victorian Bar was very divided in its thoughts about legal education.

When Maine began to take an interest in legal studies in the 1840s he would have heard all about these developments, and he also would have known that criticism of purely practical training was becoming stronger than it had been. For example, one author, Samuel Warren, had produced a sustained plea for changes in legal education. It soon encountered savage and emotional denunciation in part of the periodical press but, in fact, this seems to have encouraged numerous people to support Warren and his ideas. Of more general importance, some lawyers were finding the development of legal education in foreign countries an embarrassment. It really was too discomforting when people pointed out that there was more interest in legal education in many American cities than there was in London. Change was required not just because the old method of training was defective; it was also needed in order to preserve the profession's self-respect in the course of public debate about the law. This was, after all, a time when informed non-legal journals were calling for public investigations into institutions such as the Universities of Oxford and Cambridge, and when there was also increasing interest in the training of doctors and other professional men.[15]

[15] For these debates see Cocks, *Foundations of the Modern Bar*, particularly chapter 3. Samuel Warren wrote a number of books including *A Popular and Practical Introduction to Law Studies* (London, 1835) which was attacked in *Mag. and Rev.*, vol. 20 (1838), article 1, p. 239.

In response to the growing concern with these matters, Parliament set up a committee with the express task of investigating legal education.[16] When lawyers were called to provide it with evidence it was possible for the solicitors to point out in self-satisfied tones that they had already introduced a form of examination. But for the universities, and the Bar itself, the report, and the evidence which preceded it, could only be described as a major embarrassment. London University emerged with some credit for having at least attempted to start modern law degrees; these courses were still (though only just) surviving and some of the London graduates such as Jessel were to achieve eminence in later years. But the law professors of Oxford and Cambridge had to admit that their posts were, for the most part, sinecures of little importance for the study of English law or almost anything else. Maine might have attempted to show that he was something of an exception to the rule and that in fact he was engaged in various forms of teaching; for example he was in charge of a course which attracted prospective clergymen.[17] But, he did not seek to shelter behind this sort of activity and he roundly and firmly condemned the current arrangements for English legal education. In this regard, his evidence was completely in accord with that which came from the most critical witnesses such as Lord Brougham. Maine's views on the state of legal training at this time make his departure from the Regius Chair of Civil Law understandable.

The Committee on Legal Education eventually concluded that there was 'no Legal Education, worthy of the name, of a public nature, in England or Ireland'.[18] During the next few years it was intended that the remedy should be found in the establishment of proper, scientific, degrees in Law at the universities and greatly improved methods of instruction at the Inns of Court. The latter development held out the greater promise at this time since legal teaching could revive in the Inns without being encumbered with the great problems associated with the reform of the ancient universities. When Maine chose to go to London rather than to remain in Cambridge he could have hoped to enjoy the support of many leading

[16] See *Report from the Select Committee on Legal Education*, 25 August 1846, House of Commons Proceedings, p. 686.

[17] For a reference to this course see C. A. Bristed, *Five Years in an English University* (New York, 1852), p. 252. But Bristed does not consider the development of Maine's ideas.

[18] *Report from the Select Committee on Legal Education*, and see *Legal Studies*, no. 1, March 1982, at p. 1 (P. Stein).

barristers (such as Bethell and Brougham) in an attempt to develop new courses designed to improve the standing of barristers. Even if he failed to build an equity practice in London, he could at least take part in a revolutionary development in legal education.[19]

When Maine began to prepare his lectures for the Council of Legal Education, it was obvious that he was determined to develop a remarkable course of instruction. In considering his use of science and history we saw that he required his students to make extensive use of original texts and obtain a wide acquaintance with secondary material. From the specific point of view of education it is significant that all the requirements were published in the legal press without any sort of apology or qualification. It was as if they were to be as obvious a part of legal training as the associated courses in common law or real property.[20]

Yet, it was still unclear whether such a form of jurisprudence was merely a desirable type of study for the cultured gentleman or whether it was to be regarded as being a technical prerequisite for good practice. It is easy to find both views in much of what Maine himself wrote between, say, 1853 and the publication of *Ancient Law* in 1861. He seems to have taken a great personal pleasure in his studies, and for him it was obvious that the customs of ancient Greece were of intrinsic interest. But, on balance, his approach to jurisprudence at this time was much more earnest than any appeal to mere pleasure would suggest. The ideas he put before the Royal Commission on the Inns of Court in 1854 indicate very clearly that it was not just the introduction of examinations for barristers which Maine desired.[21] Even at this early stage he wanted the sort of course which would produce what men such as Brougham called an enlarged understanding of the law – an understanding which took the mind far beyond the mere technicalities of statutes and cases.

Such views were supported in numerous publications of the day. The new and very successful journal, the *Law Times*, in the course of discussing scientific law had published numerous editorials and reviews which condemned the mere 'red-tapists' who gave lawyers such a bad name. The dogmatic attachment to 'black-letter' law was held responsible for the fact that English lawyers were so often failures in

[19] Very brief indications of the way his thoughts had been developing may be found in references to English and Roman law in the announcement for the lectures of Michaelmas Term, 1848, in *Law Times*, vol. 11, p. 22.

[20] See, for example, *Law Times*, vol. 25 (1855), p. 231.

[21] *Report of the Commissioners*, pp. 97–102.

politics; they would never grasp the larger, more informed, perspective which was required for any proper understanding of public life. Edward Cox as the editor of the *Law Times* wrote a lengthy work on advocacy which had, as one of its themes, a concern with the liberal ideas which not only enlightened the would-be barrister but also were of assistance to him in a very precise way when he did his job.[22] Advocacy was the art of persuasion, and if a young man was to persuade the minds of his fellow citizens he had to understand something of the way their brains worked. Everything was of relevance to legal practice; the good advocate needed a knowledge of psychology, philosophy, literature, history, economics, politics, and even music. Cox was unusually thorough in articulating his views, but his sentiments were widely shared and could be found in other periodicals such as *The Jurist* and John Austin's *Province of Jurisprudence Determined* which had, of course, been read by Maine. It has been shown in another study that Austin's fascination with the relationship between theory and practice dominated his (Austin's) thoughts at certain times during the early 1830s.[23] When this is linked to Austin's very strong interest in Roman Law, and his enduring concern with the problems of codification, it is easy to see why Maine could be writing in the mid-1850s with such enthusiasm for the immediate relevance of ancient legal systems. One only has to supplement Austin's concern with Maine's conviction that law had to be explained in historical terms to see that the latter might expect Roman and English jurisprudence to become increasingly alike because of the possibility – as Maine saw it in the mid-1850s – of an attempt to codify the common law.[24] It is true that by 1861, in *Ancient Law* itself, Maine had modified his stance somewhat: the almost breezy optimism about the prospects for codification along Roman lines had departed. But in the mid-1850s there was nothing surprising about such an apparently robust belief. At the time concerned he had a clear and firm conviction that a good lawyer was, of necessity, a competent student of jurisprudence; and jurisprudence was a good guide to the specific problems of legal practice. It follows that the prevailing fashions of legal thought,

22 Edward Cox, *The Advocate* (London, 1852). Various parts of the book were reprinted to the point of tedium in numerous editions of the *Law Times*.

23 Cocks, *Foundations*, chapter 2. But a different emphasis is to be found generally in Morison's, *John Austin*.

24 These themes are touched upon in 'Roman Law and Legal Education' in *Cambridge Essays* (1856) reprinted in *Village Communities* (4th ed.) (London, 1881), pp. 330–87.

and the logical consequences of Maine's own beliefs about the relationship between legal theory and legal practice, reinforced his conviction that the views of practitioners had to be given an important role in jurisprudence. It was necessary to provide an extensive and scientific analysis of legal work.

3

ANCIENT LAW

Maine was thirty-nine years old when *Ancient Law* was first published in 1861, and the reader of its pages soon gains an impression that the book is the product of sustained reflection and the gradual development of generalisations over a period of time. The style of writing, just as much as the content of the book itself, suggests from the start that it is not so much a work of logic as an attempt at synthesis in which the author finds a place for many of the concerns which have been considered in the preceding chapters. Yet the breadth of these concerns has never been adequately reflected in the 'orthodox' response to *Ancient Law*. We have seen that the conventional interpretation begins with the observation that Maine reacted against the analytical statements of the utilitarian jurists; for the most part he did this by revealing that their notion of law was not of universal application but related almost exclusively to industrial societies where, for example, sovereign power could be clearly identified. Maine revealed the full extent to which Bentham and Austin had been misguided when he explained law in the sort of evolutionary terms which were so attractive to mid-Victorians. The phases which he revealed have been described in different ways by different commentators but, in most cases, six stages have been recognised in his treatment of the Indo-European societies which were of primary concern to him. Initially there were merely personal laws imposed by individuals who justified such orders by reference to divine sanctions. These laws were succeeded by customs and, in the course of time, these customs fell under the control of a minority such as an aristocracy. Eventually, there was a revolt against the minority and, under new social and political conditions, codes were created and developed. A few societies were capable of further progress and in the course of moving from systems which conferred rights by reason of 'status' to those which allocated them in accordance with 'contract' it was possible to see three distinct and successive agencies of change in the form of fictions, equity, and legislation. The context of these complicated developments was explored at length by Maine and this in turn involved him in writing in some detail about certain ancient civilisations.

But if this conventional view is to be accepted it would have to be conceded that there was a strange contrast between many of his early interests and what he wrote in his first book. Of course he was always concerned with the failings of utilitarian jurisprudence, and the evolution of different types of law. But if his previous thoughts were to be any guide to the themes of *Ancient Law* the book would also address other major problems such as the role of science as an instrument for improving legal analysis; the capacity to explain law by reference to fashionable subjects such as philology; the significance for jurists of the problems confronted by legal practitioners; the duties of those involved in legal education at a time of rapid social change, and so on. Implicit in this was the undoubted fact that during the 1850s he was writing for legal practitioners and the educated layman just as much as for those with an interest in the details of jurisprudence. Given his wide range of interests, many of which had involved him in public debate, it was unlikely that he would suddenly narrow his concerns when he wrote a book on law. It was much more probable that such a book would reflect his sustained involvement in arguments about, say, law reform and the training of modern barristers.

Therefore the best approach to an understanding of *Ancient Law* begins with the question: which audience or audiences was he addressing when he wrote the book? Was he writing for the layman, or the lawyer, or the jurist or all three? If his book is read in the light of what he might have wished to say to these groups different themes from those associated with the conventional view emerge, and *Ancient Law* may be seen as a synthesis of his previous concerns rather than as a concentrated exploration of just a few of them. It also proves to be of greater jurisprudential interest.

'ANCIENT LAW' FOR THE 'INFORMED PUBLIC'

Amongst historians it is well known that A. V. Dicey almost had an obsession with the relationship between law and public opinion. He wanted the public to understand the lawyers; he wanted the lawyers to understand the public; and he sought to illustrate the relationship between the two, in both its creative and destructive forms, by charting the history of nineteenth-century common law and legislation. In his lectures on *Law and Public Opinion* (1898) he developed ideas which have since been much criticised but which, at the same time, have formed a point of reference, perhaps *the* focal point of reference, for the attempt to understand modern legal history.[1]

This has done much to obscure the earlier efforts of legal theorists to explore the relationship between law and public opinion, and this is particularly so in regard to Maine's works. Just because he thought that law did not produce social change, so much as react to it, he said, in terms which were to become so familiar in the works of Dicey, that there could be a dangerous gap between law and fashionable thought. Law could not always keep pace, as it were, with sentiment and therefore there was always a possibility of antagonism between law and opinion. Worse still, opinion itself might be said to have a life of its own and as such it never could be used as an infallible guide to social reality. 'Everybody', wrote Maine, who is 'conversant with the philosophy of opinion is aware that a sentiment by no means dies out, of necessity, with the passing away of the circumstances which produced it. It may long survive them; nay it may afterwards attain to a pitch and climax of intensity which it never attained during their actual continuance.'[2]

Public opinion, then, was important in the development of the law but it was unlikely to yield any very obvious explanations for legal change. It was a proper subject for analysis by legislators but by itself

[1] The most recent summary of sources concerned with Dicey and modern legal history may be found in D. Sugarman's review of Cosgrove, *The Rule of Law: Albert Venn Dicey, Victorian Jurist*, in *Modern Law Review*, vol. 46 (1983), no. 1, p. 102.

[2] *Ancient Law: Its Connection with the Early History of Society and its Relation to Modern Ideas* (London, 1905), p. 223, chapter 7. I have used numerous editions in the course of trying to interpret this work but, for the sake of the reader's convenience and consistency of argument I quote from only one. The 'Popular Edition' of 1905 is the easiest to find and it is therefore the source of the quotations. However, since many of my arguments relate to the early development of Maine's thought it has been necessary to check the quotations against the first edition of 1861. The continuity which this reveals is striking; indeed to Maine's contemporaries (and others who read *Ancient Law* after his death when Pollock in particular was responsible for the printing of further editions) this continuity was notorious because it seemed to suggest that Maine (and Pollock) hardly felt obliged to respond to the numerous criticisms of Maine's views about patriarchal society. Fortunately, although there are many small changes between one edition and another the overall length of the book frequently remained much the same at about 399 pages and references to quotations in one edition usually serve as a good guide to the same references in other editions. (For a typical change relating to a small detail compare the analysis of the Greek intellect at p. 75 of the 1861 and 1875 editions.) To make cross-references easier between the different editions the references to chapters are also given.

it hardly served to account for the features of modern society. This measured, thoughtful approach to the topic was of considerable use to Maine since it enabled him to discuss matters of public concern without becoming entangled in any particular theory as to the public's general role in legal development. *Ancient Law* is full of references to topical phenomena which are carefully related to legal issues without at the same time being attached to any single, obvious, theory of legal change.

For example, he said that

> the rigidity of primitive law, arising chiefly from its early association and identification with religion, has chained down the mass of the human race to those views of life and conduct which they entertained at the time when their usages were first consolidated into a systematic form. There were one or two races exempted by a marvellous fate from this calamity, and grafts from these stocks have fertilised a few modern societies. . .[3]

Or, again, there were times when the role of opinion, even specialised professional opinion, might be explained in terms of great generalisations. For example, 'one of the rarest qualities of national character is the capacity for applying and working out the law, as such, at the cost of constant miscarriages of abstract justice without at the same time losing the hope or the wish that law may be conformed to a higher ideal'.[4]

These observations hint at a much broader concern on Maine's part; they point towards an interest not only in public opinion and its uncertain relationship with the law; they reveal an enthusiasm for the discussion of just those topics which were likely to interest the public and make his work more popular than, say, Austin's *Province of Jurisprudence Determined*.

In other words, it seems that public opinion is discussed in part because it is of relevance to legal history, and in part because it is one of a number of topics which is of interest to the non-specialist reader. There are in fact large sections of *Ancient Law* which are difficult to explain other than in terms of a desire on Maine's part to appeal to non-lawyers as well as legal specialists and scholars. For instance, he took an obvious delight in discussing the very fashionable subject of capital punishment. He argued that

> like every other institution which has accompanied the human race down the current of its history, the punishment of death is a necessity of society in

[3] *Ibid.*, pp. 77–8, chapter 4. [4] *Ibid.*, p. 75, chapter 4.

certain stages of the civilising process. There is a time when the attempt to dispense with it balks both of the two great instincts which lie at the root of all penal law. Without it the community neither feels that it is sufficiently revenged on the criminal, nor thinks that the example of his punishment is adequate to deter others from imitating him. The incompetence of the Roman Tribunals to pass sentence of death led distinctly and directly to those frightful Revolutionary intervals, known as the Proscriptions . . . No cause contributed so powerfully to the decay of political capacity of the Roman people as the periodical abeyance of the laws; and, when it once had been resorted to, we need not hesitate to assert that the ruin of Roman liberty became merely a question of time.[5]

This sort of delight in sweeping generalisations about races, laws, peoples, nations, and certain particular ideas or concepts such as capital punishment is one of the most persistent characteristics of *Ancient Law*. Maine is not simply compiling a scrap-book of incidental remarks which have some sort of controversial, colourful, appeal. There is an indication that such matters may be related to much grander themes, and when these are revealed it is apparent that they, too, seem calculated to appeal to the lay reader and are notable for being lively and debatable.

It is particularly clear that Maine relished the opportunity to write about popular moral issues. When he was not discussing the hanging of criminals he was claiming that

the truth is that the stable part of our mental, moral and physical constitution is the largest part of it, and the resistance it opposes to change is such that, though the variations of human society in a portion of the world are plain enough, they are neither so rapid nor so extensive that their amount, character, and general direction cannot be ascertained.[6]

In other words Maine believed he could accurately observe man's moral development (or the lack of it) in the same way that he could trace mental and physical phenomena. We should not be surprised, therefore, when we encounter an analysis in *Ancient Law* which suggests that certain human beings are not fully capable of coping with any sort of rule. 'It is a characteristic', he thought, 'both of uneducated minds and of early societies, that they are little able to conceive a general rule apart from the particular application of it with which they are practically familiar. They cannot dissociate a general

[5] *Ibid.*, pp. 389–90, chapter 10. [6] *Ibid.*, p. 117, chapter 5.

term or maxim from the special examples which meet them in daily experience.'[7]

This was more likely to meet with an interested response on the part of the lay reader than, say, Austin's analysis of sovereignty. What Maine may be taken to be doing at this point is to attempt moralistic, even arrogant, judgments about man's state, and these judgments are presented within the context of a discussion about progress – itself a topic which was likely to have popular appeal. However, as with the complicated relationship between law and public ideas, he never claimed that he had fully explained the occurrence of progress; he never arrived at a final, all-inclusive generalisation. It was possible for him to point, in rather cautious terms, to the prerequisites for a modern theory of progress: 'an indispensable condition of success is an accurate knowledge of Roman law in all its principal stages'.[8] Also, and more predictably, 'no one is likely to succeed in the investigation who does not clearly realise that the stationary condition of the human race is the rule, the progressive the exception'.[9] Some judgments, of limited application, could be made with confidence: when considering a large section of the human race Maine concluded that 'in China . . . progress seems to have been there arrested because the civil laws are coextensive with all the ideas of which the race is capable'. But, in the final analysis, 'the difference between the stationary and progressive societies is . . . one of the great secrets which inquiry has yet to penetrate'.[10]

In regard to all the chief problems of 'progress' Maine is singularly reticent. He certainly knows what can prevent progress, as is made abundantly clear, for example, when he points to the dangers of having no death penalty. But most of what he writes about progress itself is particularly full of self-qualification or expressed in the vaguest terms relating to national character, race, and so on. In so far as Maine is precise in this context he writes about progress with reference to analogies or parallels. Thus when he comes to discuss the phases of law in the 'journey of progress' he talks of the transition from the use of fictions to the creation of equity and, in the final stages, the use of legislation.[11] It is noticeable that these categories of law do not lead him into a detached analysis of substantive law itself. Instead

[7] *Ibid.*, p. 275, chapter 8.
[8] *Ibid.*, p. 24, chapter 2.
[9] *Ibid.*
[10] *Ibid.*, p. 23, chapter 2.
[11] *Ibid.*, p. 25, chapter 2 for a general discussion of these ideas.

they are the vehicles for colourful but very general comparisons between different phases of legal history in England and elsewhere. They look, almost, as if they might be the key to unlocking the mechanism of progress, but Maine is content, at the crucial points, to fall back upon mere description rather than explanation. Predictably, he ends with accounts of those stages which happen to be found in advanced, progressive societies. Large parts of *Ancient Law* are devoted to comparisons of social and legal circumstances which are never explained but which are, at the same time, related to a general theory of progress which seems at first sight to explore causal relationships while in reality it simply does not do this. Such a response need not be taken as a suggestion that Maine was attempting to paint a more colourful picture than his subject warranted: it is more likely that it points instead, once again, towards Maine's concern for the lay reader and his desire to explain law with reference to ideas which would be intelligible and interesting to the non-specialist. He was, as it were, dressing up in lively terms what he saw as descriptive truths.

This approach had a double advantage since it not only rendered legal progress interesting, but also enabled Maine to pronounce in vivid phrases upon the dramatic *failures* to achieve legal progress. In considering the heritage of classical Greece he wrote that

> there are two special dangers to which law, and society which is held together by law, appear to be liable in their infancy. One of them is that law may be too rapidly developed. This occurred with the codes of the more progressive Greek communities, which disembarrassed themselves with astonishing facility from cumbrous forms of procedure and needless terms of art, and soon ceased to attach any superstitious value to rigid rules and prescriptions. It was not for the ultimate advantage of mankind that they did so, though the immediate benefit conferred on their citizens may have been considerable . . . The Greek intellect, with all its mobility and elasticity, was quite unable to confine itself within the straight waistcoat of a legal formula . . . it confounded law and fact . . . questions of pure law were constantly argued on every consideration which could possibly influence the mind of the judges. No durable system of jurisprudence could be produced in this way.[12]

To the modern mind, the extent to which Maine relates almost every topic he discusses to the concept of progress is quite extraordinary. For instance, he wrote that when aristocracies 'became universally the depositaries and administrators of law'[13] it was apparent that the old custom whereby the judgments of the patriarchal chieftain were

[12] *Ibid.*, pp. 75–6, chapter 4. [13] *Ibid.*, p. 11, chapter 1.

attributed to superhuman dictation still showed itself 'here and there in the claim of a divine origin for the entire body of rules, or for certain parts of it, but', Maine adds, 'at this stage the progress of thought no longer permits the solution of particular disputes to be explored by supposing an extra-human interposition'.[14] Or, again, Maine thought that different social responses to law deserved different places on the ladder of progress. For example: 'The severance of law from morality, and of religion from law, [belongs] very distinctly to the *later* stages of mental progress.'[15]

Maine's concern with progress in general, rather than with the precise nature of progress or the mechanism of progress, is almost brutally persistent. The concern with progress is all the more significant just because Maine wrote so fluently, and the references to 'advance' are easily read and make a cumulative rather than immediate impression. In fact it is helpful to adopt an almost childish device and to underline them in important passages.

> The Roman Code was merely an enunciation in words of the existing customs of the Roman people. <u>Relatively to the progress of the Romans</u> in civilisation, it was a <u>remarkably early</u> code, and it was published at a time when <u>Roman society had barely emerged</u> from that intellectual condition in which civil obligation and religious duty are inevitably confounded. Now a <u>barbarous society</u> practising a body of customs, is exposed to some especial dangers <u>which may be absolutely fatal to its progress in civilisation</u>. The usages which a particular community is found to have adopted in its <u>infancy</u> and in its <u>primitive</u> states are generally those which are on the whole best suited <u>to promote</u> its physical and moral well-being; and, if they are retained in their integrity <u>until new social wants have taught new practices, the upward march of society is almost certain</u>. But unhappily there is a <u>law of development</u> which ever threatens to operate upon unwritten usage. The customs are of course obeyed by multitudes who are incapable of understanding the true ground of their expediency, who are therefore left inevitably to invent superstitious reasons for their <u>permanence</u>. <u>A process then commences which may be shortly described by saying that usage which is reasonable generates usage which is unreasonable. . .</u>[16]

It is easy to see why Maine has often been taken to have explained legal change in terms of progress. It is easy to ignore his occasional and very blunt assertions that the mechanisms of progress are, in the last analysis, mysterious and that the process occurs rarely. There are so many sentences in *Ancient Law* which concern themselves with when

[14] *Ibid.*, p. 12, chapter 1. [15] *Ibid.*, p. 16, chapter 1.
[16] *Ibid.*, pp. 18–19, chapter 1.

progress occurs and yet they never, in fact, actually explain how general progress happens. The specialist thinks, say, of numerous references to the actual process of alterations to old customs while the lay reader enjoys the observations on those things which render 'the upward movement of society . . . almost certain'. There is, overall, the strongest possible impression of law being understood and explored in terms of social progress understood scientifically, historically, philosophically and with especial reference to law, and this is so despite the fact that Maine himself was prepared to admit to having the most serious doubts about the matter.

It is in this context that his grand theme of 'status to contract' needs to be seen. The words status and contract are linked in explicit and forceful terms halfway through the work. 'The movement of the progressive societies has been uniform in one respect. Through all its course it has been distinguished by the gradual dissolution of family dependency, and the growth of individual obligation in its place':[17] and, a little later, he concludes that 'the movement of the progressive societies has hitherto been a movement *from Status to Contract*'.[18]

Of course, there are other references to this famous idea. 'Ancient Law, it must again be repeated, knows next to nothing of Individuals. It is concerned not with Individuals, but with Families, not with single human beings, but groups.'[19] Or again there is

> one peculiarity invariably distinguishing the infancy of society. Men are regarded and treated not as individuals, but always as members of a particular group. Everybody is first a citizen, and then, as a citizen, he is a member of his order – of an aristocracy or a democracy, of an order of patricians or plebeians; or in those societies which an unhappy fate has afflicted with a special perversion in their course of development, of a caste. Next, he is a member of a gens, house, or clan; and lastly, he is a member of his family . . . His individuality was swallowed up in his family.[20]

Just because there were so many aspects of the development of status 'the history of jurisprudence must be followed in its whole course, if we are to understand how gradually . . . society dissolved itself into the component atoms of which it is now constituted – by what insensible gradations the relation of man to man substituted itself for the relations of the individual to his family, and of families to each other'.[21]

[17] *Ibid.*, p. 168, chapter 5.
[18] *Ibid.*, p. 170, chapter 5.
[19] *Ibid.*, p. 258, chapter 8.
[20] *Ibid.*, p. 183, chapter 6.
[21] *Ibid.*, p. 185, chapter 6.

After he had arrived at this analysis of status and contract Maine applied it to numerous aspects of legal history; it may be found, for example, in some of his writing on wills as when he observed in the course of a complicated analysis of 'Ancient and Modern Ideas Respecting Wills and Successions' that 'the view of a Will which regards it as conferring the power of diverting property from the Family, or of distributing it in such uneven proportions as the fancy or good sense of the Testator may dictate, is not older than that later portion of the Middle Ages in which Feudalism has completely consolidated itself'.[22] But such observations did not constitute the most vigorous or most extensive applications of the doctrine to be found in *Ancient Law*. Instead, the most forceful remarks are to be discovered in just those sections which may reasonably be seen as having been written primarily with the lay reader in mind. It is significant, for instance, that Maine explores the moral implications of the idea of progress.

> There are few general propositions concerning the age to which we belong which seem at first sight likely to be received with readier concurrence than the assertion that the society of our day is mainly distinguished from that of preceding generations by the largeness of the sphere which is occupied in it by Contract. Some of the phenomena on which this proposition rests are among those most frequently singled out for notice, for comment, and for eulogy. Not many are so unobservant as not to perceive that in innumerable cases where old law fixed a man's social position irreversibly at his birth, modern law allows him to create it for himself by convention; and indeed several of the few exceptions which remain to this rule are constantly denounced with passionate indignation. The point for instance, which is really debated in the vigorous controversy still carried on upon the subject of negro servitude is whether the status of the slave does not belong to bygone institutions, and whether the only relation between employer and labourer which commends itself to modern morality be not a relation determined exclusively by contract.[23]

Maine pursued the moral implications of the distinction between status and contract with determination. He went out of his way – in the sense that he deviated from what we would regard as more obvious arguments – to relate the morality of contract to the more controversial moral notions of everyday life in England. He was particularly worried at the idea that his theory of contract flew in the face of modern ethical beliefs. He believed that a society based on contract was a society in which, of necessity, individuals had come to adopt high moral standards, and these standards, he believed, enabled them to trust each other in the course of commercial and other dealings. Yet

[22] *Ibid.*, pp. 223–4, chapter 7. [23] *Ibid.*, pp. 304–5, chapter 9.

Maine had to concede that in the Victorian society of his day there were large-scale frauds which ruined individuals and families who had committed their savings to famous banks. He responded by admitting that he was faced

> by the spectacle of frauds, unheard of before the period at which they were observed, and astonishing from their complication as well as shocking from their criminality. But the very character of these frauds shows clearly that, before they became possible, the moral obligations of which they are the breach must have been more than proportionately developed. It is the confidence reposed and deserved by the many which affords facilities for the bad faith of the few, so that, if colossal examples of dishonesty occur, there is no surer conclusion than that scrupulous honesty is displayed in the average of the transactions which, in the particular case, have supplied the delinquent with his opportunity.[24]

This rather strained argument does something to reveal the extent to which Maine was prepared to go in relating his analysis of law to popular notions of his day. At the very point – status to contract – which has been most explored by the later, scholarly, readers of *Ancient Law*, we find that Maine himself is primarily concerned not with detailed academic analysis but rather with the relationship between his legal ideas and the thoughts of the informed non-specialist reader.

For the modern student of jurisprudence there are two possible reactions to this. Either Maine has to be seen as a jurist with a serious weakness when exposed to the opportunity to write about popular ideas which might enhance his public reputation. Or else, Maine's effort to write in this way constituted an especial contribution to the development of English jurisprudence: he enabled the law to be explained in terms of ideas which could be understood and appreciated by laymen and in doing so transformed certain beliefs about law.

Unfortunately, it has to be said that there is some evidence to support the first contention. Maine enjoyed journalism at least as much as jurisprudence. Also, there was a certain restlessness about the young Maine's academic life: the man who was happy to go on to administrative work in India had already turned his back on a Regius Chair at Cambridge and become involved in the lively debates about legal reform which characterised the 1850s. The merely academic analysis of law was too constricting for his tastes.

However, the journalistic instincts were never in command. Maine

[24] *Ibid.*, pp. 306–7, chapter 9.

set out to relate his popular ideas to his purely legal work: morality did play a different role at different times in the evolution of law; progress might (by definition) be desirable but, in his eyes, it was also an essential instrument for understanding and comparing different laws; status and contract were more than terms which accorded with popular debate – to Maine they seemed to characterise the chief phases of the law where it had, somehow, been pushed or pulled into the civilised world.

If this does not sound convincing, it is helpful to go further and compare Maine's approach with that of the chief English legal theorist of early Victorian times, John Austin. There is in fact much more than merely legal analysis in Austin's work, *The Province of Jurisprudence Determined*.[25] As the title suggests, the author was concerned with the frontiers of his subject and he therefore had much to say about ethics, philosophy and politics. However, as anyone who has actually turned to his books knows, the obsession Austin had with very precise expression and shades of meaning resulted in long chapters which are very difficult to read. Maine must surely have been well aware of this; he may have felt that although Austin had achieved something remarkable for jurisprudence he had failed to express himself in such a way as to carry the topic into any but the highest levels of political debate. The sombre reputation which Austin had acquired, and the possibility that this had also influenced the vision of jurisprudence entertained by the more informed members of the public, does much to explain the popular content of *Ancient Law*.

But even if this is correct it still leaves untouched the question of how a concern with intelligibility to the layman influenced the content, as distinct from the style, of Maine's analysis of law. It did so in more than one way. He was encouraged to turn towards historical jurisprudence just because it was a more popular subject for discussion than analytic, Benthamite legal philosophy. Maine was anxious to show that legal debate need not be confined to legal minds; there was no need for modern society to relinquish such control as it had over the development of the law to highly technical specialists. Instead of the complex analysis of Austin with its focus upon the idea of a command (which Maine, of course, found unsatisfactory), or the complacent assumption of practitioners and judges that the virtues of existing law were self-evident (which Maine found risible), there was the prospect of redefining law in terms of a debate carried on by

25 See, for numerous indications of this, Morison, *John Austin*.

informed citizens in response to changing social circumstances. The focus of attention shifts, therefore, from the courts to a much broader understanding of law as the expression of values on the part of educated minds. Instead of thinking in terms of either commands or red-robed judges, the students of legal theory had to define law as a facet of culture and, in doing so, give it a novel content; and this was not a merely descriptive process for if law was to be explained in these terms it became necessary to consider how it should be discussed, and who should discuss it.

'ANCIENT LAW' FOR THE LAWYERS

It would be difficult to overemphasise the ambiguity of the things which Maine had to say about English law in his first book. For example, he was equivocal in his many attempts to compare Roman Law and English Law:

> It is true that in the wealth of legal principle we are considerably poorer than several modern European nations. But they, it must be remembered, took the Roman jurisprudence for the foundation of their civil institutions. They built the *débris* of the Roman Law into their walls; but in the materials and workmanship of the residue there is not much which distinguishes it favourably from the structure erected by the English judicature.[26]

It really is difficult to know how to interpret such statements. Is he praising the common law, or condemning it?

However, in one matter relating to the lawyers themselves, Maine was much less equivocal. When he wrote of the judiciary, he stated

> Now, it is quite true that there was once a period at which the English common law might reasonably have been termed unwritten. The elder English judges did really pretend to knowledge of rules, principles, and distinctions which were not entirely revealed to the bar and to the lay-public. Whether all the law which they claimed to monopolise was really unwritten, is exceedingly questionable; but, at all events, on the assumption that there was once a large mass of civil and criminal rules known exclusively to the judges, it presently ceased to be unwritten law. . .[27]

Maine was at least as insistent as Bentham in attacking what he saw as the absurd, almost mystical, claims of the judiciary to be the only group of British society which understood the law. He was always

[26] *Ancient Law*, p. 40, chapter 2. [27] *Ibid.*, p. 13, chapter 1.

ready to attack the idea that there was something special about the common law because it was unwritten. 'At the present moment', he observed,

> a rule of English Law has first to be disentangled from the recorded facts of adjudged printed precedents, then thrown into a form of words varying with the taste, precision, and knowledge of the particular judge, and then applied to the circumstances of the case for adjudication. But at no stage of this process has it any characteristic which distinguishes it from written law.[28]

This desire to attack the courts and the bogus claims (as he saw them) of the old judiciary was linked to Maine's enthusiasm for codification. It is particularly clear in this context that Maine saw the possibility of codifying the law as having the great advantage of abstracting legal debate from the monopolistic claims of certain lawyers. In other words, just as Maine wrote about the law in such a way as to open it up for public analysis he did not flinch at this point from demanding an appropriate change in the ways of English lawyers. His determination even led him towards a form of unqualified praise for just those theories which he usually disparaged – theories which did at least challenge the otherwise unquestioning acceptance of the ideas adhered to by practitioners. In discussing legal theory he wrote of a time when 'legal theories were more abundant than at present – theories which, it is true, were for the most part gratuitous and premature enough, but which nevertheless rescued jurisprudence from that worse and more ignoble condition, not unknown to ourselves, in which nothing like a generalisation is aspired to, and law is regarded as a mere empirical pursuit . . .'[29]

This form of qualified approval for all types of legal theory as an antidote to professional short-sightedness posed problems for Maine, particularly when he came to write about Blackstone. In a few places in *Ancient Law* he was notably respectful towards the *Commentaries*. On one occasion he even compared some of his ideas with those of Savigny. But in other places the attitude is very different. 'In all the literature which enshrines the pretended philosophy of law, there is nothing more curious than the pages of elaborate sophistry in which Blackstone attempts to explain and justify the exclusion of the half-blood.'[30] In a more determined mood he condescended to observe that

[28] *Ibid.*, p. 14, chapter 1.
[29] *Ibid.*, p. 175, chapter 6.
[30] *Ibid.*, p. 152, chapter 5.

Blackstone was 'always a faithful index of the average opinions of his day'.[31] Since Maine had rather a poor opinion of even the best of eighteenth-century English lawyers this was something of an insult. Of more significance for present purposes is the fact that he could be at least as free in his criticism of attempts to justify the law on the part of nineteenth-century lawyers. In respect of one branch of the law he wrote that

> it is easily seen by English lawyers that English equity is a system founded on moral rules; but it is forgotten that these rules are the morality of past centuries – not of the present – that they have received nearly as much application as they are capable of, and that though of course they do not differ largely from the ethical creed of our own day, they are not necessarily on a level with it . . . Many writers of treatises on equity, struck with the completeness of the system in its present state, commit themselves expressly or implicitly to the paradoxical assertion that the founders of the chancery jurisprudence contemplated its present fixity of form when they were settling its first basis . . . Equity has its place and its time; but I have pointed out that another instrumentality is ready to succeed it when its energies are spent.[32]

The reference to 'another instrumentality' which is 'ready to succeed' reveals that, as *always* when Maine is considering a body of law or the beliefs of a group of practitioners, he is viewing them in the context of progress and making moral judgments – often unfavourable – as he does so. The other 'instrumentality' in question is legislation, and it could hardly escape the readers' attention that this new body of law was not wholly under the control of the lawyers at the time at which it was created: ideally, it was, of course, the product of informed public opinion reflected in the beliefs of Members of Parliament.

Maine's treatment of English lawyers led him to attack their beliefs about legal fictions. In this context, he gave the term 'fiction' a sense

> considerably wider than that in which English lawyers are accustomed to use it, and with a meaning much more extensive than that which belonged to the Roman *fictiones* . . . I employ the expression 'Legal Fiction' to signify any assumption which conceals, or affects to conceal, the fact that a rule of law has undergone alteration, its letter remaining unchanged, its operation being modified . . . At a particular stage of social progress they are invaluable expedients for overcoming the rigidity of law . . . We must not suffer ourselves to be affected by the ridicule which Bentham pours on legal fictions whenever he meets them. To revile them as merely fraudulent is to betray ignorance of their peculiar office in the historical development of law. But at the same time it would be equally foolish to agree with those theorists who,

[31] *Ibid.*, p. 231, chapter 8. [32] *Ibid.*, pp. 69–70, chapter 3.

discerning that fictions have had their uses, argue that they ought to be stereotyped in our system. There are several fictions still exercising powerful influence in English jurisprudence which could not be discarded without a severe shock to the ideas, and considerable change in the language, of English practitioners; but there can be no doubt of the general truth that it is unworthy of us to effect an admittedly beneficial object by so rude a device as a legal fiction. I cannot admit any anomaly to be innocent, which makes the law either more difficult to understand or harder to arrange in harmonious order.[33]

Maine therefore invents his own 'fictions', gives them a place in legal progress, castigates Bentham for his failure to understand the creativity of fictions in their conventional form, and then turns upon practitioners for their respect for such fictions despite their 'beneficial object'. Having invented a category of law Maine has, as it were, to fight very hard in order to accommodate its potential uses with his other ideas. Even if it is possible to reconcile these statements through arguing that Maine is using the word 'fiction' in different senses, it is difficult to see precisely what he means.

In the final analysis, some of Maine's remarks about the lawyers become more than ambiguous; they become contradictory. It is necessary to recall in emphatic terms that Maine did not see the law itself as the great agent of progress. It often was a prerequisite for social progress; after all, 'it binds society together'. But it was not the law itself which produced change. As we saw in the Introduction, Maine believed that in progressive societies at least,

social necessities and social opinion are always more or less in advance of Law. We may come indefinitely near to the closing of the gap between them, but it has a perpetual tendency to reopen. Law is stable; the societies of which we are speaking are progressive. The greater or less happiness of a people depends on the degree of promptitude with which the gulf is narrowed.[34]

These ideas paint a bleak picture for future lawyers and judges. Once again, the idea that the common law and the ways of the Bar are in some sense self-justifying or definable in terms of tradition is out of the question. Instead the lawyer has a much humbler role; his chief task is to see that the law is changed as quickly as possible in order that the gap between legal practice and public criticism does not become too wide. The lawyer does not impose law upon society; society reveals to him the constant need for him to change his ways.

Maine could have gone on to try to develop a place for lawyers in

[33] *Ibid.*, pp. 25–7, chapter 2. [34] *Ibid.*, p. 24, chapter 2.

this scheme of social change which gave them a more elevated role without, at the same time, challenging the logic of his theory of progress. Forty years later, when theoreticians were far more interested in defending the common law than they had been in mid-Victorian times, Dicey provided a reinterpretation of this aspect of Maine's thought. Just as both men were concerned at the undesirable consequences of a gap developing between law and public opinion, so they also wrote enthusiastically of the pressing need for harmony: and this was more than a quest for general harmony between opinion and law since both men used the word harmony in the same sort of context.[35] But for Dicey, the lawyer – be he practitioner or judge – was not merely a servant of public opinion. Dicey had no intention of defending the traditions of the common law and the powers of English lawyers in terms which suggested that tradition conferred upon them self-evident virtues. However, in Dicey's view lawyers could be defended in terms of their utility. For him their chief usefulness lay in the fact that their lives were dominated by the practical demands of everyday work and not the grand theories which so often misled their continental brothers. The practical experience of the courts gave senior lawyers and judges the capacity for sound judgment in slowly relating the demands for, say, the reform of property laws concerning women to the technical difficulties involved in changing the law itself. The lawyers would usually exercise their proper role by *slowing down* or simply blunting the influence of popular ideas upon the law. There were only a few times when they should act in *advance* of public opinion. In other words, Dicey wanted harmony but he was prepared to take bigger risks in producing disharmony if the public was so ill-informed as to demand changes which conflicted with the sound judgments of the trained and experienced legal mind. For Dicey, lawyers had an important role in public life which was, at least in part, self-directing.[36] For Maine such autonomous power was intolerable – the importance of lawyers lay in their capacity to carry out the bridging act demanded by public opinion. But both were writing about the same problem; both were trying to define the proper social role for lawyers.

[35] For general concern on Dicey's part see his *Law of the Constitution* (London, 1885), p. 356 and *Law and Public Opinion* (London, 1898), Lectures 4 and 5. For similar concern on Maine's part see *Ancient Law*, chapter 2. For precise parallels, see *Law and Public Opinion*, Introduction to 2nd ed. (London, 1904), p. xxviii, and *Ancient Law*, p. 25, chapter 2.

[36] See Cocks, *Foundations of the Modern Bar*, chapter 9.

Both Maine and Dicey had an enduring fascination with the ideas and ways of French lawyers. Dicey attempted to set them up as straw men in order to justify his defence of the English common lawyers: at certain times in his life he attributed to them ideas which he could, without much difficulty, have discovered to be very different from those which they in fact held. Maine also enjoyed generalisations at their expense and he used these assertions to buttress his own notions about what made for a good lawyer and a good legal profession. Typically, in considering French law Maine started by emphasising the importance of ideas. 'The part played by jurists in French history, and the sphere of jural conceptions in French thought, have always been remarkably large . . .' He went on to observe, for example, that

> the lawyers of France immediately formed a strict alliance with the Kings of the house of Capet and Valois, and it was as much through their assertions of royal prerogative, and through their interpretations of the rules of feudal succession, as by the power of the sword that the French monarchy at last grew together out of the agglomeration of provinces and dependences.

Again and again Maine returns to the importance of ideas. The lawyers could only acquire such power because there was 'a great enthusiasm for generalisation and a curious admiration for all general propositions' which was accompanied by an enormous respect for written texts of law. It followed that

> when the French kings had brought their long struggle for supremacy to a successful close . . . the situation of the French jurists was peculiar, and continued to be so down to the outbreak of the Revolution. On the one hand, they formed the best instructed and nearly the most powerful class in the nation . . . Their judicial tact, their ease of expression, their fine sense of analogy and harmony, and (if they may be judged by the great names among them) their passionate devotion to their conceptions of justice, were as remarkable as the singular variety of talent which they included . . . But, on the other hand, the system of laws which they had to administer stood in striking contrast with the habits of mind which they had cultivated. The France which had been in great part constituted by their efforts was smitten with the curse of an anomalous and dissonant jurisprudence beyond every other country in Europe.[37]

For Maine, with his persistent interest in the analysis of the relationship between a style of life and the ideas associated with it, this could only lead to dangerous behaviour;

> the speculative opinions of the lawyers and their intellectual bias was in the

[37] For these references to French law and history see *Ancient Law*, pp. 80–4, chapter 4.

strongest opposition to their interests and professional habits. With the keenest sense and the fullest recognition of those perfections of jurisprudence which consist in simplicity and uniformity, they believed, or seemed to believe, that the vices which actually infested French law were ineradicable.

From this point he embarked upon a protracted analysis designed to show, amongst other things, that these tensions produced a most undesirable consequence in that it turned French lawyers into 'passionate enthusiasts for Natural Law'.[38]

His analysis of French legal ideas is extraordinarily extensive given the fact that he was, ostensibly, writing about ancient law. It highlights his concern with modern developments and provided a vehicle for him to express once again his ideas about the proper role for lawyers. Ideas are of the first importance; they determine the role of law in society. In particular the ideas of the lawyers are important, and it is essential that these ideas do not become, as it were, detached from the reality of the law which they administer. If legal practice and legal theory draw apart the consequences are undesirable for both.

A logical response to this would lead to the conclusion that Maine was giving lawyers a more positive role here than he does elsewhere. He did not suggest that they should simply enforce those laws which happen to be accepted by a particular community: he obviously wanted them to view such regulations with a critical eye and, if possible, improve them. But in all probability this does not conflict with the other things he has said about lawyers in *Ancient Law*: it seems rather to suggest once again that the lawyer as lawyer should not let his professional interests distort or warp the law; but the lawyer as citizen may of course play a role in the development of appropriate social ideas which should be reflected in the law. This view would at least be consistent with what Maine was saying about legal education: it was essential to raise the training of lawyers above the level of mere technique and to give them a sense of their place in history.

In writing about French law Maine emphasised once more the bold outlines of his theories concerning the role of the professional in modern society. Professional conventions and beliefs were not in some way self-justifying: they had to be justified by reference to external non-professional criteria. The values of everyday practice were not self-evident. Law and legal practice were the focal point of a battle between competing ideas, and, if a man was going to be a good lawyer, he had to begin with an understanding of this fact.

[38] *Ibid.*, p. 85, chapter 4.

Certainly, the philosophy of law was no longer to be a series of inconsequential comments about the virtues of the common law. But nor was it to be presented in terms which demanded radical political reforms (in the manner of Bentham) or in terms which made it almost incomprehensible and therefore irrelevant and unattractive to the non-specialist (in the manner of Austin). Instead, we see once again that good law was to be the expression of educated and cultured minds perpetually in search of the most creative and constructive method of bridging the ever-growing gap between old law and new opinion. Law was such that, by itself, the legal mind could never make good law.

'ANCIENT LAW' FOR THE THEORISTS

The appeal of *Ancient Law* for theorists was obvious. Quite apart from his attempts to limit the power of the legal profession, Maine was providing a novel blend of science and history and applying it to law. Also, in his more detailed arguments, he was developing ideas about jurisprudence which demanded some sort of response from other mid-Victorian jurists. For example, he had a concern with the problems of anachronism and objectivity in the history of legal thought. His interest in accurate, and even 'scientific', historical judgment appears to have made him very much aware of the dangers involved in using modern ideas as a guide to the understanding of the law of another age,[39] and his interest in this problem led him to express a most forceful dissent from the approach of Bentham and Austin. It is well known that he claimed they had failed properly to understand certain aspects of law such as sovereignty because of their failure to come to terms with history. It is less well known that this attack was based only in part on their tendency to ignore history. He was just as critical of the fact that, on the occasions when they did try to use history, they made serious errors of judgment in taking for granted their capacity to relate the legal systems of the past to the ideas of eighteenth- and nineteenth-century Britain. Maine thought that Bentham in particular had, at times, *attempted* legal history; it was just that he was scornful of Bentham's historical judgment.

For instance, he observed that Bentham believed that 'societies modify and have always modified, their laws according to modifications of their views of general expediency'. Maine responded to this by saying that

[39] See, generally, *Ibid.*, p. 236, chapter 7; pp. 310–11, chapter 9.

it is difficult to say that the proposition is false, but it certainly appears to be unfruitful. For that which seems expedient to a society, or rather to the governing part of it, when it alters a rule of law, is surely the same thing as the object, whatever it may be, which it has in view when it makes the change. Expediency and the greatest good are nothing more than different names for the same impulse which promotes the modification, and when we lay down expediency as the rule of change in law or opinion, all we get by the proposition is the substitution of an express term for a term which is necessarily implied when we say that a change takes place.[40]

However, in other paragraphs Maine was more blunt and went far beyond a criticism of Bentham. He saw that

there is such widespread dissatisfaction with existing theories of jurisprudence, and so general a conviction that they do not really solve the questions they pretend to dispose of, as to justify the suspicion that some line of enquiry, necessary to a perfect result, has been incompletely followed or altogether omitted by their authors.

Again, the problem of anachronism is crucial to the philosopher of law. The fault of past theorists is that

they take no account of what law has actually been at epochs remote from the particular period at which they made their appearance. Their originators carefully observed the institutions of their own age and civilisation, . . . but when they turned their attention to archaic states of society which exhibited much superficial difference from their own, they uniformly ceased to observe and began guessing.[41]

As always with Maine this form of argument was of immediate relevance to Victorian legal thought. He did not seek merely enhanced historical understanding; instead he used the new truths as an argument in his discussion about the need for reform. In his own moralistic phrases, he admonished his readers with the idea that 'the grand source of mistake in questions of jurisprudence is the impression that those reasons which actuate us at the present moment, in the maintenance of an existing institution, have necessarily anything in common with the sentiment in which the institution originated'.[42]A concern with anachronism was always of importance to Maine in both the purely historical and the more polemical aspects of his work.

There was another persistent concern of Maine's in *Ancient Law* which was of as much relevance to the problems of legal theory and which engaged his feelings to an extent that few other topics could

[40] *Ibid.*, p. 118, chapter 5.
[41] *Ibid.*, pp. 118–19, chapter 5.
[42] *Ibid.*, p. 189, chapter 6.

rival. His thoughts about the various uses to which the law of nature had been put by social theorists were expressed in the strongest terms. He devoted two whole chapters to, respectively, the *Law of Nature and Equity* and *The Modern History of the Law of Nature* and there are references to the notion throughout the book.

The Law of Nature confused the Past and the Present. Logically, it implied a state of Nature which had once been regulated by natural law; yet the jurisconsults do not speak clearly or confidently of the existence of such a state, which indeed is little noticed by the ancients except where it finds a poetical expression in the fancy of a golden age.

The more recent analysts had failed completely to understand the concept:

in truth modern speculations on the Law of Nature betray much more indistinctness of perception and are vitiated by much more hopeless ambiguity of language than the Roman lawyers can be justly charged with. There are some writers on the subject who attempt to evade the fundamental difficulty by contending that the code of Nature exists in the future and is the goal to which all civil laws are moving, but this is to reverse the assumptions on which the old theory rested, or rather perhaps to mix together two inconsistent theories.[43]

As always, Maine is very concerned with the practical damage which may result from the acceptance of these bad ideas.

The doctrines and institutions which may be attributed to it are the material of some of the most violent controversies debated in our time, as will be seen when it is stated that the theory of Natural Law is the source of almost all the special ideas as to law, politics, and society which France during the last hundred years has been the instrument of diffusing over the western world.[44]

If there was any man for whose ideas he had an unequivocal hatred it was Rousseau: he had turned the theory of natural law upside down. The contemplation of the law of nature had been replaced by thought about the state of nature and for this Rousseau was largely responsible.[45] From this point Maine becomes emotional.

It is not worth our while to analyse with any particularity that philosophy of politics, art, education, ethics and social relations which was constituted on the basis of a state of nature . . . But though the philosophy founded on the hypothesis of a state of nature has fallen low in general esteem, in so far as it is looked upon under its coarser and more palpable aspect, it does not follow that

[43] *Ibid.*, pp. 73–4, chapter 4. [44] *Ibid.*, p. 80, chapter 4.
[45] *Ibid.*, p. 88, chapter 4.

> in its subtler disguise it has lost plausibility, popularity, or power. I believe, as I have said, that it is still the great antagonist of the Historical Method; and whenever . . . any mind is seen to resist or contemn that mode of investigation, it will generally be found under the influence of a prejudice or a vicious bias traceable to a conscious or unconscious reliance on a non-historic, natural condition of society or the individual . . . Looking back, however, to the period at which the theory of the state of nature acquired the maximum of political importance, there are few who will deny that it helped most powerfully to bring about the grosser disappointments of which the first French Republic was fertile. It gave birth, or intense stimulus, to the vices of mental habit all but universal at the time, disdain of positive law, impatience of experience, and the preference of *a priori* to all other reasoning . . . its tendency is to become distinctly anarchical.[46]

Maine's anger had more than one source. He found the old continental arguments about natural law a futile exercise. He wanted to ensure that if he did persuade English legal theorists to take a greater interest in history he did not, at the same time, lead them towards arguments about what the past had proved to be 'Natural'. In addition, his distrust of *a priori* reasoning was exceptionally strong and he could be expected to attack it with vigour when it appeared in any fashionable doctrine. As we have seen, he is most careful not to make any reference at the start of *Ancient Law* to the doctrine of 'status to contract' – the principle is only 'discovered' after a great deal of material has been considered. A disregard for experience and 'sober research' was, as he saw it, characteristic of all those violent and anarchical political movements of modern times which so worried Maine when he turned to journalistic writing; and it would have been surprising if these feelings had not done at least something to influence the content of *Ancient Law* at this point.

Modern critics have given very little attention to Maine's lengthy excursion into the legal theories associated with the law of nature. Presumably the lack of interest arises in part because natural law was hardly of interest to English lawyers between the time at which Maine wrote and the mid-twentieth century; his concern with the topic – in so far as it was mentioned at all – was seen as being incidental to his interest in, say, the social context of law. The highly selective quality of this modern perspective is apparent when one reads the references in modern textbooks of jurisprudence to Maine's determined attack on the failings of Austin and Bentham. In fact in *Ancient Law* itself his comments on these writers are *much* less frequent and *much* more

46 *Ibid.*, pp. 89–92, chapter 4.

conciliatory than his remarks on natural law; the student of legal philosophy would entirely miss the most vigorous and lively passages of *Ancient Law* if he thereby was led to ignore Maine's assault on natural law in legal argument. It concerned Maine more than any of the utilitarian theories.

The best way of explaining the full length of Maine's analysis of natural law, and at the same time of accommodating it within the evolution of his own jurisprudential ideas, is to return once again to his capacity to write in such a way as to make legal philosophy intelligible and even a source of pleasure to the layman. In this context the debate about natural law had obvious advantages since it could easily be related to topics of widespread interest such as the influence of French ideas or the dangers of merely theoretical reasoning. At the same time he could talk in very scholarly terms of the role of the law of nature in Greek thought and Roman jurisprudence – he could even draw appropriate contrasts with the modern notions of the common law. All of these issues could be related to each other in his attempt to produce scientific results which reflected diligent historical research rather than prejudice; for Maine the very idea of the law of nature presupposed bad, unscientific and unhistorical reasoning – it rested on misinterpretations of Roman Law and the most fanciful notions of man's early state. It was a very convenient instrument for showing how the scholarly destruction of erroneous legal theories could take place in terms which were immediately comprehensible to the informed reader who nevertheless lacked a legal training. Good legal theory enabled law to be expressed in ways which made it comprehensible to properly educated citizens.

A SYNTHESIS

In considering Maine's use of Victorian ideas about science, history, philology, and legal education it has become apparent that it would be wrong to attribute to his early life any self-conscious, deliberate attempt at interdisciplinary writing in the modern academic sense of the term. Once he had decided to write a work on jurisprudence his circumstances were such that it would have been difficult for him even to have conceived of law and legal change within the confines of modern academic categories. It would have been odd for him to do other than range across the subject matter of what is now anthropology, history, the history of ideas, legal history, statute law, case law, custom, and so on. And he could do this without any of the methodological self-consciousness apparent in some modern interdisciplinary work.

It was the *way* he discussed matters just as much as *what* he discussed which was important. He avoided the 'elaborate sophistry' of Blackstone.[47] He did not require the reader to jettison as irrelevant or pernicious large numbers of everyday historical and cultural assumptions in the manner that was demanded by Bentham's interpretations of utilitarianism. Bentham's ideas, at least in the limited form in which they were available to the nineteenth-century reader, were expressed with clarity, but most of them were scarcely presented in such a way as to appeal to the layman. They certainly did not, for the most part, contain a sympathetic attempt to relate legal theory to ideas about the Greeks, the Romans, science, history, evolutionary progess and the like. The contrast with Austin is even more vivid. Maine concentrated upon writing lucidly about just those topics which were likely to interest a wide readership.

Also, it can be seen that it would be a mistake for us to concentrate exclusively upon the idea which, to a greater extent than any other, has now become associated with the content of *Ancient Law*. Obviously, the discovery of a change from status to contract within progressive societies was of great importance both to Maine and his early readers. But in considering Maine's achievement as a whole even these matters are much less striking than the way in which the book was written. A large amount of source material was integrated into arguments which attempted to respond to ideas about history, science, evolution, politics and philosophy. It was not methodically related to some single theory of progress.

The synthesis which Maine attempted contained acute strains, but some of its closely woven themes persisted from first to last and it is these which need to be brought to the fore once again. In particular he was anxious to show that the proper role for a lawyer during an era of rapid change was modest and passive: the lawyer had no sort of right to plead that only he understood the law; on the contrary it was his humble task to assist others in expressing new ideas in new legal terms and thereby to prevent a great gap developing between law and social opinion. Informed laymen should understand and direct the development of the law. If it really was the case that only the lawyers understood the law, then the law was bad and social harmony was endangered.

[47] *Ibid.*, p. 152, chapter 5.

This analysis of the proper role for the lawyer accorded with Maine's beliefs as to the proper role for the jurist. It was the task of the latter to ensure that the law was expressed in a form that was as clear and as simple as was possible. But Benthamite clarity by itself was not enough; in addition the law had to be explained in terms of cultural developments, past and present, and the explanation had to be presented in such a way as to engage the interest and informed criticism of the educated reader. Always, the law was too important to be left to the professional lawyers.

So, the synthesis of ideas and arguments which Maine presented in *Ancient Law* was remarkable, but, at the same time, it was most delicately balanced. There was no reason to believe that he could forever sustain his careful mixture of interests in science and history, legal evolution and social stability, philosophical speculation and political opinion. The extraordinary thing was that at one time in his life he had been able to achieve some sort of synthesis within the covers of a single book. For the early 1860s at least, it looked as if Maine had proved – and proved in a scientific manner – that jurisprudence should play a vital role in the understanding of society and the proper management of social change. It was as if he had written a legal manual for the guidance of good citizens.

Just because the synthesis was so delicately balanced it was likely to fall victim to attacks from numerous directions with critics focusing on isolated issues. For some, *Ancient Law* would be associated with a few specific and very controversial ideas rather than with Maine's general method of argument. Others, with more justification, would observe that Maine had not even attempted to provide definitive answers to many of the chief problems which he discussed. For example, he had not explained progress, legal or otherwise; and for all the faults which he had observed in utilitarian theory his precise opinion of Bentham and Austin was not yet apparent. Maine had shown how certain jurisprudential questions *might* be answered by having regard to historical facts, but he himself had not yet answered the questions.

By allowing his interests to range so widely, and by ensuring that his ideas would appeal to a substantial readership, Maine had already done much for English jurisprudence. He had given it an identity which was independent of both professional thought and the theories of the utilitarians. In itself, the creation of this identity was a significant achievement; and it was all the more striking because it had been accomplished without any sustained theoretical analysis as to the nature of law. Taken as a whole, the impressive but strange nature of *Ancient Law* as a work of jurisprudence is well illustrated by two facts. Its breadth of vision ensured that it is of some relevance to almost any school of legal theory, past or present. But nowhere in the book did Maine seek rigorously to apply some explanatory theory to *all* of his observations, and as a result although we speak easily of Benthamite or Austinian jurisprudence there is no such thing as a 'Mainian' theory of law.

4

AFTER *ANCIENT LAW*

INDIAN VILLAGES AND ENGLISH UTILITARIANS

An enthusiasm for Indian topics formed a consistent theme to Maine's writing: between the time of his early contributions to the *Saturday Review* in the mid-1850s and the publication of his last book in 1884, he wrote about the subcontinent in vivid terms. This fascination was in part the product of the subject's intrinsic interest; but in part, too, it was the product of Maine's pleasure in attacking the parochialism of his fellow Victorians: and this was so whether their prejudices arose out of some form of national intolerance, or a narrow vision of the common law, or religious dogmatism, or simple ignorance on any matter of any sort. For example, of Buckle's *History of Civilisation* he observed that the author

> has derived all the distinctive institutions of India and the peculiarities of its people from their consumption of rice. From this fact, he tells us, that the exclusive food of the natives of India is of an oxygenous rather than a carbonacious character, and it follows by an inevitable law that caste prevails, that oppression is rife, that rents are high; and that custom and law are stereotyped. The passage ought to be a caution against over-bold generalisation; for it unfortunately happens that the ordinary food of the people of India is not rice.[1]

In contrast, Maine was much more cautious in his use of generalisations relating to India. His colourful pronouncements were linked to qualifications and references to what was not yet known. His hesitant explanation of caste as a product of certain developments in trades and crafts was so embarrassingly simple that he himself wished to emphasise the oddity and inexplicability of its origin as an 'extraordinary calamity' in the history of Indian life and thought. In this context he was very much aware of the dangers inherent in any

[1] 'The Effects of the Observation of India on Modern European Thought', Rede Lecture, 1875, reprinted in *Village Communities* (London, 1885), pp. 213–14.

dogmatic use of his own discussion of status and contract as providing the major signpost on the route to progress. Faced with a great population of people whom he frequently found to be of the highest intelligence, and whose social arrangements were indisputably of the most sophisticated kind, he could only wonder at the inability of himself and other social analysts to explain the failure of such a society to achieve what he regarded as 'progess'. India, more than any other subject, prevented Maine from generalising with confidence about the actual mechanisms of evolutionary change, and, when he arrived in India for the first time in 1862, his sensitivity to information from sources outside his own culture could have been expected to produce further work which might have enabled him to cope with the unresolved problems of *Ancient Law*.

His response to the realities of Indian village life has given rise to a detailed debate amongst modern anthropologists and historians, and their initial concern has been to discover what Maine actually said about this topic because it is difficult to provide a wholly coherent account of his thoughts. For example, Louis Dumont has pointed out that the 'village community' of *Ancient Law* was a rather odd creation.[2] In essence, for Maine, such communities were at once an organised patriarchal society and an assemblage of co-proprietors. In later years this was modified to the extent that in *Village Communities* Maine wrote that 'I shall have hereafter to explain that . . . the Indian village communities prove on close inspection to be not simple but composite bodies, including a number of classes with very various rights and claims'. In the same lectures Maine added the rather

[2] L. Dumont, 'The Village Community from Monro to Maine', in *Contributions to Indian Sociology* (Dec. 1966–7), at, for example, p. 82. See also: J. W. Burrow, '"The Village Community" and the Uses of History in Late-Nineteenth Century England' in N. McKendrick (ed.), *Historical Perspectives* (London, 1974); and C. J. Dewey, 'Images of the Village Community: A Study in Anglo-Indian Ideology', *Modern Asian Studies*, vol. 6 (1972), p. 310. For consistent criticism of Maine's powers of observation in India see C. Drekmier, *Kingship and Community in Early India* (Stanford, 1962). Note the scarcity of references to Maine in J. D. M. Derrett, 'The Administration of Hindu Law by the British', *Comparative Studies in Society and History*, vol. 4 (1961–62), pp. 10–52; and the dismissive attitude in D. Rothermund's contribution to D. A. Low (ed.), *Soundings in Modern South Asian History* (London, 1968) p. 132. For a much more flattering view of Maine's ideas (albeit on a high level of generalisation) see D. Thorner, 'The Comparative Method of Sir Henry Maine' (1951), in *The Shaping of Modern India* (Delhi, 1980), p. 249 at p. 258. I am indebted to Pramit Chaudhuri for this reference. For other enthusiastic uses of Maine in an Indian context see B. S. Cohen, 'From Indian Status to British Contract', *Journal of Economic History*, vol. 21 (1961), pp. 613–28 at p. 628 and M. Singer and B. S. Cohen, *Structure and Change in Indian Society* (Chicago, 1968), p. 19.

tantalising statement that the village community 'is found, on close observation, to exhibit divisions which run through its internal framework . . . The most interesting division of the community may be described as a division into several parallel social strata.'[3] But with few exceptions these thoughts are not developed.

As Dumont was careful to show, Maine for the most part simply failed to provide the promised explanation. Lively remarks about plans for further work were followed by silence. This is important in any assessment of Maine's thought since many have been impressed by Maine's capacity to integrate his interpretation of the village as an organised patriarchal society, and an assemblage of co-proprietors, into his general theory that the infancy of law is distinguished by the prevalence of co-ownership, the intermixture of personal with proprietory rights, and the confusion of public and private duties.

Faced with a lack of empirical evidence in his work some attacks by modern critics concerned with Maine's response to Indian realities have been brutal and his references to an 'extraordinary calamity' or the inexplicability of progress have served as no defence. Dumont himself has shown that Maine's limited attempts to justify his views about India are contradictory. Maine was not only able to detect a village 'brotherhood' which formed 'a sort of social hierarchy'; he also in places expressed the belief that the village structure was non-hierarchical and based on democratic, egalitarian or even communistic principles. Maine's use of these terms barely withstands any sort of analysis: the word 'brotherhood' refers at times to the whole village population and at other times to the more powerful members of the village who, allegedly, had the rights of co-owners in land. It is as if Maine could not forsake a Western tendency to make nice distinctions between political units and forms of ownership in land: and in his case it is particularly clear that these distinctions became confused and were never properly related to the available evidence.

It can at least be said that at times Maine recognised the deficiencies of his sources. He saw the 'Revenue Settlements' as being a valuable source of information for many purposes, but he believed that they could only be understood in the light of 'the oral statements of experienced Indian functionaries' who nevertheless, Maine conceded, were often at variance with each other over the correct in-

[3] *Village Communities*, pp. 234 and 176 respectively. For the impact of *Village Communities* see Max Muller, *India: What Can It Teach Us?* (London, 1892), p. 48.

terpretation of the evidence.[4] Despite this admission, Maine seems to have made no great effort to improve on his sources. In this regard he simply failed to take full advantage of his stay in India, and it followed that he was never confronted with the sort of facts which could have moved him beyond the perspectives of *Ancient Law*. Instead, he seems to have become more and more determined to sustain his old belief in a particular vision of the Indo–European village community. In a damning observation, Dumont concludes his own analysis with the remark that Maine 'hardly ever looked at the Indian village itself, instead it always had to be seen as a counterpart to Teutonic, Slavonic or other institutions'.[5] As a result Indian society was interpreted by Maine in such a way as to reveal appropriate analogies with western societies, and the overall picture of the village community on the subcontinent is full of inconsistencies and thoroughly unconvincing. For all his hesitation, he would have been well-advised to have adopted a more cautious attitude towards the ideas of Buckle.

However, none of these attacks on him does anything to diminish the significance of India for his thought in general. To some extent at least such views serve to emphasise the point that Maine, despite his protestations to the contrary, was playing an important role in the development of specifically British ideas about India. As a participant in an essentially British discussion it is necessary to have in mind his possible role in the evolution of utilitarian thought relating to the subcontinent. Certainly on his return to England Maine was full of indignation when he wrote about the indiscriminate application of utilitarian ideas to Indian problems. In his study of *The English Utilitarians and India*, the late Professor Stokes concluded that Maine's principal achievement was 'to challenge the dominion exercised by abstract ideas over the English mind; a dominion which he attributed to the abstract analytical method of the Utilitarians'.[6] There are colourful examples of this challenge to be found throughout Maine's works. For instance they may be seen in his remarks about the unintended, and often undesirable, consequences of simply imposing an administratively tidy system of courts upon an ancient civilisation.

[4] Dumont, 'The Village Community from Monro to Maine', pp. 84–5.

[5] *Ibid*., p. 85.

[6] E. Stokes, *The English Utilitarians and India* (Oxford, 1959), p. 312. But perhaps Stokes sensed that Maine's response to utilitarianism and India was an intricate and unexplored matter: both the brevity and suggestiveness of his remarks about Maine are striking.

However Maine's response to utilitarian ideas in India was more complicated than this suggests. For him, the most unjustified and destructive of the English abstract ideas which blighted the development of Indian law was the simple and thoroughly ill-informed belief in the capacity of the English common law to provide legal remedies for all people in all places. It was exasperation at the uncriticial praise which was given to purely English law which drove Maine to write at such lengths about the impact of courts upon the development of custom. For him, it was futile to suggest that any sort of court could have other than a profound impact upon customary change: the very fact that a common law court might be respectful of custom, and thereby prepared to recognise it, led inexorably to what Maine described as a hardening of custom itself. Custom enforced by courts was not the same as custom which changed in ways which were free from legal interference; in particular the latter spontaneous methods were likely to be much more flexible. Modern anthropology has attuned our minds to the controversial and complicated significance of 'imposed law' for societies dominated by what western eyes see as being custom. It is easy for us to take Maine's protests for granted; but viewed in the context of their time they have a more strident quality and point to the fact that in an Indian context Maine had at least as much fear of the common law as he did of utilitarianism.

It is possible to go further and show that in some contexts he had great hopes for utilitarian ideas in India. They accorded much more nicely than the common law with his thoughts about codification. As early as 1863, when considering the legal education of civil servants he wrote: 'we will hope that the growing intricacy and technicality of Indian law will be obviated by the true remedy, the development of clearly written statute law, and the introduction of a code or substantive body of fundamental rules'.[7] Given this sort of approach to legal reform, utilitarianism had two advantages: it demanded that the law be stated in clear terms which could be understood beyond the confines of the legal profession; and it was admirably suited to the requirements of a legal system which, it was to be hoped, would reflect contractual rather than status values. Of course, both of these assumptions are viewed today as being highly controversial and much more complicated than they might appear to be at first sight. But for

[7] Sir M. E. Grant Duff, *Life and Speeches of Sir Henry Maine: a Brief Memoir* (London, 1892), p. 308.

the moment such considerations are irrelevant. What matters in the present context is that Maine did not set out to save India from the tyranny of abstract utilitarian thought. He was much more concerned about what he saw as being the tyranny of the common law: and for him the very idea of utility itself could do much to undermine a belief in the common law and provide a suitable substitute.

That this should have been so is not surprising if one considers the example of Maine's successor as Legal Member of the Viceroy's Council. James Fitzjames Stephen was greatly interested in the lessons which Indian experience could give to British political thought and, in particular, he sought to use the example of India as an antidote to what he saw as being the misguided enthusiasms to be found in the later works of J. S. Mill. Those of Stephen's ideas which eventually were published in book form as *Liberty, Equality, Fraternity*[8] were written on the return voyage from India in response to the ideas which Mill had expressed in *On Liberty* and *Utilitarianism*. Stephen himself had carried both of these books by Mill in his travelling library, and his reaction to them is a clear and lively reflection of his experience of the problems and opportunities of imperial government.

In his recent book on the man, James Colaiaco is at pains to emphasise the significance of India in Stephen's thought and through numerous examples he shows that Stephen himself was correct when, in 1872, he wrote that 'India has been a sort of second university course to me . . . There is hardly a subject on which it has not given me a whole crowd of new ideas.'[9] For Stephen these new observations provided more than enough evidence to prove just how wrong-headed Mill's ideas were; and, admittedly, in some respects they also revealed that certain utilitarian justifications for the political and social reconstruction of India were impracticable. Utility however was still the test for good law; it was just that utility was now to be related to the virtues of imperial rule and was to bolster the capacity of the British to, say, control feuding between Hindus and Muslims.

[8] James Fitzjames Stephen, *Liberty, Equality, Fraternity* (edited by R. J. White) (Cambridge, 1967). First published in London, 1873. But Stephen's lively remarks about India have done something to obscure the fact that we will never fully understand his thought until we have a study of his beliefs concerning the proper role of legal practitioners in Victorian society. The latter might do more to explain his thought than any amount of writing about the subcontinent.

[9] Stephen to Emily Cummingham, 7 May 1872, quoted in Colaiaco, *James Fitzjames Stephen*, p. 120, fn. 72.

Laws which kept the peace were useful: and for Stephen that was more or less the end of the matter.[10]

This is yet another indication that the response of English Victorian jurists to utilitarian thought was extraordinary in its range and variety: Dicey, for example, adopted a different view when he developed the links between utilitarianism and practical individualism. Certainly, in respect of their Indian writings it is not reasonable to regard either Maine or Stephen as opponents of the abstract analytical approach even if the latter gave it a formidably crude application. Stephen simply disdained the specific liberal content which (as Stephen saw it) Mill had sought to impose upon the alternative 'manly' vision of utility which suited the robust needs of Empire. From the 1860s onwards, Maine just disregarded Mill for the most part, and praised utilitarianism as a guide to clear-headed thinking for the imperial administrator.[11] Both distrusted liberalism; both delighted in providing 'proofs' against democracy; both loved efficiency and put utilitarian arguments to autocratic uses.

But in Maine's work there is a very different tone which does not delight in intemperate assertions about moral, racial and religious superiority. Such observations fill large paragraphs of Stephen's analysis and they have been restored to prominence in modern times by the Hart-Devlin debate concerning law and morality. In contrast, despite a few unpleasant asides about certain ethnic groups, Maine showed little enthusiasm for such judgments and they never formed a necessary part of his arguments about what made for good government and good law. All races and nations deserved good and competent governments; and no group of people anywhere on earth could hope to achieve such an objective through democracy. The best hope for humanity lay in the mutual tolerance of educated and mature minds – and, under appropriate circumstances, such minds could be found in numerous contrasting societies.

For Maine the future of India did not consist of British officials conferring alien benefits upon an inferior subject group. It was, ideally, a joint enterprise between enlightened men of goodwill; and these men might come from any section of the population. Also,

10 On the liberal and authoritarian elements of utilitarianism in an Indian context at this time see *Ibid.*, p. 99. Perhaps my analysis oversimplifies: see, for example, *Ibid.*, p. 107.

11 For Mill's strange use of some of Maine's ideas see the Introduction by S. Collini in J. M. Robson (ed.), *J. S. Mill: Essays on Equality, Law, and Education* (Toronto and Buffalo, 1984), pp. xlvi–ii in particular.

despite the grandeur of the imperial machine, it was to a necessary extent an inherently modest enterprise. The mechanisms of progress were imperfectly understood and the impact of British rule was itself far beyond the control of even the most efficient Viceroy. Once a court had been created, or a custom sustained by means of legal sanctions, or a legal system had come to be linked in certain ways to novel forms of economic activity, the full development of Indian life and thought was no longer under the control of any government. 'We . . . change because we cannot help it. Whatever be the nature and value of that bundle of influences called Progress, nothing can be more certain than that, when a society is once touched by it, it spreads like a contagion.'[12] The spread might have some of the qualities of a disease, but on occasion the result could be highly beneficial, as when new forms of ownership developed: 'Nobody is at liberty to attack several property and to say at the same time that he values civilisation. The history of the two cannot be disentangled.'[13]

In Maine's view, the British had special responsibilities in India. If they are 'too slow, there will be no improvement. If they are too fast there will be no security.' They have an especial duty to manage the relationship between their own and less powerful cultures: 'the British rulers of India are like men bound to make their watches keep true time in two longitudes at once'.[14]

A sense of Britain and India participating in a shared adventure which had fallen upon both societies by chance is given a particularly forceful expression in the final part of his Rede lecture of 1875 – the same lecture in which he had so castigated the views of Buckle. Having identified the Greeks as the people who created the principle of progress he was happy to engage in his favourite sort of generalisation.

> Except the blind forces of Nature, nothing moves in this world which is not Greek in its origin. A ferment spreading from that source has vitalised all the great progressive races of mankind, penetrating from one to another, and producing results accordant with its hidden and latent genius, and results of course often far greater than any exhibited in Greece itself. It is this principle of progress which we Englishmen are communicating to India. We did not create it. We deserve no special credit for it. It came to us filtered through many different media. But we have received it, so we pass it on. There is no reason why, if it has time to work, it should not develop in India effects as wonderful as in any other of the societies of mankind.[15]

[12] From the Rede Lecture of 1875 reprinted in *Village Communities*, pp. 237–8.
[13] *Ibid.*, p. 230. [14] *Ibid.*, p. 237. [15] *Ibid.*, p. 238.

Obviously, there was more in this than rhetorical delight. For Maine there was something noble in passing on the 'principle of progress' even if, ultimately, it could not be explained. It is necessary for us to remember, too, that he was probably in need of such motivation during the time when he was actually working in India. Holdsworth has pointed out that Maine was involved in the production of 209 pieces of legislation! Other writers on India have remarked on Maine's failure to make any great impression as Legal Member of the Viceroy's Council, but much of this might be accounted for by the exhausting tedium of the everyday work with which he was confronted.[16]

At least it can be said that he never let the discomforts of hard work reduce his accounts of his own motivation to bigoted references to national superiority with a strong, associated hint of self-sacrifice for the sake of helping inferiors. When we contrast the warmth of his sentiments with the bleak dogmatism of Stephen we come much closer to understanding the place of India in much of Maine's thought. The latter could never have written as Stephen did, that 'Our law is, in fact, the sum and substance of what we have to teach them. It is, so to speak, the Gospel of the English, and it is a compulsory gospel which admits of no dissent and no disobedience.' Instead, for Maine, India was the scene of careful administration and lively speculation about the creative and destructive aspects of the relationship between East and West. It was not primarily the scene of deep research into Asian history; it is significant that he never even tried to become a scholar of Sanskrit.[17] Still less was it the place where he attempted anything like a sustained study of the social realities of Indian village life; on his own admission he still relied on secondary authorities in these matters and, again on his own admission, these were often contradictory and inadequate as supports for his more adventurous generalisations. Most important of all, India was not the place that enabled Maine to show that Utilitarianism was an imperfect guide to constructive social change because it ignored history. Bentham's legacy was far too valuable as a justification for legal reforms in which Maine believed for him even to consider a wholehearted attack

[16] Holdsworth, *A History of English Law*, vol. 15, p. 362. In contrast, consider the total failure to mention Maine in Sir Benjamin Lindsay's *Law, Modern India and the West* (edited by L. S. S. O'Malley (Oxford, 1949)). Stephen has always attracted more attention in this context. But it can be argued that Maine arrived in India at a crucial moment of its legal history: see W. McCormack, 'Caste and the British Administration of Hindu Law', *Journal of Asian and African Studies*, vol. 1 (1966), pp. 25–32 at p. 25.

[17] But 'useful work can be done without Sanskrit': J. D. M. Derrett, *The Concept of Property in Ancient Indian Theory and Practice* (Gronigen, 1986), p. 2.

upon utilitarian theory in this context. Therefore India provided Maine with illustrations of great variety and colour, but it did not change his views about law or social change or scientific understanding. The ideas of the man who returned to England in 1869 remained remarkably undisturbed by the experience of Calcutta and the innumerable villages of the subcontinent.

It follows that his response to India has often misled those who have analysed his thought and, in reality, the strange truth is that most of his experiences need to be ignored if his writings on the subcontinent are to be understood. Given the fact that there often was something open-minded and generous about the early ideas which Maine developed before he went to India it is perhaps no bad thing that they were to endure through his actual experience of Imperial rule. But of course one consequence of this was that he failed to develop his jurisprudential thought in reaction to his actual experience of the communities about which he had already written. In the next section we will see that for his jurisprudence the most significant of his responses to Indian realities arose out of neither his sight of Indian villages nor his uses for utilitarianism in an alien context but rather out of his meetings with Indian lawyers; and even here his reaction was to be dominated by political and not theoretical considerations. It was to introduce contradictory elements into his thought about law.

INDIAN AND ENGLISH LAWYERS

Maine's lack of interest in the challenge which the facts of Indian communities posed for his early thought points to a general indifference on his part towards the development of new ideas. He sometimes repeated the issues which he had raised in *Ancient Law*, but he did not attempt a further exploration of their jurisprudential significance. Instead, in the years following 1861, he concentrated much of his attention upon reconciling the ideas which he had already considered with the new discoveries of continental scholars who were investigating early systems of land tenure and the like. He was concerning himself more and more with purely historical arguments rather than with their role in legal philosophy.

There are a number of possible explanations for this. Even his friends described Maine as being somewhat lazy, and in so far as he never enjoyed very good health they defended his occasional lack of application. Also, the systematic analysis of something as intricate as, say, the jurisprudential significance of the relationship between law and history was all the less likely to attract his enthusiasm when he was involved in the preparation of new laws for India or the introduction of new courses for undergraduates at Oxford. Between the publication of *Ancient Law* in 1861 and Maine's death in 1888 he would have been unable to give his undivided attention to jurisprudence even if he had wished to do so.

However, the most important cause of his declining commitment to developing new thoughts about law was of an intellectual nature. When, in writing *Ancient Law*, he developed the theme that jurisprudence should be written in a way which was immediately comprehensible to the layman, the legal practitioner and the jurist, he was expressing ideas which accorded with much of fashionable legal thought. Codification was seen as an instrument for replacing the obscurities of the common law with clear statements of legal principle which could be criticised by both the layman and the lawyer. In the second half of Maine's life, however, many of these assumptions were to change, and in the late 1870s support for the common law was to revive with such force that his ideas about law and legal change were to look anachronistic.

His difficulties with changes in legal thought first became apparent when he went to India. In the course of the 1860s many English lawyers sensed that the India of the late nineteenth century was to be blessed or cursed (depending on the point of view of the Victorian observers) with a great number of lawyers. There were already indications that this was to have important political consequences. The Hindus of the coastal presidencies were much readier to exploit vocational opportunities than the Muslims of the interior and as a result the two groups were developing in very different ways under the Raj. Above all, the English lawyer in India was always faced with the challenging fact that the native lawyers were in a strong position to advance their national cause not only in the courts but in the press and elsewhere. Law was an obvious instrument of colonial politics.[18]

Despite the continued warnings of all the medical men whom he consulted about his health, Maine spent much of his time in Calcutta,

[18] For a more detailed study of lawyers in nineteenth-century India see Anil Seal, *The Emergence of Indian Nationalism* (Cambridge, 1968), particularly at pp. 123–30: n.b. at p. 129: 'Forming an independent status group, confident in their new skills to conduct the constitutional dialogue with their rulers, lawyers marched in the van of politics in later nineteenth-century India, just as they had for centuries managed the politics of revolt in the Occident.'

and there he soon found that the increase in the number of lawyers attending the new university was being discussed. It seems that between 1864 and 1868, 114 studied law, whereas between 1869 and 1873, 443 did so.[19] These numbers would seem tiny to a twentieth-century observer, but it appeared to those involved that there might be no end to the increase, and it reflected similar developments in other parts of India where it was clear that the graduates concerned were taking to legal practice. Most of them had become pleaders and it was not long before they were involved in politics.[20]

Years later, in 1886, Maine himself could remark in unpleasant tones that as far as India as a whole was concerned there was 'a certain incongruity in the notion of some 4,500 of the dominant Baboo caste claiming to give the law to 180 millions of souls'.[21] But in the 1860s he had been both more alarmed and more constructive. In 1866 he spoke of

> the great addition . . . which is due to the numbers and influence of the Native Bar. Practically, a young educated Native, pretending to anything above a clerkship, adopts one of two occupations – either he goes into the service of Government, or he joins the Native Bar . . . the Bar is getting more and more preferred to Government service by the educated youth of the country, both on the score of its gainfulness and on the score of its independence.[22]

This development caused him more concern than information about villages or arguments about utilitarianism.

He considered the matter in some detail in his public speeches.[23] Perhaps, he admitted, there was a need for at least a few more lawyers and, also, it was clear to him that many of those who read law were going to become very astute lawyers indeed. But against this he had to set what he saw as their almost obsessive delight in mere technicality for its own sake. It seemed to Maine that the Indian students of law were developing a fine grasp of legal detail, and a remarkable capacity for subtle argument, but at the same time they were failing to see that

[19] *Ibid*. Seal shows that interpreting these figures is a complicated matter. And for the university in general see 'Address to the University of Calcutta' (March 1864), reprinted in *Village Communities*, p. 241. It seems that Maine also may have had in mind all graduates (not just law graduates) who went on to become lawyers: see *Ibid*. (March 1865), p. 256. Barristers were a small minority leading a movement to law jobs which resulted in there being almost 14,000 lawyers in the three Presidencies by the late nineteenth century: see Seal, *The Emergence of Indian Nationalism*, p. 123.

[20] Seal, *The Emergence of Indian Nationalism*, pp. 129–30.

[21] *Ibid*., p. 177. [22] *Ibid*., p. 124.

[23] See *Village Communities*, pp. 240–95.

good legal practice demanded more than this. Just what this extra component was to be in the Indian context is rather difficult to identify: it seems that for Maine it consisted in part of standards of good conduct, but it also seems to have involved the idea that law should never be applied in a purely mechanical fashion – it demanded a certain maturity of judgment and, as it were, a rounded awareness as to the proper purpose of law. Otherwise advocates would tend to prefer 'subtlety to breadth'. It was true that

> technicalities are absolutely indispensable to lawyers, just as the ideas of form, of proportion, and colour have to be thrown into a technical shape before they can give birth to painting or sculpture. A lawyer cannot do without technical rules, any more than a sculptor or painter; but still, it is universally true that a disposition to overrate technicalities, or to value them for their own sake, is the characteristic mark of the journeyman, as distinguished from the artist. A very technical lawyer will always be a third-rate lawyer.[24]

All this sounds vague, but it represents a significant development in Maine's thought. He was being forced to turn his attention away from the purely scientific analysis of law and towards a much more traditional understanding of what made for good legal work. In retrospect it is easy to see how this could lead Maine away from his public criticism of the Inns of Court to a much more moderate understanding of the proper role of a professional lawyer. At one stage of his Indian lectures, he spoke of reasonableness and commonsense rather than breadth of knowledge as the answer to excessive technicality.[25] From this position it is possible to see how the English common law tradition with its avoidance of grand generalisations, its respect for professional corporate life, and its interest in standards of character could be used to bolster a concern with sound judgment. In substance, a fascination with legal logic was to be tempered with a respect for maturity; and there was to be praise for an understanding of law acquired as much through experience as through intellectual analysis.

There is evidence that Maine tried to arrange for more Indian lawyers to attend the Inns of Court and thereby presumably to acquire

[24] *Ibid.*, p. 259.

[25] *Ibid.*, p. 260: 'But still, after all, the grand criterion of legal matters is common sense, and if you are inclined to employ an argument, or to draw an inference, or to give an opinion which does not satisfy the test, which is out of harmony with experience and with the practical facts of life, I do not say, reject it absolutely, but strongly suspect it, and be sure that the presumption is heavily against it.'

more than purely technical knowledge of the law.[26] But it is clear that he still had a general dislike for the Inns and, in any event, he must have doubted whether such institutions could provide the answer to the legal problems of Imperial India. The number of Indians who could afford to make the journey to England and the Inns of Court would always be small. Whatever his full thoughts on the matter, many of the foreign lawyers who did in fact visit the Temple became prominent nationalist politicians – Gandhi himself is an obvious example from a later generation. Probably, Maine never accommodated his imperial ideas to his notions of good legal practice.

Almost at the start of his penultimate address to the students of Calcutta University he made a revealing remark when he informed his audience that 'in contrasting England and India, in comparing the East and the West, we must sometimes bring ourselves to call evil good, and good evil. The fact is, that the educated Native mind requires hardening.' This statement was part of an argument designed to show that whereas the West was lacking in the 'culture of the imagination' the East has suffered because 'the imagination has run riot'.[27] At this point he was talking about the devotion of Indian students to the Arts in general rather than to law in particular: he was never to suggest that ingenuity and subtlety in handling purely technical legal issues amounted to 'imagination', and he was always sharply critical of the Indian legal mind at those points where it did not look beyond the ideas of the 'journeyman'. At its most general, Maine seems to have thought that East and West could help each other by providing a remedy for each others' defects. It is as if he believed that an impractical and too sophisticated East could be reminded of important realities and everyday problems by Westerners who had a due regard for facts: and it followed, of course, that the West underestimated the importance of imagination and could benefit from Eastern wisdom. Obviously, all of this is very vague but it does go a little way to explain how Maine could argue for one approach to thinking in the East, and a totally different approach in the West. Like

[26] *Law Times*, vol. 44 (1867–8), pp. 112–13, Maine's sudden attempt to talk of the moral qualities of the Inns met with ridicule: 'The moral elevation of which Maine speaks as arising out of contact with the members of the Inns is a fiction of the learned Doctor's orientalised imagination. At the moment the Inns are places of uncomfortable probation and intense idleness.'

[27] See 'Address to the University of Calcutta', in *Village Communities* (4th ed., 1881), p. 275. This edition contains additional material which is useful but which does not affect the present arguments about the context of his beliefs.

so much else that he wrote, it emphasises the importance of ideas, and suggests that he experienced intellectual unease in the face of well-established conventions wherever he found them. Certainly the inference is odd: India needed the Inns of Court but England did not.

His temporary enthusiasm for the Inns of Court in a colonial role proved to be very short-lived and produced no theoretical writing in which he even attempted to reconcile his hostility to the common law with momentary respect for its institutions. He soon returned to his older critical views, but began to express them in a different way. In the past he had been fully prepared to become involved in public arguments about the proper training and regulation of barristers and was happy to be seen as one of the more extreme reformers of the legal profession as a whole. Yet after his return to England in 1869 he avoided becoming heavily involved in public debate about the Bar and its social duties. He still wrote for the public press on a wide variety of issues: more than one authority has shown that Maine wrote numerous articles for the leading periodicals of the time; and yet very little of what he now wrote seems to have been of immediate relevance to the legal profession.[28] His desire to avoid such a topic seems uncharacteristic when it is realised that discussion about lawyers was extremely fashionable at the time concerned. In the 1870s the Bar was confronted with the most radical reforms it was to experience in the whole of the nineteenth century. Throughout these years the Judicature Acts were a topic of constant public interest, and they were of particular concern to barristers because practitioners believed that the legislation could ruin their livelihoods through changes in the distribution of courts and the rules relating to venue. Many of those who wrote were highly critical of the Bar and its influence; there was even serious discussion as to whether the Inns of Court should be abolished and there were intense and successful demands for the introduction of compulsory examinations for barristers.[29] Yet Maine said nothing about this in the newspapers and periodicals.[30]

His apparent desire to avoid open commitment in these matters was

[28] See, Feaver, *From Status to Contract*, bibliography, and M. M. Bevington, *The Saturday Review* (New York, 1966).

[29] See Cocks, *Foundations of the Modern Bar*, chapters 6 and 8.

[30] Or did he? There are *numerous* references to the legal world in the *Saturday Review* of these years and some occasional paragraphs (but not whole articles) read a little in Maine's style. Perhaps the experts are wrong and Maine was just careful to suppress any evidence of his journalistic writing on the law. (Maine had an earlier dispute, in 1861, with some others involved with the *Saturday Review* but this may have been forgotten by the 1870s.)

probably linked to changes in his ideas about the public presentation of legal theory. Although he avoided considering the rights and wrongs of legal practice in the press he certainly did not avoid such discussion in his works of scholarship. However, the observations now took a different form. After his experiences of the 1860s, the equivocal observations about life at the Bar and the achievements of barristers began to vanish from the pages of his works. The elegant paragraphs which – even when critical – could so easily make for relaxed conversation amongst the more cultured sort of barristers, became a thing of the past. Increasingly, he failed to say favourable things about any aspect of the Bar and its professional life, and when he did find something commendable – such as the Bar's role in discovering facts during a trial – he made the point with restraint.

Whereas he had been quite open and hopeful in the 1850s when he made suggestions for the reform of professional life, by the early 1870s his criticisms were inserted in rather unexpected places in his major books and, at times, they have about them a savage and destructive bitterness. The fact that these observations were to be surrounded by chapters devoted to, say, the primitive laws of Europe or India must have done much to save Maine public embarrassment, but it did nothing to modify the hostile tone which he adopted when he actually discussed English lawyers. In short, it seems as if he was presenting his ideas in the one way that would enable him to avoid acrimonious public debate in the periodical press. But these attacks upon the Bar were to remain consistent and may be found in all the chief works of his later years. It follows that he was not only avoiding public disapproval; he was also saying something about the relationship between jurisprudence and professional practice. He no longer attempted to integrate the two topics into his general analysis of law: it seems that he no longer saw any potential for a fruitful dialogue between English practitioners and English jurists.

These problems were increased by the difficulties which Maine encountered in his capacity as a teacher of law at Oxford and Cambridge. The degrees concerned with English law were regarded as an experiment when they first began at the ancient universities in the mid 1850s, and friends involved in their development kept Maine informed of what was happening when he was in India. There was surely an echo of this when he informed the prospective lawyers of Imperial India that, although some good things could be said in favour of the ancient universities of England, they also deserved criticism for their opposition to new ideas. In his view, they were particularly inept at responding to the occasional need to change what was being taught to undergraduates.[31] At this time Maine must have been interested in the fact that the new degrees took the form of combined courses in law and history. Bryce and others with an interest in the history of law were involved in the attempt to develop legal studies in Oxford during this time, and it would have been only natural for them to turn to Maine for support in their attempt to advance the idea that law should be understood primarily in historical terms.

However, by the end of the 1860s, their approach to the new undergraduate degrees was encountering more and more difficulties.[32] It seems that neither the historians nor the lawyers were enthusiastic about the union of their respective disciplines, and this discontent was being mentioned in the public press. (It was a pity that they could not foresee the future achievements of those who had already taken the new degree. From a comparatively small number of pupils these courses were to produce men of the calibre of Phillimore the international lawyer, Parry the composer, and Green the philosopher.) Maine must have known that the mixed degree was unpopular and it is possible – we simply do not know – that he may have had misgivings when, after his return to England in 1869, he accepted an invitation to become the new Corpus Professor of Jurisprudence at Oxford. Certainly, it seems that he insisted upon the fact that the new job would not involve living in Oxford itself; he regarded London as more pleasant and more important. To some extent at least he may have accepted the Oxford post for financial reasons, for although he had been able to acquire some investments, and had managed them well, it seems they were not yet sufficient to give him a private income.[33]

[31] See *Village Communities* (4th ed., 1881), 'Address to the University of Calcutta', p. 242: 'Their weak side has been intolerance of new subjects of thought; their strong side has been their impatience of superficiality.'

[32] Some of the difficulties are referred to in Feaver, *From Status to Contract*, at, for example, pp. 111–12. For a lively account of some aspects of what was happening as a whole at Victorian Oxford see C. Harvie, *The Lights of Liberalism* (Harmondsworth, 1979).

[33] Feaver does not explore all the educational problems which confronted Maine, but he does reveal some very practical considerations which may well have been relevant. In 1888, when Maine died, his personal estate was valued at almost £50,000; however it is quite possible that twenty years earlier Maine may have been short of money: see *From Status to Contract*, p. 307, fn. 20.

If Maine did have fears about what the new appointment was to involve they were soon to be amply justified. He had to come to terms with the fact that at both Oxford and Cambridge it was still believed that the union of law and history had 'proved more barren than had been expected'. For example, it was said that at Cambridge

> the budding barrister regards the 'getting' up of a certain specified period of history as an unmitigated nuisance, interfering unwarrantably with his willing devotion to Coke and Blackstone, while the obvious necessity of requiring only a limited knowledge of special portions of 'Modern History' from all candidates in the joint Tripos has produced a dead level of mediocrity in the historical performance of the large majority of men.[34]

When the change came, Maine's problems were well expressed, albeit inadvertently, by someone who pointed out with reference to Cambridge that 'while professional Law is rightly sent away to its own place in a School of its own, the historical aspect of Law, Constitutional Law, and the Principles of General Jurisprudence are to find their place in the Historical Tripos'.[35] This was, in fact, a serious exaggeration for there was still a considerable quantity of both jurisprudence and legal history to be found in the law syllabus at both Oxford and Cambridge. But it pointed clearly to a preference for studies in which more and more attention was being given to the analysis of certain parts of the common law.[36] Generally, there was a suspicion in the fashionable press at this time that the University of Oxford was 'laudably anxious to increase in every way its hold on the busy classes' and that as a result it was responding to the requirements of those who wished to become, say, solicitors; and such men, it was thought, wished for more vocational forms of study than those which had been available.[37]

For different reasons the 'senior' part of the profession, the Bar, was also likely to be unsympathetic towards the ideas of men such as Maine. Educational reform was becoming a much less fashionable issue in the highest reaches of the profession. With the outstanding exception of Lord Selborne, there were few barristers of any emi-

[34] One of the best records of academic opinion on these topics is the *Saturday Review*. For the present quotation see vol. 34 (1872), p. 9. For a general study see Bevington, *The Saturday Review*.

[35] The *Saturday Review*, vol. 35 (1873), p. 11.

[36] In this connection see F. H. Lawson, *The Oxford Law School 1850–1865* (Oxford, 1973), pp. 29, 34–5, 39, 44, 48–9, 55, 84, 91.

[37] The *Saturday Review*, vol. 42 (1876), p. 434.

nence who sought to sustain the radical tradition established by men such as Brougham.[38] Maine can have had few hopes for the future.

Feaver, in his study of Maine, argues that at this stage of his work Maine had an enthusiasm for the subject of Roman law which led him to try and use it, in Maine's own words, as a means 'to connect legal studies with other academical studies'.[39] Certainly, there is evidence to show that Maine believed that Roman Law had a constructive educational role in the scheme of degrees which was emerging.[40] It is easy to imagine that he hoped it could be used, as it were, to dilute the study of statutes and cases. However, there is no evidence in his written work of an attempt to develop his own studies of Roman law, and his lectures now contained fewer references to the topic than they had done in the past. The probable explanation for the comparative lack of personal interest lies in the inability to relate Roman law to professional debates and law reform in the manner of the 1850s when changes at the Inns of Court and the possibilities of codification were fashionable topics. Roman law was no longer associated with such issues. Its divorce from professional concerns was insisted upon by a writer in the *Saturday Review* who observed that

> as one of the chief objects of legal education is to enlarge the views and extend the knowledge of English lawyers, it was thought that the best instrument for attaining the end was to encourage the study of Roman Law. On the principle of doing a thing very heartily if it is done at all, the study of Roman Law was not only encouraged, but every sixpence given by way of pecuniary reward to successful students was devoted to recompense proficiency in Roman Law. To be able to go high in Roman Law a student must be a good Latin Scholar and be able to read German and French commentators with ease. He must also be willing to go into numerous antiquarian details which are totally unconnected with the general history or theory of law. Nine students out of ten are thus excluded from any hope of getting any tangible reward, however hard they may work. Nor is this all. The study of Roman Law is in this way kept apart from that of English law. One does not illustrate the other. The study of Roman law becomes antiquarian and technical; the study of English law is pursued as if anything but the lowest acquaintance with the elements of Roman law need not be wished for.[41]

Sentiments such as these were widespread and they show very clearly the extent to which Maine's intellectual world was being challenged

[38] The revival of 'traditional' thought about education at the Bar is considered in Cocks, *Foundations of the Modern Bar*, chapter 8.

[39] Feaver, *From Status to Contract*, p. 112.

[40] *Ibid.*

[41] The *Saturday Review*, vol. 38 (1875), p. 72.

by the 1870s. It explains again why he seems to have lost hope of any radical change in the methods of legal education. Insofar as the academic world had power over the teaching of law it was already losing interest in Maine's overriding concerns. The attempt to use the imagination with a view to revealing the interconnected quality of different laws in different places and at different times was being replaced with what were, to Maine, narrower concerns. When his circumstances are considered there is nothing surprising about the fact that he tried to obtain a knighthood soon after he arrived at his new position. As he put it in a letter to a friend, 'I am not at all sure that it would not add to my influence at Oxford'.[42] It must have been a considerable relief for Maine to learn in 1871 that he would henceforth be 'Sir Henry'. He had achieved considerable repute in academic circles but he had forsaken his earlier, more controversial involvement in fashionable discussion about legal education.

All of the difficulties which someone of Maine's views had to confront during these years could only be expected to produce what was, in fact, reflected in Maine's life and work. A withdrawal from public debate about legal ideas was accompanied by intense, even emotional criticism of new forms of legal thought. For Maine, both the profession and legal education were in need of radical change. Both were in need of more far-reaching alterations than were likely to be produced by the Judicature Acts and the public debates which they encouraged. None of the likely reforms was designed wholly to deprive the profession of its control over the law, and none of them was likely to give rise to the sort of non-technical courses in legal education which were dear to Maine's heart. Given these bleak prospects, and the tendency for the new law degrees to avoid all forms of controversy, it is hardly surprising that Maine said less and less about legal education. He had to accept that the preservation of 'pure' law degrees was the best he could hope to achieve, and it must have been very obvious to him that he would never see English legal studies of the sort he had hoped for in his youth.

It was, then, to be expected that Maine slowly ceased to concern himself with the grand Victorian projects for reform in the world of lawyers. In 1877 he accepted an invitation to become the master of Trinity Hall in Cambridge and, despite its long association with the teaching of civil law, and despite his own affection for the college, he

[42] See Feaver, *From Status to Contract*, pp. 124–5: quoting a letter to Grant Duff, 8 April 1871.

seems to have done nothing to develop new forms of study when he arrived there.[43] With the exception of Lightwood, there appears to have been nobody at Trinity Hall who would have wished to help Maine to sustain the older and more adventurous forms of legal analysis which had characterised the 1850s. In one way, there is something sad about Maine's appointment to the Whewell Chair of International Law in 1887. International law was one of the very few legal subjects which had been taught at the ancient universities before the 1850s.[44] It was as if nothing had changed.

In a crude sense everything concerned with legal education had gone wrong for Maine. He had achieved public recognition, but he himself must have sensed that his ideas were already unfashionable by the mid-1870s. A concern with the scientific analysis of law was in decline. There was much less interest in explaining all aspects of law in both historical and philosophical terms. The Bar was asserting traditional values just when these values were (according to Maine) in need of heavy criticism. Legal education was becoming more closely linked to the study of the common law.

In many ways it would be appropriate to call Maine an early-Victorian jurist rather than simply a Victorian jurist. As far as education was concerned, by about 1875 there was something anomalous about the man's books and his beliefs; and if in later years he was quiet on the subject of legal education it was surely because he sensed that his ideas would be regarded as strange and unacceptable. It could only be expected, therefore, that his thoughts about legal education would play an important but, at the same time, inconsistent part in his writings on jurisprudence. Like his beliefs about the irrelevance of method, the nature of Indian communities, and the problems of practising lawyers, they are of importance in any attempt to under-

[43] There are no indications of any such initiatives in Charles Crawley, *Trinity Hall, 1350–1975* (Cambridge, 1976), pp. 86–7, 113, 146–52. Note the lack of interest in H. E. Malden, *Trinity Hall* (London, 1902), pp. 225–6, 254–6. For Lightwood see Enid Campbell, 'German Influences in English Legal Education and Jurisprudence in the Nineteenth Century', *University of West Australia Law Review*, vol. 4 (1959), pp. 357–90. In reality Maine was now more interested in contemporary politics than jurisprudence.

[44] Maine's posthumous contribution to the literature of international law was undistinguished and (it seems) soon to be ignored by his supporters. See *International Law: the Whewell Lectures* (ed. F. Pollock and F. Harrison) (London, 1888). (However, there were American and French editions and Holdsworth says of these lectures that 'Their chief value lies in his analysis of the case of *R. v. Kegan* (1876) 2 Ex. Div. 63, and his treatment of the question of the relation of English Law to International Law': see *A History of English Law*, vol. 15, p. 366.)

stand his later writings on legal topics. They suggest a varied and, at times, confused response to the questions which he had left unanswered in *Ancient Law*. Above all, they point towards a failure to develop new jurisprudential ideas in the years which followed the publication of *Ancient Law* in 1861. But this is a controversial suggestion which requires detailed justification in the chapter which follows: it will be suggested that Maine achieved little for jurisprudence in the four well-known works which followed his first book.

5

THE DECLINE OF A JURIST

'VILLAGE COMMUNITIES'

Most commentators on Maine see his works of the 1870s as an elaboration of the ideas to be found in *Ancient Law*. They stress the element of continuity in Maine's thought, and point out that he was now attempting to relate some of his old ideas to the work of other scholars at Oxford who were engaged in comparative social studies. For example, we know that at this time Maine was interested in Max Muller's more recent work with comparative philology, E. B. Tylor's studies in anthropology, William Stubbs' historical writings and Andrew Lang's treatment of mythology.

It is easy to see why a work like *Village Communities*, published in 1871, can be seen in this light. Much of it is taken up with a comparison between the origins of European property law and Maine's previous ideas about Indian systems of land holding. He had given his first series of Oxford lectures in 1870 and by working on the book during the summer of that year he had made his lectures, and two additional articles, suitable for publication in the following spring. As before, the explanatory theme designed to hold together his various ideas was the transition from forms of joint ownership arising out of status relationships to individual ownership reflected, to an ever increasing extent, in the development of contractual rights. In this respect the actual content of Maine's analysis had changed – in particular there was much more attention being given to English feudalism – but the interpretation remained, in all essentials, quite what it had been.

However, in respect of jurisprudence there was a significant break with earlier ideas. Despite his emphasis upon the importance of legal history, he was now more accommodating and more respectful towards the legal theorists who had ignored the lessons of the past. He went even further than he had done in *Ancient Law* in stressing the extraordinary significance of Benthamite thought for the development of modern Britain. Linking together his concern with the ancient and the modern he claimed that 'the Roman *jus gentium* was gradually sublimated into a moral theory which, among theories not laying claim to religious sanction, had no rival in the world till the ethical doctrines of Bentham made their appearance'.[1] In part this sweeping claim reflected Maine's determination to find nothing very impressive within the theories associated with the French Revolution. But chiefly it was a response to the fact that Maine was in some ways interested in utilitarian ethics, whilst he was at the same time saddened by Bentham's lack of concern for evolutionary development.

Village Communities does in fact contain indications that Maine was trying to work his way towards some form of reconciliation between competing schools of jurisprudence. He was quite capable of beginning remarks about legal philosophy with an attack upon utilitarian theorists whose ideas he then proceeded to use, rather unexpectedly, with a view to furthering his historical analysis of law. For example, in considering Indian custom, he wrote that

> So long as that remarkable analysis of legal conceptions affected by Bentham and Austin is not very widely known in this country (and I see no signs of its being known on the Continent at all), it is perhaps premature to complain of certain errors, into which it is apt to lead us on points of historical jurisprudence. If, then, I employ the Indian legal phenomena to illustrate these errors, I must preface what I have to say with the broad assertion that nobody who has not mastered the elementary part of that analysis can hope to have clear ideas either of law or of jurisprudence.[2]

These words merit attention. Once again it is clear that Maine was not unequivocally set upon the destruction of utilitarian jurisprudence; he wanted to use it himself and he often saw his task as correcting its abuse rather than attacking its lack of historical analysis.

From this hesitant beginning, he went on to outline the essentials of the utilitarian theory. Its adherents believed, he said, that

[1] *Village Communities in the East and West, Six Lectures Delivered at Oxford, to which are added other Lectures, Addresses and Essays* (London, 1889), p. 194, Lecture 6. Because it contains additional material which is useful (but not such as to affect the present arguments about the context of his beliefs) I have referred at this point to the edition of 1889 which is now commonly found in a 1974 reprint by Arno Press: fortunately the American editions published by H. Holt followed their British counterparts.

[2] *Ibid.*, pp. 66–7, Lecture 3.

a law . . . is a command of a particular kind. It is addressed by political superiors or sovereigns to political inferiors or subjects; it imposes on those subjects an obligation or *duty* and threatens a penalty (or *sanction*) in the event of disobedience. The power vested in particular members of the community of drawing down the sanction on neglects or breaches of the duty is called a Right.[3]

But from this assertion Maine moved quite suddenly towards the sort of criticism which is more frequently associated with his best known writing. He revealed the shortcomings of Austin and Bentham when their ideas are applied to ancient forms of social arrangement. 'Without the most violent forcing of language', he claimed,

it is impossible to apply these terms, *command, sovereign, obligation, sanction, right,* to the customary law under which the Indian village communities have lived for centuries, practically knowing no other law civilly obligatory. It would be altogether inappropriate to speak of a political superior commanding a particular course of action to the villagers . . . Nor, in the sense of the analytical jurists, is there *right* or *duty* in an Indian village community; a person aggrieved complains not of an individual wrong but of the disturbance of the order of the entire little society. More than all, customary law is not enforced by a sanction . . . Under the system of Bentham and Austin, the customary law of India would have to be called morality – an inversion of language which scarcely requires to be formally protested against.[4]

From this high point of criticism Maine soon turns, yet again, to qualified enthusiasm for Benthamite notions. They are, he argues, applicable to certain villages where there is a chief exercising powers which make him a sort of hereditary judge. Also, speaking more generally, it was much easier to relate the utilitarian theory to codified Brahminical law. The recognition that English legal analysis had at least some uses in the study of Indian society, led him on to a different and imaginative application of Bentham's ideas to the actual processes of legal change. He began to use Bentham's ideas to explain development and not merely to typify social states. He observed that

the fact which has greatest interest for the jurist is one which has been established by the British dominion of India, and which could not probably have been established without it. It may be described in this way. Whenever you introduce any one of the legal conceptions determined by the analysis of Bentham and Austin, you introduce all the others by a process which is apparently inevitable. No better proof could be given that, though it be improper to employ the terms *sovereign, subject, command, obligation, right,*

[3] *Ibid.*, p. 67, Lecture 3. [4] *Ibid.*, pp. 67–8, Lecture 3.

> *sanction,* to law in certain stages of human thought, they nevertheless correspond to a stage to which law is steadily tending and which it is sure ultimately to reach.[5]

It seems that the reader may assume that this form of utilitarian legal theory is the most suitable framework for the development of contractual relations in a society which is leaving status behind. Maine is arguing that if contractual relations triumph, so too does Benthamite jurisprudence.

Oddly, this type of jurisprudence is even capable of precise application in solving historical problems. In considering the influence of the English upon the legal development of India, Maine always stressed the extent to which the changes which were introduced came about unintentionally.

> The English never therefore intended that the laws of the country should rest on their commands, or that these laws should shift in any way their ancient basis of immemorial usage. One change only they made, without much idea of its importance, and thinking it probably the very minimum of concession to the exigencies of civilised government. They established Courts of Justice in every administrative district.[6]

The consequence of this was the transformation of usage and custom, because in seeking to maintain and enforce traditional ways these courts used new methods.

> Usage, once recorded upon evidence given, immediately becomes written and fixed law. Nor is it any longer obeyed as usage. It is henceforth obeyed as the law administered by a British Court, and has thus really become a command of the sovereign. The next thing is that the vague sanctions of customary law disappear. The local courts have of course power to order and guide the execution of their decrees, and thus we have at once the sanction or penalty following disobedience of the command. And with the command and with the sanction, come the conceptions of legal right and duty.[7]

Maine goes on to remark that he is now speaking of 'practical consequences' rather than some form of logic inherent in the processes of legal change. But it is surely beyond dispute that it was the elements of Benthamite jurisprudence that enabled him to identify the pattern of legal development in modern India. A supposedly *a-historical* or even *anti-historical* theory of law is used by Maine in order to understand an *historical* event. Perhaps we should not be too surprised at this; we have seen again and again how Maine had a delight in paradox.

Village Communities also revealed that he was producing further

[5] *Ibid.*, pp. 69–70, Lecture 3.
[6] *Ibid.*, pp. 70–1, Lecture 3.
[7] *Ibid.*, p. 72, Lecture 3.

ideas about practising lawyers. In particular he was interested in writing at greater length about English barristers and judges.

Without any disparagement of the many unquestionable excellences of English law – the eminent good sense frequently exhibited in the results which it finally [*sic*] evolves, and the force and even the beauty of the judicial reasoning by which in many cases they are reached – it assuredly travels to its conclusions by a path more tortuous and more interrupted by fictions and unnecessary distinctions than any system of jurisprudence in the world.[8]

This lack of enthusiasm for the English legal mind in action was easily linked to strong opinions about the proper education of lawyers. He observed that

the student who has completed his professional studies is not unnaturally apt to believe in the necessity, and even in the sacredness, of all the technical rules which he has enabled himself to command; and just then, regard being had to the influence which every lawyer has over the development of law, it is useful to show him what shorter routes to his conclusions have been followed elsewhere as a matter of fact, and how much labour he might consequently have been spared.[9]

In other words the scholar should soon see that the glorification of much of England's technical law was misplaced: an enlarged understanding of other legal systems would save students from unnecessary effort. Of course, Maine did have some good things to say about practitioners; he recognised that at times the work of historians had to be qualified by the judgment of those who worked in the courts. For example he thought that the ideas of Professor Nasse of Bonn were such that they 'required revision from an English professional lawyer'.[10] However, such remarks are hardly representative of his thought, which was becoming increasingly assured in its attacks on English practitioners. He denounced 'the extravagant estimate universally set by English lawyers upon their own system, until their complacency was rudely disturbed by Bentham'.[11] He derided those in India (including many non-Europeans) who sought unthinkingly to apply the law imported from Westminster Hall; not only was much of it inappropriate in such a context – even within its own terms it hardly merited 'the complacent encomiums on its perfection which [were] heard from English judges'.[12] It is impossible to miss the tone of suspicion and disrespect for English lawyers in so much of what he

[8] *Ibid.*, p. 5, Lecture 1.
[9] *Ibid.*, p. 6, Lecture 1.
[10] *Ibid.*, pp. 11–12, Lecture 1.
[11] *Ibid.*, p. 37, Lecture 2.
[12] *Ibid.*, p. 38, Lecture 2.

says. Moving back and forth between Indian and English topics he expressed dislike of the 'spirit' which the lawyers introduced into the administration of Indian law and went on to talk of 'the contagion, so to speak, of the English system of law – the effect which the body of rules constituting it produces by contact with native usage'.[13] It seems that Maine could not endure the arrogance, as he saw it, of English lawyers because this produced an unquestioning attitude towards the use of the common law in India. It was simply assumed that it must be ideal for universal application. It contributed to the 'wholesale and indiscriminate borrowing from the English law . . . For myself,' Maine continued, as he remarked upon the destruction of unwritten customary law, 'I cannot say that I regard this transmutation of law as otherwise than lamentable.'[14]

Also, lawyers had damaged social interests during previous historical epochs as when, for instance, they had developed a great number of minute rules on a few highly specialised topics. Certain parts of ancient Irish law contained, for Maine, a quite extraordinary amount of detail: it was 'so vast', wrote Maine, 'that I cannot but believe that much of it is attributable to the perverted ingenuity of a class of hereditary lawyers'.[15] But Maine could never put his present concerns entirely to one side and again and again he returned with something like disdain to the ideas of English barristers. Even when he was considering an ostensibly scholarly issue such as the significance of the Norman invasion for the history of English property law he could not restrain himself from criticism. With a hint of condescension he points out that 'the technical theory' of the modern law could, understandably, lead the legal mind to the belief that the Conquest was responsible for a great 'interruption' and the creation of interests in realty which were known to the nineteenth-century lawyers. But it was all the less excusable for practitioners to ignore facts with which they 'were occasionally well acquainted' and which should lead them to break away from the technical perspectives and revise their notions: for instance they should not ignore evidence pointing towards the long continuance of joint cultivation and associated customs. In particular they should not ignore this after the subject had been discussed in public – as it had been by many, including, of course, Maine himself.[16]

[13] *Ibid.*, p. 74, Lecture 3.

[14] *Ibid.*, pp. 75–6, Lecture 3.

[15] *Ibid.*, p. 81, Lecture 3.

[16] He makes many such remarks about the beliefs which English lawyers had as to the history of real property law: see, for example, *Ibid.*, p. 83, Lecture 3.

It would be easy to extend the list of examples of Maine's disrespect for the products of the English legal mind. He hated the 'abundant technicalities' it produced and was always quick to observe 'legalistic' attempts to give a 'forced technical meaning' to words.[17] Fortunately, in writing about these matters Maine supplemented his criticism with positive suggestions. Even more than when he had written *Ancient Law*, he sought to show that there was a worthwhile alternative to the common law. 'Why is it', he asks rhetorically in *Village Communities* 'that the English mode of developing law by decided cases tends less to improve and liberalise it than the interpretation of written law by successive commentators? Of the fact there seems no question.' Such an observation gave him the opportunity to discuss the virtues of codified law, and he proceeded to observe that 'even where the original written law is historically as near to us as are the French Codes, its development by textwriters is on the whole more rapid than that of English law by decided cases'.[18]

He considered a number of explanations for the contrast between the civil and common law systems in their response to the need for progress. The commentator concerned with a code had no 'distinct check' upon his writing and 'the natural limitations on the precision of language' gave him a certain liberty. In addition he had the great advantage of dealing continuously with a whole branch of law, and, knowing it as well as he did, he could take his own course by exploiting the inconsistencies between the *dicta* of his predecessors. By contrast, 'the reason why a Bench of Judges, applying a set of principles and distinctions which are still to a great extent at large, should be as slow as English experience shows them to be in extension and innovation, is not at first sight apparent'. For Maine, however, the mystery does not last long: 'Doubtless', he thought,

> the secret lies in the control of the English Bench by professional opinion – a control exerted all the more stringently when the questions brought before the courts are merely insulated fragments of particular branches of law. English law is, in fact, confided to the custody of a great corporation, of which the Bar, not the Judges, are far the largest and most influential part. The majority of the corporators watch over every single change in the body of principle deposited with them, and rebuke and practically disallow it, unless the departure from precedent is so slight as to be almost imperceptible.[19]

Maine's obvious sense of frustration with the common law and the ways of English lawyers did not stop at this point. He sought very

[17] *Ibid.*, p. 170, Lecture 5.
[18] *Ibid.*, p. 48, Lecture 2.
[19] This argument may be found at *Ibid.*, pp. 48–9, Lecture 2.

deliberately to mute their influence, at least in the development of Indian law, through the introduction of codes: 'the cure can only consist in the enactment of uniform, simple, codified law, formed for the most part upon the best European models'. And he was just as insistent upon the same sort of remedy in England itself. He provided a sustained plea for the destruction of the traditional methods of English law by means of using scientific jurisprudence.

> I must ask you to believe that the very small place filled by our own English law in our thoughts and conversation is a phenomenon absolutely confined to these islands. A very simple experiment, a very few questions asked after crossing the Channel, will convince you that Frenchmen, Swiss, and Germans of a very humble order have a fair practical knowledge of the laws which regulate their everyday life. We in Great Britain and Ireland are altogether singular in our tacit conviction that law belongs as much to the class of exclusively professional subjects as the practice of anatomy. Ours is, in fact, under limitations which it is not necessary now to specify, a body of traditional customary law; no law is better known by those who live under it at a certain stage of social progress, none is known so little by those who are in another stage. As social activity multiplies the questions requiring judicial solution, the method of solving them which a system of customary law is forced to follow is of such a nature as to add enormously to its bulk. Such a system in the end beats all but the experts; and we, accordingly, have turned our laws over to experts, to attorneys and solicitors, to barristers above them, and to judges in the last resort. There is but one remedy for this – the reduction of the law to continuous writing and its inclusion within aptly-framed general propositions. The facilitation of this process is the practical end of scientific jurisprudence.[20]

At this point Maine writes with feeling. In his condemnation of English legal thought itself he is more explicit, more downright, than he was in *Ancient Law*. The only possible conclusion that the reader may draw from his words is that he sought to use jurisprudence as an instrument to procure a revolution in the world of English lawyers. He wished to destroy their autonomous world – he wished to deprive them of the right exclusively to control the growth of the country's law through any claim they might make on the grounds that they were experts. The tone has changed and become more abrasive: and the reasoning has changed and become more explicit.

In considering *Ancient Law* we saw how concerned Maine was about the capacity for law to become separated from the society it was supposed to reflect: he believed that there were times when the law stood in outright opposition to changing ideas and as a result the

[20] *Ibid.*, pp. 59–60, Lecture 2.

whole fabric of society was endangered. This sort of analysis brought very clearly to the fore Maine's radical conservatism and his acute concern with what he observed to be the rapidly changing conditions of Victorian England. If British society was to avoid great, sudden and revolutionary upheaval it was essential that the law should be altered and made to reflect more accurately new public ideas. Only this could produce ordered change.

In modern conditions the existence of the common law was unjustified: scientific analysis would classify it as customary law and such a type of law was wholly inappropriate when 'social activity multiplies the questions requiring judicial solution'. The increasing number of legal issues inevitably produced so much complexity in the law that it 'beats all but the experts';[21] and once it was the exclusive preserve of the experts it was no longer capable of being understood by the majority of citizens who would, therefore, proceed totally to disregard their country's legal traditions and develop ideas which would be further and further detached from the values of the lawyers. Under modern circumstances the common law and its traditions were, of necessity, a source of constant and most serious instability in society. Scientific jurisprudence showed that codified law managed to express legal notions in terms which could be understood and debated by the public at large. After debate they would be changed in response to new ideas by commentators who could consider the departments of law as a whole and were not inhibited by professional opinion.

Unfortunately, Maine did not now provide a precise analysis of what it is that he meant by scientific jurisprudence. Instead, he simply devoted more time to the roles of other modern writers on legal history. His response to the works of Freeman, Von Maurer and Nasse are frequently most respectful. In this regard, the iconoclasm of *Ancient Law* has gone, and the work of the various scholars is compared and contrasted, often with a judicious sense of balance. The scholarship concerned with the history of western Europe is placed, as it were, beside the present reality of the East. 'It is not too much to say that the phenomena observed in the East, and those established in the West by historical research, illustrate one another at every point. In India these dry bones live.'[22] The reader is invited to see how erroneous have been certain historical theories of property law – in particular the much-despised ideas of English lawyers must be put to

[21] Both quotations may be found at *Ibid.*, p. 60, Lecture 2.
[22] *Ibid.*, p. 148, Lecture 5.

one side – but he is not given to understand that some all-embracing explanation of legal phenomena is likely to be achieved or is even possible.

Instead, behind the reinterpretations of Bentham and the attacks on the common law, there is a self-conscious doubt about the values of his own methods. It was in *Village Communities* that he qualified the Comparative Method in a number of ways. It was here that he expressed concern as to the proper use of the words 'Comparative Jurisprudence'. The Comparative Method could produce 'wonderful results' but he would be making 'a very idle pretension' if he suggested that the method could achieve the results with jurisprudence which it had accomplished in philology. To emphasise this important point: 'to give only one reason' for the diversity in 'the phenomena of human society, laws and legal ideas, opinions and usages, are vastly more affected by external circumstances than language. They are much more at the mercy of individual volition, and consequently much more subject to change effected deliberately from without.'[23]

By the end of *Village Communities* Maine had turned this restrained approach to legal theory to his own advantage. Perhaps with a sense of mischief – for it was a diversion – he observed that 'Political Economists often complain of the vague moral sentiments which obstruct the complete reception of their principles.'[24] Predictably, he saw these sentiments as arising out of rules of conduct which had been expelled from the law itself, but lingered on in sentiment and practice. In particular he argued that the 'Rule of the Market', in which it is assumed that an individual has some sort of right to obtain the 'best price', cannot be justified in terms of an 'original and fundamental tendency of human nature'.[25] It was only produced as status gave way to contract. The Rule of the Market 'only triumphs when the primitive community is in ruins'.[26] Maine recognised that there may even be modern efforts to fix prices by tariff; 'such attempts are justly condemned as false political economy, but it is sometimes forgotten that false political economy may be very instructive history'.[27] Even if Maine was now less confident about his jurisprudential judgments, he clearly saw that his doubts concerning the capacity to generalise might be applied with advantage to the political economist's vision of human nature. Once again he was intent upon attacking the would-be expert.

[23] *Ibid.*, pp. 6–8, Lecture 1.
[24] *Ibid.*, p. 195, Lecture 6.
[25] *Ibid.*, p. 197, Lecture 6.
[26] *Ibid.*
[27] *Ibid.*, p. 191, Lecture 6.

By the 1870s the science of jurisprudence was no longer what it had been for Maine. The claim, or at least the hope, that it might arrive at a grand synthesis of historical and contemporary observations is put quietly to one side. Instead there is a new respect for the analytical achievements of Bentham and Austin and, insofar as these need to be modified by historical understanding, the modifications are not such as to enable the jurist to reduce them to a rule. The complexities are too great, 'the possibilities practically infinite'.

This reduces the philosophical status of scientific jurisprudence but it does not detract from its immediate practical utility. On the contrary, as Maine explicitly states, it is an instrument 'for procuring the reduction of the law to continuous writing and its inclusion within aptly-framed general propositions'. It is this process which will enable all citizens, even those 'of a very humble order' to have 'a fair practical knowledge of the law which regulates their everyday life'. It is now the means by which the law may be prized away from the experts – from the lawyers – and returned to the public. We are beginning to see how in seeking to render the law clear Maine was also seeking to change its content; he was even attempting the utter destruction of the common law. Scientific jurisprudence was no longer aimed at some ultimate truths, but it still could play a vital role in the development of good law.

In some respects, admittedly, this accords with *Ancient Law*. Particularly at a time of rapid social change the practising lawyer has a humble, passive role; and the especial task of the jurist is to contribute to social harmony by the clarification of legal principle, the development of codes, and the discussion of law in such a way as to make legal debate comprehensible to the lay mind. What had now changed was his confidence in the synthesis of ideas which characterised *Ancient Law*. Quite simply, he was no longer sure of his capacity to produce some all-embracing theory which could account for the totality of legal phenomena. In 1861 Maine had believed he was on the way to more wide-ranging and successful forms of analysis but by the 1870s this belief was gone, and the relationship between the various elements in his lectures was not clear. By the 1870s it is not too difficult to isolate these elements and consider separately, say, his response to new ideas in legal history and his assault upon notions associated with, say, the common law. The former would look more scholarly than many of the more argumentative passages of *Ancient Law*; and the latter would look more polemical than many of the more restrained parts of *Ancient Law*. It was now difficult to see how the grand attempt at the synthesis of these elements which had been characteristic of *Ancient Law* could possibly be sustained. It was as if the horizons of Maine's jurisprudence had begun to contract.

'THE EARLY HISTORY OF INSTITUTIONS'

The full title for this, his third book, is *Lectures on the Early History of Institutions*, and as its title and date of publication (1875) suggest it was another product of the lectures he had delivered at Oxford in the years following his appointment as Corpus Professor of Jurisprudence. The Preface contains the claim that Maine was attempting 'to carry further in some particulars the line of investigation pursued by the Author in an earlier work on *Ancient Law*'.[28] In pursuit of this objective the initial chapters are dominated by a long and detailed historical analysis in which he attempted to respond to the recent work of other scholars; his lectures now contain references to Sohm, Le Play, Morgan, McLennen, Tylor and many others. Despite an obvious respect for their achievements Maine did not feel compelled to transform his old views about social change in the light of the new information which they had made available. At times his tone is insistent, even shrill. In the course of emphasising his previous ideas, he claimed that 'it is one of the facts with which the Western world will some day assuredly have to reckon, that the political ideas of so large a portion of the human race, and its ideas of property also, are inextricably bound up with the notions of family interdependency, of collective ownership, and of natural subjection to patriarchal power'.[29] There even was continuity in the way he sought to turn upon those who discuss very modern and fashionable issues without regard to their historical background. For example, in considering the property rights of married women, he attacked his fellow Victorians when they responded to this topical subject by suggesting that it was some sort of novelty; on the contrary, as Maine emphasised, it was one of the oldest forms of right known to legal thought.[30]

But for all the colourful emphasis upon continuity, a significant part of Maine's new lectures was taken up with a subject which previously had received scant attention in Victorian England. He was

[28] *Lectures on the Early History of Institutions* (London, 1875), p. vii.

[29] *The Early History of Institutions*, pp. 2–3. Maine was now committed to the long and unconvincing defence of his patriarchal theories; see Feaver, *From Status to Contract*, particularly at pp. 142–3 and chapter 13.

[30] *Ibid.*, chapter 11, 'The Early History of the Settled Property of Married Women', particularly at p. 306.

very concerned with showing that the ancient laws of Ireland – the brehon laws – were a source of great historical interest and provided instructive material for an understanding of legal change. He wrote with a feeling which amounted to joy when he discussed the translation of the records relating to these laws: the recent work which had been done, and which was still being done, with these Irish texts had put at his disposal a previously closed system of law. He spoke of the possibility of regarding the Irish laws as a code; 'if its authenticity could be fully established, this ancient Irish code would correspond historically to the Twelve Tables of Rome, and to many similar bodies of written rules which appear in the early history of Aryan societies'.[31] Sensing, perhaps, that he had been carried away by his own pleasure he soon qualified this until, ultimately, he restored his initial view after an elaborate argument in which he talked of 'Kernels' of written law common to different systems and of contrasting 'accumulations' formed upon them in different places.[32] In any event, whatever their precise origin, Maine argued that the laws which were known and which now had been translated, were of immense value to the scholar.

The brehon laws are in no sense a legislative construction, and thus they are not only an authentic monument of a very ancient group of Aryan institutions; they are also a collection of rules which have been gradually developed in a way highly favourable to the preservation of archaic peculiarities.[33]

As ever, Maine's enthusiasm took him towards controversial observations with strong political overtones. In considering Irish legal history he was led to insist upon the importance of centralised government for the development of modern legal ideas. It was just this form of government which Ireland was lacking at a crucial stage in its legal history when the old brehon laws could have been transformed into something distinctively modern.

If the country had been left to itself, one of the great Irish tribes would almost certainly have conquered the rest. All the legal ideas which, little conscious as we are of their source, come to us from the existence of a strong central government lending its vigour to the arm of justice would have made their way into the brehon law; and the gap between the alleged civilisation of England and the alleged barbarism of Ireland during much of their history, which was in reality narrower than is commonly supposed, would have almost wholly disappeared.[34]

[31] *Ibid.*, p. 10, chapter 1.

[32] *Ibid.*, pp. 10–12, chapter 1.

[33] *Ibid.*, p. 11, chapter 1.

[34] *Ibid.*, pp. 54–5, chapter 2.

Maine was also, of course, anxious to relate all this new information to his ideas about lawyers and in particular to his theories about English lawyers. As before, he attacked the parochialism of the English legal mind. With condescension he stated that 'it is not, perhaps, as often noticed as it should be by English writers on law that the method of enunciating legal principles with which our Courts of Justice have familiarised us is absolutely peculiar to England and to communities under the direct influence of English practice'.[35] Predictably, he went on to point out that even such powerful persuasive authorities as the texts of the Roman *Corpus Juris* and the unofficial writings of famous lawyers hold, at most, a secondary place in the estimation of the English judges and Bar. In tones of some exasperation he remarked that he had 'found it difficult to make foreign lawyers understand why their English brethren should bow so implicitly to what Frenchmen term the "jurisprudence" of a particular tribunal'.[36]

Suddenly, however, Maine qualified his remarks. It was true that only legislative rearrangement and restatement could cure the English law of the injury which it had received from its own methods; but in doing this the new law would 'fully disclose the stores of common sense which are at present concealed by its defects of language and form'. Maine emphasised 'one of the most honourable characteristics of the English system,' which was to be found 'in its extreme carefulness about facts'. In this respect Maine's praise was almost unlimited. 'Nowhere else in the world is there the same respect for a fact, unless the respect be of English origin. The feeling is not shared by European contemporaries, and was not shared by our remote ancestors.'[37] He even brought himself to agree with the views of barristers: 'I quite concur', he wrote, 'in the ordinary professional opinion that its view of facts and its modes of ascertaining them are the great glory of English law'.[38]

It was, surely, the very notion of finding himself in agreement with professional ideas which immediately drove Maine from this point to reconsider his most fundamental beliefs about law reform. In sad tones he said he was afraid that 'facts must always be the despair of the law reformer'.[39] At one time it had been thought that reforms in the

[35] *Ibid.*, pp. 46–7, chapter 2. [36] *Ibid.*
[37] *Ibid.*, p. 48 chapter 2. [38] *Ibid.*, pp. 48–9, chapter 2.
[39] *Ibid.*, p. 49, chapter 2.

law of evidence would ensure that questions of fact ceased to present any serious difficulty: or, in any event, Maine himself believed that Bentham had expressed such a view. Yet now, Maine thought, 'inquiries into facts became more protracted and complex than ever';[40] and his response was not to reassess Bentham's ideas but momentarily to forsake reform itself.

> The truth is that the facts of human nature, with which Courts of Justice have chiefly to deal, are far obscurer and more intricately involved than the facts of physical nature, and the difficulty of ascertaining them with precision constantly increases in our age, through the progress of invention and enterprise, through the ever-growing miscellaneousness of all modern communities, and through the ever-quickening play of modern social movements.[41]

Maine is here introducing into his analysis ideas which are by his past standards most unorthodox. He admits that there are limits to the possibility of law reform, and he justifies this concession to those who oppose change by pointing to 'the facts of human nature'. Thus by 1875 Maine was beginning to lose his old and unequivocal faith in certain forms of legal change and in the capacity of anybody to make scientific judgments about human nature and history.

It is because of this that no very clear picture of law and lawyers emerges from the pages of *The Early History of Institutions*. Admittedly, he is concerned with the way in which the lawyers have made the law much more intricate than it need have been. For example, this explains some of his interest in the ancient Irish laws when they were, in a sense, a part of culture.[42] It was only much later, when the law had fallen into the hands of a hereditary group of lawyers, that it became obscure by reason of its detail and nice distinctions.

But criticisms and observations such as these are no longer linked to a coherent argument. At times, Maine made remarks about English law which follow his old disdain for the profession but, by reason of their random placing, they are difficult to relate to any general analysis of legal practice. He retained his old contempt for the style of certain English law books and he still could not resist making this disrespect public.[43] He praised Hatherley, a Lord Chancellor of recent date, for a

[40] *Ibid.* [41] *Ibid.*

[42] *Ibid.*, p. 14, chapter 1. This is one of the points at which Maine observes that in certain eras law is a form of poetry.

[43] *Ibid.*, p. 17, chapter 1.

particular decision, and as elsewhere, he remarked upon 'the care with which an English Court of Justice sifts the materials brought before it',[44] but he did not relate this sort of observation to his ideas about the distinct glory of English courts being found in their capacity to ascertain facts. Once or twice he remarked with some impatience upon the conservatism of English lawyers. Once or twice he emphasised their great concern with the past. As before he still criticised the incapacity of English lawyers to change their law when change was needed. As before, he emphasised the importance of 'Fictions' in legal history: 'almost everybody can observe that, when new circumstances arise, we use our old ideas to bring them home to us; it is only afterwards, that our ideas are found to have changed'. And he could not resist the temptation to add, in less than flattering terms that 'An English Court of Justice is in great part an engine for working out this process.'[45] Fictions, special pleading, the importance of professional ideas, and all the other legal topics to be found within his earlier works are present, but it is so much more difficult to relate them to any interpretation which provided a general explanation for legal behaviour. In particular, he was less interested in understanding the relationship between lawyers' ideas and public opinion.

He was less concerned with the coherence of everything he wrote and more concerned with particular problems. Even when he interested himself in only a few themes, he was no longer so concerned with the relationship which they had to each other. At times the reader has an impression of an urbane and widely-informed author taking his audience through a series of topical subjects with a slightly inconsequential but pleasant and, in places, lively commentary. By itself this was not necessarily any bad thing: insofar as his audience could be expected to include many lawyers, Maine may have intended his lectures to alert them to the existence of ideas outside the law. It was as if he was now engaged in a series of lectures upon very general and unrelated topics.

For example, Maine had an intense dislike of fanatics and those who, as he saw it, blighted public life with the rigid imposition of dogmatic beliefs. He was always a great hater of modern nationalism. He was most anxious to trace the long and violent process whereby

[44] *Ibid.*, p. 4, chapter 1: the case in question was *Warrick v. Queen's College, Oxford*, 6 L.R., Ch. App., 716. The context of this case in the law of real property is considered in a forthcoming study by the present writer: 'Jaded Victorian Advocates: the Case of De La Warr v. Miles'.

[45] *Ibid.*, p. 229, chapter 8.

'common territory' was substituted for 'common race' or 'kinship'. For Maine this development was easy to relate to some modern societies: in considering the concept of the English race and the presence of men of English origin in America and Australia, he observed that the notion of consanguinity 'is extremely diluted, and quite subordinated to the newer view of the territorial constitutions of nations'.[46] But in respect of other modern societies Maine's reasoning had to be more elaborate. He acknowledged that in his day 'the older conception of national union through consanguinity has seemed to be revised by theories which are sometimes called generally theories of Nationality, and of which particular forms are known to us as Pan-Sclavism and Pan-Teutonism'. This revival was explained by Maine as 'a product of modern philology'; it had grown out of the assumption that linguistic affinities proved community of blood. In response, he argued somewhat ingeniously that 'wherever the political theory of Nationality is distinctly conceived, it amounts to a claim that men of the same race shall be included, not in the same tribal, but in the same territorial sovereignty'.[47]

In retrospect it is particularly noticeable that there was a possible link between these ideas and some of the nationalist notions in the German historical jurisprudence with which Maine was acquainted. If he had explored this relationship Maine would surely have had much more than an influence upon the quality of English political debate at this stage of his life; he also would have done more to change the history of English jurisprudence. He would have presented a very clear European alternative to utilitarian legal theory. Speaking very generally, the ideas of German scholars were received with great respect in English academic life at this time, and Maine might have been able to further his cherished ambition of relating legal study to other forms of intellectual inquiry by using their jurisprudential methods. But it seems that he was never tempted. No doubt he was repelled by the vagueness of arguments concerned with nationalism; they were too like the absurd generalisations practised by those other thinkers who had a misguided enthusiasm for the 'Law of Nature'. Also, he could easily have seen how they might be used to defend an institution such as the common law from the legislative reforms of Parliament; such an ancient form of law might be defended on the grounds that it was in some vague sense the 'natural' expression of the

[46] *Ibid.*, p. 74, chapter 3. [47] *Ibid.*, p. 75, chapter 3.

ways of the English people. Maine simply regarded such notions as an affront to civilised jurisprudence. Indeed at other times he went, as it were, in the opposite direction. 'Happily', he observed, 'it is a distinct property of the Comparative Method of investigation to abate national prejudices.' He went on to state his belief that 'the government of India by the English has been rendered appreciably easier by the discoveries which have brought home to the educated of both races the common Aryan parentage of Englishmen and Hindoo'.[48] In other words this form of scholarship pointed, as Maine saw it, to the need to ignore national boundaries rather than to emphasise their importance. He felt that 'wherever we have any knowledge of a body of Aryan custom, either exterior to or but slightly affected by the Roman Empire, it will be found to exhibit some strong points of resemblance to the institutions which are the basis of the brehon law'. Of this latter body of Irish law, Maine observed that

> it has some analogies with the Roman law of the earliest times, some with Scandinavian law, some with the law of the Sclavonic races, so far as it is known, some (and these particularly strong) with the Hindoo law, and quite enough with old Germanic law of all kinds, to render valueless, for scientific purposes, the comparison which the English observers so constantly institute with the laws of England.[49]

Whatever its validity by the standards of modern scholarship there is a certain grandeur about Maine's sweeping determination to use 'science', in the form of the comparative method, as an instrument for attacking the prejudices of his own countrymen and establishing foundations for mutual respect between different nations.

This sort of concern with popular views has to be kept very much in mind when considering the last two lectures which, with the other eleven, make up *The Early History of Institutions*. At first sight they seem to be different in content and argument from the other part of the work since they consist almost entirely of an analysis of John Austin's ideas and only incidentally continue Maine's earlier exploration of new research into ancient law. On closer inspection however, the last two lectures do accord with the themes of the others. They begin with a denunciation of just the sort of legal history which Maine so disliked. Laying stress upon his suspicion of the ideas of the English Bar he observed that

> the historical theories commonly received among English lawyers have done

[48] *Ibid.*, pp. 18–19, chapter 1. [49] *Ibid.*, pp. 20 and 19, chapter 1.

so much harm not only to the study of law but to the study of history, that an account of the origin and growth of our legal system, founded on the examination of new materials and the re-examination of old ones, is perhaps the most urgently needed of all additions to English knowledge.[50]

It is fair, or at least logical, to conclude from this that Maine believed that the lawyers had produced misconceptions about England of such dimensions that their erroneous ideas amounted to the greatest defect of English knowledge as a whole. However, strangely, having said this, Maine turned completely from the issue and began an analysis of utilitarian jurisprudence. Presumably he felt that he had already said enough to substantiate such a judgment about the lawyers' abuse of history; and he thought he now could turn his attention to the defects of English legal philosophy as a sort of supplement to his purely historical investigations.

In any event, it is immediately clear that Maine wanted to go further than he had ever done before in the direction of finding a coherent and useful place for Austin's ideas in the study of jurisprudence. In part this was because Austin's ideas had come to occupy an important position in the teaching of law and it would have been odd for a professor of jurisprudence such as Maine to ignore his works: when speaking at Oxford, Maine pointed out that the *Province of Jurisprudence Determined* has 'long been one of the higher class books in this University; and, taken together with other lectures . . . it must always, or for a long time to come, be the mainstay of the studies prosecuted in this Department'.[51] But in part Maine was attracted to the subject by an increasingly strong belief in its intrinsic merits. He praised both Austin and Bentham for their avoidance of *a priori* reasoning and their determination to concentrate upon 'strict scientific process' allied with observation, comparison and analysis. For him, their merits were such that they deserved attention even if the reader did not agree with their particular conclusions: their vigorous reasoning and careful writing made for a good training – 'they are indispensable, if for no other object, for the purpose of clearing the head'.[52]

We have seen that the flowing style of *Ancient Law* may well have been to a significant extent the product of a reaction against the work of Austin: in the 1850s and 1860s Maine wrote in a popular way just

[50] *Ibid.*, p. 342, chapter 12.
[51] *Ibid.*, p. 345, chapter 12.
[52] *Ibid.*, p. 343, chapter 12.

because he was alarmed at the failure of Austin properly to explain his ideas to the educated public. Now, however, he made an attempt to rehabilitate Austin even in this context: he explained Austin's 'peculiarities' of style as a product of the author's extreme interest in Bentham and Hobbes with whom he had, as it were, 'a perpetual commerce of thought'. Maine thought that the chief problem presented to the mind by a reading of Austin lay not in style but rather in 'the shape in which the conceptions of law, right, and duty are presented to it'.[53] Unfortunately, this unexpected distinction between style and shape seems obscure and Maine failed to elaborate upon it. Perhaps he meant that individual arguments of Austin could be understood, but the premises upon which they were founded were not always clear. Certainly, there is a hint that this was what Maine intended in his later observation that Austin, like some of the 'greatest writers on Political Economy', did not state his 'assumptions or postulates' with sufficient fullness.[54] For Maine this was particularly regrettable because he believed that when these assumptions were made clear Austin's arguments became much more convincing. Indeed, given the premises, they were valid; if the starting points were accepted 'the great majority of Austin's positions follow as of course and by ordinary logical process'.[55]

Having advertised Austin's achievements, and having to his own satisfaction given him a secure place in the proper education of lawyers, Maine proceeded in a much more critical manner to relate Austin's ideas to the analysis of ancient society. The reader has already been warned by Maine of the fact that this may lead to an emphasis upon some of Austin's ideas to the exclusion of others; Maine had already described Austin's concern with the laws of God as 'singular' and had hinted at a capacity to detach them from the rest of his work. Now, however, he proceeded to a fuller consideration of Austin's ideas with an analysis which began with sovereignty – and this was so despite the fact that this was the last topic considered by Austin. Indeed Maine felt compelled to explain why Austin did not begin with the topic, and he embarked on a very unconvincing explanation in terms of Austin's desire to respond to the ideas of Blackstone and Bentham.

After introductory remarks Maine therefore starts a commentary

[53] *Ibid.*, p. 345, chapter 12.
[54] *Ibid.*, p. 347, chapter 12.
[55] *Ibid.*, p. 346, chapter 12.

on Austin's ideas by inverting the latter's order of topics, and giving the greatest prominence to just the sort of subject which was most likely to prove vulnerable to historical criticism. The emphasis was no longer upon what we might call the formal analysis of concepts such as duty; it was, instead, focused upon ideas which may be related to readily perceived political and social facts. The result was easy to predict. Austin was praised for his full examination of the conceptions dependent upon the notion of sovereignty in the form of positive law, sanction and right, etc. But he was found lacking in his failure properly to consider 'the origin of Government and Sovereignty'. Maine pointed out that Austin barely entered on this inquiry, 'indeed he occasionally, though perhaps inadvertently, uses language which almost seems to imply that Sovereignty and the conceptions dependent on it have an *a priori* existence'.[56] For Maine this is indefensible; unless we investigate the social reality we cannot decide 'in what degree the results of the Austinian analysis tally with facts'. He went on to emphasise the point. 'There is, in truth, nothing more important to the student of jurisprudence than that he should carefully consider how far the observed facts of human nature and society bear out the assertions which are made or seem to be made about Sovereignty by the Analytical Jurists.'[57] In other words, Maine claims that the most important issue in the jurisprudence of the day lies in a consideration of the context of one particular analytical notion. Austin's work is turned (almost literally) upside down and then, as it were, forced to answer questions which the jurist did not set himself to answer.

The result of this investigation was a foregone conclusion. The analytical jurists made 'unhistorical' assumptions; the Austinian view of sovereignty is simply the result of 'Abstraction'. At the same time however, Maine did not turn from his initial praise; he wished, as always, to stress the value of the work done by the analytical jurists. He was particularly critical of their attempts to relate the concept of sovereignty to direct or indirect force, but he accepted that such an approach has some sound philosophical merits. The Austinian notion of sovereignty

> is arrived at by throwing aside all the characteristics and attributes of Government and Society except one, and by connecting all forms of political superiority together through their common possession of force. The elements neglected in the process are always important, sometimes of extreme impor-

[56] *Ibid.*, p. 356, chapter 12. [57] *Ibid.*, p. 357, chapter 12.

tance, for they consist of all the influences controlling human action except force directly applied or directly apprehended; but the operation of throwing them aside is, I need hardly say, perfectly legitimate philosophically, and is only the application of a method in ordinary scientific use.[58]

Austin's approach had some of the qualities of sound mathematical reasoning. It is just that when a topic such as sovereignty is considered the defects of such an approach are liable to become apparent; 'the pupil of Austin may be tempted to forget that there is more in actual sovereignty than force, and more in laws which are the commands of sovereigns than can be got out of them by merely considering them as regulated force'.[59]

All this provided Maine with the foundations for more wide-ranging remarks about customs and conventions in which he proved, without much difficulty, how impossible it was to relate Austinian notions to numerous historical phenomena. It culminated, however, in an attempt to rearrange Austin's ideas which was so extreme that the modern reader might be forgiven for wondering at first if Maine intended his words to be taken seriously. In speaking of the second, third and fourth lectures of the *Province of Jurisprudence Determined* Maine remarked that they are occupied with an attempt to identify the law of God and the law of Nature with the rules required by the theory of utility. 'The lectures', he continued, 'contain many just, interesting, and valuable observations; but the identification, which is their object, is quite gratuitous and valueless for any purpose.'[60] In this extraordinary and brief sentence Maine dismisses from consideration what one can only assume Austin took to be an essential and substantial part of his analysis. In short Maine has deliberately produced a 'new' Austin who seems most unlike the 'old' Austin. The order of the latter's argument is inverted; large parts of his writing are omitted altogether; and what remains is praised for its technical accomplishment in philosophical terms but condemned for its failure to relate to the facts of legal history.

This brutal surgery seemed to cause Maine no alarm whatsoever. In his next and final lecture he continued to mix praise for the analytical jurists with rather pompous corrections to their assumptions about the past. Bentham and Austin are put in their time and place as firmly as the notion of sovereignty itself; neither could have conceived of

[58] *Ibid.*, p. 359, chapter 12.
[59] *Ibid.*, p. 361, chapter 12.
[60] *Ibid.*, p. 369, chapter 12.

their particular brand of jurisprudence without having lived in the modern state with its characteristic forms of sovereignty. Fortunately, just because of this, their theories did reflect some of the reality of the age in which they lived. They were 'able to frame a juridical terminology which had for one virtue that it was rigidly consistent with itself, and for another that, if it did not completely express facts, the qualifications of its accuracy were never serious enough to deprive it of value and tended moreover to become less and less important as time went on'.[61] In retrospect there is something almost amazing about these words of Maine: history revealed the inadequacy of Austin as a guide to legal phenomena but it would, at the same time, bring reality closer and closer to Austin's vision of the law. History required that the future lay with the ideas of those who ignored history.

It was the oddity of this that drove Dicey in *Law and Public Opinion* to observe:

> It is difficult, for example to say whether Maine does or does not accept Austin's analysis of sovereignty as sound, if it be taken as an account of the fully developed idea of sovereignty as it exists in a modern civilised state such as England; but it is quite clear that he attaches an importance to the historical growth of conceptions, such as sovereignty or law, which was unknown to Austin, and to the school of Bentham.[62]

Presumably, it was an awareness of his own ambiguity which led Maine himself to place a novel emphasis upon the fact that law had a history of close association with two notions, order and force. Before the time of the analytical jurists law implied order more than all other things.

In particular law was inextricably linked to the laws of science: by quoting Blackstone he stressed how law could be explained as a rule of action, it could be applied to all kinds of action, whether animate or inanimate, rational or irrational – 'Thus we say, the laws of motion, of gravitation, of optics or mechanics, as well as the laws of nature and of nations.'[63] However, as Maine saw it, in the work of the analytical jurists force is of primary significance. For them it is only through metaphor that the term law has been extended 'to all uniformities or

[61] *Ibid.*, p. 397, chapter 13.

[62] Dicey, *Law and Public Opinion*, p. 412.

[63] *The Early History of Institutions*, p. 371, chapter 13.

invariable successions in the physical world, in the operations of the mind, or in the actions of mankind'.[64]

Maine might have made use of this distinction by using it to illustrate still further what he saw as being the unique and very modern quality of analytical jurisprudence. He could have related it to his numerous attacks upon the law of nature by showing that the latter was the product of past circumstance and of no use or relevance to the nineteenth century. He could even have used it to argue that the common law, as a body of rules which had at times been regarded as existing independently of sovereign power, was of necessity an anachronism. But instead of this he suddenly tried to unite the two notions: 'Many persons to whom the pedigree of much modern thought is traceable, conceived the particles of matter which make up the universe as obeying the commands of a personal God just as literally as subjects obey the commands of a sovereign through fear of a penal sanction.'[65] In other words the order of nature has been regarded as determined by a Sovereign command, and, as a result, we may say – according to Maine – that order and force as terms of jurisprudence lose much of their explanatory power. In fact Maine goes on to an almost casual exploration of custom in which comparatively little use is made of the idea of order.

In short, there is a suggestion in both the tone and content of this last lecture that Maine is casting about for new ideas and failing to discover a line of inquiry which can engage his interest for any length of time. In the previous lecture he had spoken openly of the need for a new form of legal understanding: 'next to a new history of law what we most require is a new philosophy of law'.[66] The very fact that he at least considered Austin's theology was an indication of a search for a new approach. Perhaps he had fleeting hopes that the concepts of force and order would enable him to provide a synthesis of historical and analytical jurisprudence.

This discontent with jurisprudence as he now found it is all the more understandable when it is placed alongside his failure to relate his ideas about lawyers, and the practice of law, to the other elements of his work. We have seen that he claimed that he was carrying further the line of investigation pursued in *Ancient Law*, but in substance this only referred to the almost anecdotal presentation of more infor-

[64] *Ibid.*, p. 372, chapter 13. [65] *Ibid.*, p. 373, chapter 13.
[66] *Ibid.*, p. 342, chapter 12.

mation rather than the rethinking of his chief ideas. In some respects, admittedly, it is difficult to criticise him for this. The brehon laws were of great importance and it was right that he should draw them to the attention of jurists. His incidental remarks, particularly his observations on nationalism, were pleasant and civilised. But in the final analysis he now had little to offer the legal philosopher beyond obvious and repetitive remarks about historical and analytical perspectives on the law. He had come a long way from the confident pronouncements and hopes of *Ancient Law*; the process which we observed in *Village Communities* had been taken a step further. There was no longer any obvious belief in his own capacity to produce a comprehensive legal philosophy in which he could explain the relationship between different legal phenomena and, at the same time, accommodate these phenomena within laws of history and social change.

'DISSERTATIONS ON EARLY LAW AND CUSTOM'

Just as he had done in the *Early History of Institutions*, Maine began his *Dissertations*[67] of 1883 by making a claim to continuity with his previous studies;[68] and, as before, the claim could not conceal the fact that he was drawing further away from what he had said about legal philosophy in his earlier works. Tracing the precise changes in Maine's ideas is no easy task at this point because, as he himself pointed out, the new book was based upon lectures given some years before at Oxford, yet, in the course of revising them, much of their content had been 'materially altered'.[69] In regard to these alterations it is immediately apparent to the reader that Maine was now taking an

[67] *Dissertations on Early Law and Custom*, chiefly selected from lectures delivered at Oxford (London, 1883): some of the chapters (5,6,9,11) had already been published in part in the *Fortnightly Review* and the substance of chapter 8 had appeared in the *Nineteenth Century*. See 'The Decay of Feudal Property in France and England', *Fortnightly Review*, vol. 21, April 1877, pp. 460–77; 'Ancient Ideas Respecting the Arrangement of Codes', *Fortnightly Review*, vol. 25, May 1879, pp. 763–77; 'The King and his Relation to Early Civil Justice', *Fortnightly Review*, vol. 30, November 1881, pp. 603–7; 'The King and his Successor', *Fortnightly Review*, vol. 31, February 1882, pp. 180–94; 'South Slavonians and Rajpoots', *Nineteenth Century*, 2 December 1877, pp. 796–819. Feaver's bibliography in *From Status to Contract* provides a complete cross-reference for all of Maine's published work during these years. Elements of the above articles may be found in the following respective pages of *Dissertations on Early Law and Custom*: 291–328; 362–92; 160–91; 125–59; chapter 8.

[68] *Ibid.*, preface: 'The Author continues in these pages the line of investigation which he has followed in former works.'

[69] *Ibid.*

approach which differed markedly from his previous style of analysis. He clearly took still more delight than he had previously done in producing colourful turns of phrase which bear little relation to his scholarly concerns. For example, in considering the importance of the Salic rule Maine could not resist observing that 'The King of England who first invaded Ireland was a Frenchman. The King of England who united Scotland with her was a Scotchman. But the King of France was from first to last born and educated a Frenchman.'[70] And a moment later he could not refrain from talking of 'the French love of unity, the French taste for centralisation, the French national spirit'.

In places this sort of enthusiasm led Maine towards political observations of an even more direct nature than those which could be found in his previous works. In the course of considering the decay of feudal property in France and England he suddenly digressed to consider what was likely to sustain, in his own day, the institution of private property. In search of a justification for this form of ownership he pointed to the popular notion – 'to a very great extent a true one' – that 'all property has been acquired through an original transaction of purchase'.[71] He was just as happy to go on and to point out that private property was also supported by a 'general sense of its expediency', the legal rules for prescription, and 'the respect of the most permanently powerful section of every society for its institutions'. Maine was so carried away by his political preferences that he went on to praise the Victorian attempts to render more easy the sale of land previously subject to strict settlements and other impediments. He related these reforms to his great theme of status to contract by expressing his desire to see 'the purification by contract of the title to property'.[72] He must have known very well how topical these references were in 1883 when *Early Law and Custom* was put before the public. The Settled Land Act of the preceding year went some way towards giving those who occupied land under family trusts the right to sell such land even if certain other parties to the trust objected. He may also have had in mind the fairly recent legislation concerned with co-ownership which, again, made it easier to sell land when it was subjected to multiple interests.

Maine was yet more open, yet more committed, in his enthusiasm for integrating into his analysis the popular scientific ideas of the day.

[70] *Ibid.*, p. 159, chapter 5. [71] *Ibid.*, p. 325, chapter 9.
[72] *Ibid.*

With obvious delight, he sought in his remarks about primitive societies to associate Darwin's ideas, particularly those to be found in his *Descent of Man*, with the Patriarchal theory to which Maine himself was, of course, so strongly attached.[73] And he was just as enthusiastic about popular beliefs relating to 'Natural Selection'. For example, in considering the development of primogeniture he thought that 'in the beginning of history, quarrels were rife within reigning families . . . The madness of rivalry took possession of the chiefs and the people were smitten.' The explanation for what then happened was simple: 'a very ancient, possibly the most ancient method of settling these quarrels was that which has been called in our day Natural Selection'.[74] As before, in the course of such arguments, he used science to attack those who had no historical understanding of law.

In general terms he ridiculed those who thought that somewhere there was 'a framework of permanent legal conceptions which is discoverable by a trained eye, looking through a dry light, to which a rational Code may always be fitted'. Maine now felt that he could call all science in support of his own vision: 'the legal notions which I described as decaying and dwindling have always been regarded as belonging to what may be called the osseous structure of jurisprudence; the fact that they are nevertheless perishable, suggests very forcibly that even jurisprudence itself cannot escape from the great law of Evolution'.[75] Maine also made a lively use of other scholars, some of whom (such as Herbert Spencer) claimed to be scientific and others of whom (such as Fustel de Coulanges) provided him with generalisations which he could treat in a vaguely scientific manner. By the middle of *Law and Custom* the reader has no cause for being surprised when he is told that science was on the side of Maine's arguments.[76]

Perhaps Maine felt driven to such colourful generalisations just because other parts of *Law and Custom* were far from being contentious and dramatic as when they consisted of discussions about the anthropological work of Tylor or McLennan or Lewis Morgan. Much of Maine's lengthy account of 'East European House Communities'[77]

[73] *Ibid.*, for example, at p. 206, chapter 7: 'the greatest name in the science of our day is associated with it . . .'.

[74] *Ibid.*, p. 133, chapter 5.

[75] *Ibid.*, pp. 360–1, chapter 10. This is one of the points at which he does criticise Bentham and Austin for their lack of historical judgment.

[76] For example, see p. 206, chapter 7 (use of Darwinian analysis).

[77] *Ibid.*, chapter 8.

is carried on in terms which makes it strange to find it in the same book as those passages which have been mentioned above. The same may be said of his analysis of the 'Theories of Primitive Society' or his very extensive consideration of 'Ancestor-Worship' and the 'Sacred Laws of the Hindoos'.[78] For page after page there is (by comparison with his past writing) rather detailed and even (to use again one of Maine's words) 'sober' analysis.

In short it seems that Maine was as anxious as he had ever been to ensure that his works mixed scholarly analysis with fashionable observations and lively comment. But now the mixture consists not so much of regular comparisons between, say, scientific material and popular ideas, as between separate and irregular references to these very different topics. The overall content of the book is similar to that of its predecessors, but the way in which the content is presented has changed: the scholarly work does not, as it were, sit so easily beside the lively remarks relating to more worldly matters.

Admittedly, some of his sentences are still in the style of *Village Communities*. There is still the opposition to 'professional' ideas; there is still the interest in the actual creation of professional groups of lawyers and their capacity to mix legal and religious work; there is still the attempt to compare different bodies of law, as when he compares Hindu law and the English common law. But within the great range of his references there is also a new element. There are more extensive sections of analysis exclusively concerned with modern English law and its institutions. For the first time Maine considers in a little detail the growth of 'the most highly centralised system of judicial administration in the world' and makes references to English legal history as when, for example, he remarks that 'even with the addition of the new county courts, the English judicial system has another feature peculiar to itself – the fewness of the judges employed in administering justice'. Maine at one stage begins an exploration of the origins of the common law, and he claims, predictably enough, that 'It was in the main a version of Germanic usage, generalised by the King's courts and justices.'[79]

Passages such as this were associated with a novel concern for the development of English substantive law. He considered aspects of property law at length and it is noticeable that he was no longer so

[78] To be found in, respectively, *Ibid*., chapters 7, 3 and 1.

[79] A good example of the interest in English developments is to be found in *Ibid*., pp. 389–92, chapter 11. The reference to Germanic usage is at p. 190, chapter 6.

heavily concerned with its relationship to primitive institutions such as co-ownership. It is true that he saw the latest simplifications in the conveying of land as encouraging a reference to certain ancient principles of transfer, but now he went beyond these comparisons between old and new and considered modern systems for, say, the public registration of sales.[80] This appears in a chapter concerned with the classifications of property, and it is succeeded by an even longer chapter devoted to the classifications of legal rules.[81] Much of the latter is concerned with debates, not all of them of an historical nature, about the divisions proper to Roman Law but, again, there are significant references to the development of justice in England. He obviously enjoyed writing sentences such as: 'So great is the ascendancy of the Law of Actions in the infancy of Courts of Justice, that substantive law has at first the look of being gradually secreted in the interstices of procedure; and the early lawyer can only see the law through the envelope of its technical forms.'[82] He went on, rather wryly perhaps, to observe that even modern civilisations experienced reversions towards earlier conditions of thought: after all, he argued, the law reforms of the 1830s were associated with a revival of interest in strictness of pleading.

The reader of his books might reasonably expect this interest in the English legal system and English law to be accompanied by an increased interest in purely English jurisprudence. There are a number of references to the ideas of Bentham and Austin; and in accordance with his previous criticisms he observed that

> the great difficulty of the modern Analytical Jurists, Bentham and Austin, has been to recover from its hiding place the force which gives its sanction to law. They had to show that it had not disappeared and could not disappear; but that it was only latent because it had been transformed into law-abiding habit. Even now their assertion that it is everywhere present where there are Courts of Justice administering law, has to many the idea of a paradox – which it loses, I think, when their analysis is aided by history.[83]

But, considered as a whole, *Law and Custom* is remarkable for its dearth of references to jurisprudence, and in particular for its failure to consider utilitarian and positivist jurisprudence in any detail.

In part at least Maine himself explains this. At one point he referred to *Ancient Law*, noting that he said there: 'What were the motives

[80] *Ibid.*, p. 358, chapter 10.
[81] *Ibid.*, respectively chapters 10 and 11.
[82] *Ibid.*, p. 389, chapter 11.
[83] *Ibid.*, pp. 388–9, chapter 11.

which originally prompted men to hold together in the family union?' And in 1861 he had answered this by saying that 'To such a question Jurisprudence unassisted by other sciences is not competent to give a reply.'[84] Now, in 1883, he was publishing lectures some of which at least did seek to answer the question and it followed, of necessity, that he thought he had less and less to say about jurisprudence. The impression which this created in the mind of the reader was likely to be very significant; Maine's analysis of law and his analysis of anthropology were, to an increasing extent, unrelated. Indeed we may say that this was the point at which Maine, by his own reasoning, had become interested in anthropology as a distinct form of study quite separate from jurisprudence.

But Maine did not devote all of *Law and Custom* to this sort of issue. Much of it was concerned with modern developments which were just as capable of being related to the problems of legal philosophy. It seems that now he just was not so interested in exploring the relationships concerned. Perhaps the best way to explain this comparative lack of interest in legal theory is to stress his remarks about the subject in the *Early History of Institutions* where, as we have seen, he concentrated upon an interpretation of Austin's works and, at the same time, made it very clear that he wanted a new philosophy of law. Maine made no suggestion in 1883 that he had progressed towards the discovery of such a philosophy. There is even a certain self-consciousness about his references to the old schools of thought. It seems that he was aware of the fact that he had nothing new to say about jurisprudence and that he felt that comparative silence was appropriate.

However, his apparent desire to remain quiet on this topic was to be important. Now it was easy to see that Maine's thought had undergone a change since *Ancient Law* was first published. The link between various forms of reasoning was no longer as clear as it had been. The assured cross-references between jurisprudential theory and the sort of facts discussed in *Ancient Law* were a thing of the past. Just as Maine had explicitly called for a new legal philosophy and failed to find one, so, too, he now had failed to integrate the new phenomena he discussed into some general and coherent scheme for the understanding of law. To some extent at least *Law and Custom* should be seen as a response to the failure of everyone, including Maine himself, to develop the new jurisprudence which might have served to integrate

[84] *Ibid.*, again see discussion at p. 206, chapter 7.

analytical and historical information. As a result the elements in Maine's initial synthesis become yet more distinct and bear a still more awkward, less persuasive, relationship to each other. He is now much readier to discuss anthropology in something like its own terms and law becomes to an increasing extent a vehicle for political comment or anecdotal remark, or even uncritical historical observations. There is nothing violent about the change: in all save one respect – the novel lack of interest in jurisprudence – it is a matter of degree. But it is nonetheless a significant development; the Maine of 1883 believed he had little new to offer the lawyer, and almost nothing to give to the jurist. He could no longer even attempt to answer the questions he had once set himself.

'POPULAR GOVERNMENT'

Popular Government was based upon articles published in the *Quarterly Review* between 1883 and 1885, and it reveals very clearly the extent to which Maine continued to lose interest in speculative legal thought during his later years. Instead, his mind was dominated by immediate political developments – such as a further extension of the franchise – and his chief concern was to persuade his fellow Victorians that democracy threatened their greatest achievements. However, even against this unpromising background, Maine was unable to resist incidental observations upon law in its political context and these merit attention.

Much of what Maine said in *Popular Government* is topical, and it is difficult for the modern reader to put twentieth-century prejudices to one side when reading the four essays contained within the book. For example, Maine explored a theme which is common in late twentieth-century legal debate when he argued that a written constitution such as that of the United States of America provided direct lessons for English lawyers. In particular he praised it for what he saw as its capacity to thwart the socialist measures which might be attractive to a House of Commons elected by an ever increasing number of electors.[85] He was writing at a time when universal male adult suffrage had almost been achieved and his sense of alarm as to where this could

[85] *Popular Government* (London, 1885), Essay 4, 'The Constitution of the United States', reprinted by Liberty Classics, 1976. Maine responded to the critics of his essays in an article in *Nineteenth Century* (see 'Mr. Godkin on *Popular Government*', vol. 19, March 1886), but this did not contain anything of jurisprudential significance.

lead was very clear. He thought it threatened private property and the production of wealth.

> Nothing is more certain than that the mental picture which enchains the enthusiasts for benevolent democratic government is altogether false, and that, if the mass of mankind were to make an attempt at redividing the common stock of good things, they would resemble, not a number of claimants insisting on the fair division of a fund, but a mutinous crew feasting on a ship's provisions, gorging themselves on the meat and intoxicating themselves with the liquors, but refusing to navigate the vessel to port.[86]

He was particularly anxious to show that much of the American constitution was 'English' and, as such, well-adapted to English circumstances.[87] He wrote that

> there are doubtless strong conservative forces still surviving in England; they survive because, though political institutions have been transformed, the social conditions out of which they originally grew are not extinct. But of all the infirmities of our Constitution in its decay, there is none more serious than the absence of any special precautions to be observed in passing laws which touch the very foundations of our political system.[88]

And having observed this he went on to talk of 'the nature of this weakness, and the character of the manifold and elaborate securities which are contrasted with it in America . . .' In proceeding to consider these 'manifold and elaborate securities' he resorted to the experience of the past and roundly asserted that 'the great strength of these securities against hasty innovation has been shown beyond the possibility of mistake by the actual history of the Federal Constitution'.[89] Predictably, Maine's great favourite in this regard is the capacity, as he saw it, for various parts of the constitution to be used in such a way as to defend freedom of contract. For him it was this which 'has in reality secured full play to the economical forces by which the achievement of cultivating the soil of the North American Continent has been performed, it is the bulwark of American individualism against democratic impatience and Socialist fantasy'.[90]

Maine also explored other matters which have become popular in recent years; for instance he explored 'the theory of the Mandate', the

[86] *Popular Government*, p. 66, Essay 1.

[87] For example, *Ibid.*, p. 11. Maine's old friend, Lord Bryce was on the verge of publishing his study of American politics and he was somewhat alarmed at Maine's lack of understanding about America and the US constitution: see Feaver, *From Status to Contract*, at p. 254.

[88] *Popular Government*, p. 236, Essay 4.

[89] *Ibid.*, pp. 236–39, Essay 4.

[90] *Ibid.*, p. 243, Essay 4.

proper powers of political parties and the proper role of juries. In all respects he was notably pessimistic: for example, in regard to juries he concluded that 'nor is it in the least doubtful that, but for the sternly repressive authority of the presiding Judge, the modern English Jury would, in the majority of cases, blindly surrender its verdict to the persuasiveness of one or other of the counsel who have been retained to address it'.[91] Fortunately, for Maine there was the occasional gleam of light; in considering the prospects of democracy he agreed that it might succeed – it had some advantages;[92] but his more sustained view was well-expressed when he said 'we are drifting towards a type of government associated with terrible events – a single Assembly, armed with full powers over the Constitution, which it may exercise at pleasure'.[93]

It is reasonable to wonder how all of this relates to Maine's achievements as a jurist. But Maine himself made it clear that *Popular Government*, like all his books, was to be seen as a great deal more than an extensive form of journalism. Even though it was made up of articles which were first published in the *Quarterly Review* he never set out to distinguish its content from his other works. He clearly intended it to be taken as a serious contribution to legal writing, and as such its extremely polemical content strikes a jarring note.

The best way to explain this, and to assess the jurisprudential significance of what he was attempting, is to return to his old concern with clarity of exposition and literary appeal. His desire to explain the law in terms which would be understood and appreciated by the layman was as strong as it had ever been; and now it was only too obvious to Maine that if Britain was to preserve the conservative features of its 'social conditions' it would have to develop what we might call a new legal superstructure with a new political role for law and lawyers. In other words, it is of the first importance to see that, as always, in being so very conservative Maine was not being, at the same time, a supporter of the common law. As before, he was seeking to preserve the past by ridding law of its worst and least efficient features; and, as before, for Maine the common law, and the constitutional ideas which went with it, were inefficient and deserved to be superseded by a modern American constitution. This does not, of

[91] *Ibid.*, p. 107, Essay 2. This is one of the very few remarks of Maine in *Popular Government* which might be construed as a compliment to the common law. But it is a somewhat backhanded form of praise.

[92] *Ibid.*, p. 121, Essay 2.

[93] *Ibid.*, p. 136, Essay 2.

course, mean that the common law, or even, say, the Inns of Court, would vanish. Maine hardly mentions either of them now. It just meant that the common law, and the ideas of the common lawyer, would cease to dominate the whole world of law; in particular the relationship between legal thought and political life would not rest upon the idea that the common law was in some way or other the source of the citizen's liberties. In future the best law was to be preserved by clear statements of principle contained within an entrenched constitution. These principles could, of course, be understood and debated by non-lawyers; and, once again, we see that for Maine it was desirable to do everything to ensure that law did not become the possession of the lawyers as it had become under the common law. He had returned to his determined statements to this effect in *The Early History of Institutions*, but now the remedy is a written constitution rather than codification by itself.

Within a year of publication of *Popular Government*, A. V. Dicey was to publish his very influential *Law of the Constitution*.[94] In considering *Ancient Law* we have seen how there are links between the way Maine and Dicey wrote about public opinion. However, strangely enough, in contrast to this similarity in their work, there are very real differences of approach in the way the two analysed the actual relationship between law and politics. Both were concerned with harmony between the law and public thought but they sought to achieve it in contrasting ways. Dicey was acutely concerned with the difficulties of the Bar.[95] In the decades preceding the 1880s the very existence of the profession had been called in question; many eminent lawyers had openly doubted the capacity for their old ways to survive an era when the public was far more interested in legal reform than legal tradition. Dicey, unlike Maine, sensed that the public mood was changing and in the early 1880s, partly in response to this, and partly in response to his own deeply held convictions, he presented a powerful case for the virtues of professional experience. In other words he praised the common law for its capacity to produce lawyers with a knowledge of practical problems. In the everyday life of the courts they learned about human nature, and they saw that what mattered in the law was not grand-sounding declarations of principle so much as the actual enforcement of rights. Dicey's analysis was elaborate and sustained – eventually it transcended the boundaries of his consti-

[94] A. V. Dicey, *Law of the Constitution* (London, 1885).
[95] Cocks, *Foundations of the Modern Bar*, chapter 9.

tutional studies and received more extensive treatment in his separate study, *Law and Public Opinion*.[96] The radical contrast with Maine's ideas about the proper role for lawyers is easy to see. As far as Dicey was concerned, it was necessary to leave many of the most important issues in the development of the law to the lawyers. But for Maine, as before, this was not appropriate; law should reflect experience, but experience should be judged and assessed by the informed individual who might or might not be a lawyer. It was not the experience of the courts which was of primary importance; on the contrary the experience of everyday work had a bad and destructive influence upon the professional outlook. Lawyers became too concerned with technique as an end in itself and many of their practices reflected their own interest rather than the public's. Always, it was the task of the jurist to simplify law, relate it to principle, and, thereby, to open it up for public discussion. The common law, with its implicit claim to leave the creation of law in the hands of the lawyers was something which could not be justified in the light of either history or the behaviour of professional men.

As before, almost the only reason Maine can find for praising the 'Law of Nature' as a guide to jurisprudence lies in the fact that it went some way to producing better organised and more coherent bodies of law; it brought about many valuable reforms of private law 'by simplifying it and clearing it from barbarous technicalities'.[97] Also, it was in the name of clarity that Maine continued his praise for the utilitarian jurists. He praised Austin's analytical power in the latter's very conservative *Plea for the Constitution*. In approving of Austin and other writers he wrote that 'In our day, when the extension of popular government is throwing all the older political ideas into utter confusion, a man of ability can hardly render a higher service to his country, than by the analysis and correction of the assumptions which pass from mind to mind in the multitude . . .'.[98] At times Maine seems to be suggesting in the manner of Austin that clarification itself will lead automatically to an understanding of what it is that makes for good law.

However, Maine's increasingly strong and explicit conservatism presented him with great problems as far as Bentham was concerned.

[96] A. V. Dicey, *Law and Public Opinion* (London, 1904). The book is based upon lectures which were first given in 1898.

[97] For such sentiments, see, for example, *Popular Government*, p. 22, Preface.

[98] *Ibid.*, p. 78, Essay 2.

The latter's concern with clarity and 'masculine' thought was, no doubt, admirable, but now Maine went out of his way to attack Bentham's 'Greatest Happiness Principle' and he derived some humour from what he took to be his political judgment. For Maine it was clear that 'multitudes include too much ignorance to be capable of understanding their interest', and this fact 'furnishes the principal argument against Democracy'. He was adamant in this regard, and in emphasising his opinions he made it very clear that however much he might wish to prevent legal debate from becoming a monopoly of the lawyers he certainly did not intend it to become dominated by the public at large. 'The fact is', wrote Maine,

> that, under its most important aspect he [Bentham] greatly overrated human nature. He wrongly supposed that the truths which he saw, clearly cut and distinct, in the dry light of his intellect, could be seen by all other men or by many of them. He did not understand that they were visible only to the Few, to the intellectual aristocracy.[99]

Maine was being remarkably forthright. Once again we see that a vital task of the jurist is to clarify the law: Bentham is to be commended for this; and, no doubt, Maine also commended Bentham's suspicion of the lawyers and what they did with the law. But Bentham was wholly wrong in his belief that all or even many citizens would be capable of understanding the law in its clarified form. This privilege was preserved, by reason of their exalted mental competence, for the 'intellectual aristocracy'. The creation of new law is to be left in the hands of clever and educated people who need not be lawyers; and this is so because, of course, the jurists have clarified the law for them. These informed individuals plainly make up only a small part of the population, and the cynic might be forgiven for wondering whether Maine's attacks upon the lawyers have given everyday citizens any more control over the law than Dicey's exaltation of the lawyers themselves.

Maine was, no doubt, sincere in his belief as to the possible achievements of an intellectual aristocracy. Law, however clearly expressed, could only be understood in terms of what history had shown to be possible; and only a few could ever come to a proper understanding of history and thereby acquire a knowledge of say, the problems inherent in any appreciation of the relationship between law and opinion. *Popular Government* contains many indications that Maine saw this relationship as approaching a particularly difficult phase in modern

[99] These various references to Bentham are all found at *Ibid.*, pp. 102–3, Essay 2.

western life. The capacity for an educated elite to modify the law in response to change was being threatened from numerous quarters for it was not just an extended franchise which endangered harmony between society and law. Maine was particularly concerned with those whom he described as the 'Irreconcilables'.

There can be no more formidable symptom of our time, and none more menacing to popular government, than the growth of Irreconcilable bodies within the mass of the population. Church and State are alike convulsed by them; but, in civil life, Irreconcilables are associations of men who hold political opinions as men once held religious opinions . . . They are doubtless a product of democratic sentiment; they have borrowed from it its promise of a new and good time at hand, but . . . they utterly refuse to wait until a popular majority gives effect to their opinions.[100]

Reemphasising the ideas he had developed before, he stressed that the worst of these men are the nationalists: 'nobody can say exactly what Nationalism is, and indeed the dangerousness of the theory arises from its vagueness. It seems full of the seeds of future civil convulsion.'[101]

It looks as if Maine was trying to plead for the use of an intellectual aristocracy on the grounds that it could protect the people from those who would pervert the true democratic process. Such a concern on his part may be found within his writing in other places, and there are very large sections of *Popular Government* which show that he had a great distrust of almost all sections of the population. It was this lack of faith which led him to despair of achieving progress through Parliamentary democracy. For him, the electorate as a whole was profoundly conservative and quite incapable of achieving progress by itself. As Maine put it, 'one of the strangest of vulgar ideas is that a very wide suffrage could or would promote progress, new ideas, new discoveries and inventions, new arts of life'. In reality, he thought, 'the chances are that, in the long run, it would produce a mischievous form of conservatism, and drug society with a potion compared with which Eldonine would be a salutary draught'. He was most insistent upon this old argument of his and pursued it at numerous points. A wide suffrage 'would probably put an end to all social and political activities, and arrest everything which has ever been associated with liberalism'.[102]

Maine's strength of feeling and manifest sincerity arose out of his

[100] *Ibid.*, p. 49, Essay 1. [101] *Ibid.*, p. 50, Essay 1. [102] *Ibid.*, p. 57, Essay 1.

well-established conviction that, most of all, a wide suffrage would endanger scientific progress. He asked any man who disagreed with him to 'turn over in his mind the great epochs of scientific invention and social change during the last two centuries, and consider what would have occurred if universal suffrage had been established at any one of them'.[103] He proceeded to argue that if such a franchise had been established there would have been no spinning-jenny and no power-loom, no threshing machine and no adoption of the Gregorian calendar. Roman Catholics and Dissenters would have been proscribed in accordance with the sentiments of the mob – albeit different mobs on different occasions. Mr Darwin's ideas, including of course his notion of the survival of the fittest, are 'evidently disliked by the multitude, and thrust into the background by those whom the multitude permits to lead it'.[104]

There is an easy explanation for the strength of Maine's feelings upon this last point: as in his previous work, he spoke with approval of 'the springs of action called into activity by the strenuous and never-ending struggle for existence, the beneficent private war which makes one man strive to climb on the shoulders of another and remain there through the law of the survival of the fittest'.[105] The proper setting for this struggle was, needless to say, 'the sacredness of contract, and the stability of private property, the first the implement, and the last the reward, of success in the universal competition'.[106] All of this was liable to be upset by a wide suffrage. The legislative infertility of democracies springs from permanent causes. The prejudices of the people are far stronger than those of the privileged classes; they are far more vulgar; and they are far more dangerous because they are apt to run counter to scientific conclusions.'[107] For Maine, one of the strongest proofs of all in this regard seems to have been based upon his assessment of how the female mind worked. If women became involved in politics public life would soon be characterised by increased conservatism. They were the 'strictest conservators of usage and the sternest censors of departure from accepted rules of morals, manners, and fashions'.[108] Most striking of all, however, was his attempt to emphasise 'the very slight changeableness of human nature' as evidenced by prehistoric investigations. If we take these into consideration we will see, he thought, that 'like the savage, the Englishman,

[103] *Ibid.*, pp. 57–8, Essay 1.
[104] *Ibid.*, p. 59, Essay 1.
[105] *Ibid.*, p. 70, Essay 1.
[106] *Ibid.*, p. 71, Essay 1.
[107] *Ibid.*, p. 87, Essay 2.
[108] *Ibid.*, p. 149, Essay 3.

Frenchman, or American makes war; like the savage he hunts; . . . like the savage he indulges in endless deliberation . . .'[109]

This was very dangerous ground for Maine. It hinted at the immutability of social institutions such as law in a way which he would always have avoided in the past. He was plainly in some difficulties in, at the same time, attacking democracy based upon a wide suffrage, defending his old ideas about progress, remarking upon the permanent elements in human nature, and stressing – as he always had done – how much legal ideas and institutions had changed in the course of ages. In any event, his concern with relating science and history to his extreme political worries, and his numerous ideas about man and progress, culminated in some ideas which look singularly odd beside the conventions of modern jurisprudence. At one stage he resorted to using 'scientific method' to undermine the sort of reasoning associated with Bentham's science of legislation. 'Neither experience nor probability', he thought

> affords any ground for thinking that there may be an infinity of legislative innovation, at once safe and beneficent. On the contrary, it would be a safer conjecture that the possibilities of reform are strictly limited. The possibilities of heat, it is said, reach 2,000 degrees of the Centigrade thermometer; the possibilities of cold extend to about 300 degrees below its zero; but all organic life in the world is only possible through the accident that temperature in it ranges between a maximum of 120 degrees and a minimum of a few degrees below zero of the Centigrade. For all we know, a similarly narrow limitation may hold of legislative changes in the structure of human society.[110]

Bentham's reforming science of legislation has been replaced by a deeply conservative analogy.

Popular Government sold well and did very little for Maine's reputation as a scholar.[111] This surprised and disappointed him but enough has already been said to show how easy it was for reviewers, particularly those who wrote for radical journals, to emphasise its polemical content. In retrospect at least it seems unfortunate that Maine did so little to detach it from his previous jurisprudential ideas. It was true that much of it accorded with what he had said about legal philosophy in the *Early History of Institutions*: he continued to commend the achievements of utilitarian jurists in clarifying the law and he still sought – if somewhat precariously – to show how profoundly law may

[109] *Ibid.*, p. 153, Essay 3. [110] *Ibid.*, pp. 157–8, Essay 3.

[111] Feaver, *From Status to Contract*, Chapter 18, 'A Manual of Unacknowledged Conservatism' and Chapter 19, 'Final Years', particularly p. 237.

change in the course of history. But there is no new development of these two ideas. Once again, he completely ignored his own call of 1875 for a new jurisprudence. In so far as it relates to law, *Popular Government* looks like a very tired addition to ideas which he had already put before the public.

From a jurisprudential point of view the best that may be said is that he did a little more than he had already done to make law a subject of public discussion. All the articles which made up *Popular Government* were read before publication by Fitzjames Stephen. It was hardly surprising that the very conservative author of *Liberty, Equality, Fraternity*[112] found much to praise in what Maine had written, and it would be pleasant to record that Maine's later thoughts had the same influence upon the discussion of legal ideas as his friend's book. After all, as I have pointed out above, it is possible to trace the debate about the relationship between law and morality on the part of Professor Hart and Lord Devlin back to the publication of Stephen's work; Stephen was noted for his vigorous assertions about the need for the law to maintain certain moral standards and to concern itself in some instances with what many would now regard as private conduct. But it is very obvious that *Popular Government* has never started a comparable debate. Its concern with the relationship between law and politics was too crude. In *Popular Government* Maine was, for the most part, simply concerned with using the law as an instrument to further his immediate political objectives – and these were not such as to encourage jurisprudential argument on the part of himself or anyone else. Given the fact that Maine wanted *Popular Government* to be considered alongside his other works it has to be regarded as a remarkable failure. He completely failed to develop any of his thoughts about legal philosophy. It was, and it remains, a great disappointment. The attempt at synthesis which characterised *Ancient Law* has been put to one side and it was obvious now that nothing would be found to replace it.

[112] See chapter 4, fn. 8 (p. 84).

6

THE RECEPTION OF MAINE'S JURISPRUDENCE

It is a commonplace in the history of jurisprudence that later generations fasten on a few aspects of a jurist's achievement and thereby distort the nature of his work. Recent scholarship has argued very forcibly that this has happened in the case of thinkers as contrasted as St Thomas Aquinas, Hugo Grotius, Gianbattista Vico, Sir William Blackstone, Adam Smith, Jeremy Bentham and John Austin. The later use of their ideas often appears to bear little relationship either to the specific intentions of the jurists concerned, or to the very broad themes in their works which come to the fore when the reader has in mind the historical context in which their books were produced.

If Maine's thought suffered a similar fate it should come as no surprise. We have seen that his own selection of Austin's ideas was unbalanced in the extreme; it is such a strange selection that it is difficult to believe that Maine was even attempting an objective assessment and he may have expected that he himself would fare no better at the hands of others. Also, because of their references to numerous topics, there was a quality to Maine's works which made them susceptible to inappropriate quotation; the critic can choose from such a variety of themes and topics. When he died in 1888 it was likely that the reception of Maine's ideas would be full of contrasts.

HISTORICAL JURISPRUDENCE

Many writers on legal thought regard Maine as the founder of historical jurisprudence in England, but their response to his ideas has been complicated by the ambiguous way in which they themselves have employed the words 'historical jurisprudence'. Since the time of Sir William Holdsworth, there has been a tendency for commentators to suggest that as an authority on historical jurisprudence Maine 'convinced English lawyers that if they wished to understand their law they must study it historically'.[1] It has been easy to step from this position to another position in which Maine's contribution to historical jurisprudence is seen as consisting in the possible stimulus he gave to the study of English legal history. In other words historical jurisprudence is not associated with, say, specific theories about legal change and social types; instead, it is left undefined and is linked to a powerful but indeterminate belief that the legal present cannot be understood without reference to the legal past.

If this seems strange it is worth stressing that Sir Carleton Allen followed Holdsworth in taking such an approach. Allen believed that Maine had rescued the history of law from almost total neglect and, in doing this, had turned the minds of English lawyers away from some very odd ideas about the development of the common law. For Allen, by insisting upon the study of legal history, Maine had changed the concerns of legal thought to such an extent that Maine's own ideas looked, in retrospect, almost trite. He had so altered the assumptions as to what was acceptable that, in Allen's judgment 'considerable portions of *Ancient Law* have, in the course of seventy years, become almost elementary to the student of legal institutions'. As a result, Allen argued that with respect to *Ancient Law* 'so far as England is concerned, it is not too much to say that with the appearance of this book modern historical jurisprudence was born'.[2]

Given the emphasis upon legal history it is reasonable to suggest that Allen had in mind Maine's possible influence upon the remarkable work of Pollock and Maitland, *The History of English Law Before the Time of Edward I*.[3] If Maine did have a significant influence upon the study of the English legal past it would certainly have been reflected in this book. Yet, despite the fact that Maine had at least attempted some specific observations about the development of English legal history, and despite the more obvious fact that his generalisations about law as a whole could be related to the growth of the common law, there are few mentions of Maine in the work concerned. Pollock never lost his respect for Maine's ideas about primitive law. But his silence – and that of Maitland – on the topic of

[1] Holdsworth, *A History of English Law*, vol. 15, p. 366.
[2] Sir Carleton Allen, *Legal Duties and other Essays in Jurisprudence* (Oxford, 1931), essay on 'Maine's Ancient Law', p. 139.
[3] Sir Frederick Pollock and F. W. Maitland, *The History of English Law Before the Time of Edward I* (Cambridge, 1895).

Maine's thought about English law itself, point clearly to the belief that Maine's approach to the legal history of his own country left much to be desired.

In this regard, Professor Stein has set out many of the objections which the late-Victorian legal historians brought against Maine's ideas, and it is clear beyond doubt that the criticisms were justified and that they related to important issues. It was pointed out that much of what Maine had said constituted an inaccurate guide to Anglo-Saxon societies which did not consist of patriarchal clans united by agnatic relationships. It was possible to make jokes at Maine's expense when he used anachronistic terms to describe the 'Family' and likened it to a 'Corporation'. Similar things could be said about his analysis of ownership in the context of his discussion of the village community and its rights over land. After these, and other observations, it is hardly surprising that Professor Stein expressed gratitude to Sir Henry Maine 'for provoking a brilliant piece of corrective research by Maitland' when Maine's blunders concerning Bracton induced Maitland to write *Bracton and Azo* with a view to correcting a 'stupendous exaggeration'.[4]

The lack of enthusiasm for Maine seems to have gone even further than these criticisms suggest. The second paragraph of Pollock and Maitland's Introduction to *The History of English Law* is somewhat isolated from the arguments of those which surround it, and the strong, almost emotional, words produced in the course of discussing just the sort of approach which Maine had used point to a severely hostile attitude to his whole method of writing about legal phenomena. Pollock and Maitland wrote that

> it has been usual for writers commencing the exposition of any particular system of law to undertake, to a greater or less extent, philosophical discussion of the nature of laws in general, and definitions of the most general terms of jurisprudence. We purposefully refrain from any such undertaking. The philosophical analysis and definition of law belongs, in our judgment, neither to the historical nor the dogmatic science of law, but to the theoretical part of politics. A philosopher who is duly willing to learn from lawyers the things of their own art is as full as likely to handle the topic with good effect as a lawyer, even if that lawyer is acquainted with philosophy, and has used all due diligence in consulting philosophers. The matter of legal science is not an ideal result of ethical or political analysis; it is the actual result of facts of human nature and history. Common knowledge assures us that in every tolerably settled community there are rules by which men are expected to order their conduct.

[4] Stein, *Legal Evolution*, p. 110, and see generally chapter 5, 'The Aftermath of Ancient Law'.

In part, no doubt, all of this was aimed at what they took to be the wilder extremes of current historical scholarship with its emphasis upon national spirit and folk-consciousness. But Pollock and Maitland made no attempt to salvage Maine's ideas from their general attack, and it is passages such as this which explain their obvious determination to make few mentions of his name. Indeed, soon afterwards, Pollock and Maitland went so far as to refer to the fact that 'by gradual steps, as singularly alike in the main in different lands and periods, at the corresponding stages of advance, as they have differed in detail, public authority has drawn to itself more and more courses and matters out of the domain of mere usage and morals'. This was exactly the sort of problem with which Maine had been concerned, and yet, again, they make no mention of his thought.

Admittedly, Vinogradoff was to make an attempt to claim Maitland for Historical Jurisprudence, and thereby, perhaps, indirectly to suggest Maine's influence as an earlier writer on the subject. In an essay entitled 'A Master of Historical Jurisprudence' he wrote of Maitland as the man 'who was not led on by the aims of the craftsman, intent on immediate utility, nor by the instructive industry of an antiquarian; he tried to fathom the process of social life, and he knew that it was only by diving deep into the current of history that we could make the attempt'. As such, 'his attitude towards the objects of his research was thoroughly *philosophical*, not in the sense of abstract systematisation, but in the original meaning of the Greeks'.[5] However, it is most unlikely that Maitland would have enjoyed any accolade which might enable us to link his ideas with those of Maine. We have recently been reminded by Collini of Maitland's reported remark about Political Science that 'either it is history or it is humbug'; and Collini has also pointed out that Maitland was very wary of fashionable Idealism and was never any sort of disciple of Gierke despite his translation of the latter's *Die Deutsche Genossenschaftsrecht*. Gierke's 'splendid' book was 'too metaphysical' and Maitland was unimpressed by 'a sociology emulous of the physical sciences [which] discourses of organs and organisms and social tissue', and, 'among the summits of philosophy', of 'a doctrine which . . . ascribes to the State, or more vaguely, the "community" not only a real will, but "the" real

[5] Sir Paul Vinogradoff, *Collected Papers of Paul Vinogradoff* (Oxford, 1928), vol. 1, p. 265. See also *Outlines of Historical Jurisprudence* (Oxford, 1920), vol. 1, Preface (n.b., the book is dedicated to Dicey) and J. W. Jones, *Historical Introduction to the Theory of Law* (Connecticut, 1940) at, for example, p. 58.

will'.[6] No quantity of references to the Greeks could enable Vinogradoff successfully to turn Maitland into an Historical Jurist, least of all an Historical Jurist who would happily link his analysis of history with the sort of ideas to be found in either German historical scholarship or *Ancient Law* with its interest in the capacity for the physical sciences to provide a model for the study of the past.

In short, despite the claims of Holdsworth and Allen, we begin to see at this point Maine's negative role in English legal scholarship. The fact that Maine had failed to provide a coherent and persuasive synthesis of legal and philosophical enquiries must have done much to contribute to the belief that the two could, and should, be separated. It was a belief which was already finding support before Maine's death but it would have deeply shocked Maine during his early, optimistic years when he was preparing *Ancient Law*. It also would have offended theorists such as Austin and Heron; and it would greatly have disappointed imaginative public men such as Brougham and West-

[6] See S. Collini, 'Sociology and Idealism in Britain, 1880–1920', *Archives Européennes de Sociologie*, vol. 19, 1978, pp. 32–4, quoting Kitson Clark, 'A Hundred Years of the Teaching of History at Cambridge, 1873–1973', *Historical Journal*, vol. 16, 1973, p. 543 and C. H. S. Fifoot (ed.), *The Letters of F. W. Maitland* (Cambridge, 1965) pp. 86, 209; and O. Gierke, *Political Theories of the Middle Ages* (translated and introduced by F. W. Maitland) (Cambridge, 1900) p. xi. Vinogradoff himself could become somewhat entangled in his analysis of where Maitland did (and did not) follow Maine: see *Outlines of Historical Jurisprudence*, p. 147. Generally, writers on Maitland have taken contrasting approaches to assessing the possible significance of Maine. H. E. Bell's *Maitland: A Critical Examination and Assessment* (London, 1965) appears to avoid all discussion of Maine even where it would surely be appropriate (e.g. pp. 3–4); H. A. L. Fisher in *Frederick William Maitland: A Biographical Sketch* (Cambridge, 1910) praises Maitland's fortitude in the face of temptation – 'the very seduction of Maine's method, the breadth of treatment, the all-prevailing atmosphere of nimble speculation, the copious use of analogy and comparison, the finish and elasticity of style were likely to lead to ambition and ill-founded imitation' (p. 27). C. H. S. Fifoot, in *Frederick William Maitland: A Life* (Harvard, 1971) reports on Maitland's critical views of Maine and proceeds (at p. 118) to defend Maine. In his edition of *The Letters of F. W. Maitland*, Fifoot also reveals some of the less pleasant things Maitland said about Maine: for example, in a letter to Pollock in 1901 he said, 'You spoke of Maine, well I always talk of him with reluctance, for on the few occasions on which I sought to verify his statements of fact I came to the conclusion that he trusted too much to a memory that played him tricks' (see Letter 279, and note 97). In his recent study, *F. W. Maitland* (London, 1985) Professor Elton mentions Maitland's lack of respect for Maine (p. 17) and himself makes the observation that 'Anthropology directed the influential, though in the end misleading, work of Sir Henry Maine . . .' (p. 19). However, sometimes Maitland found his way to very moderate praise: in 1892 he wrote that 'It would seem as if Maine's teaching bore better fruit in France and Belgium than in England' (see H. A. L. Fisher (ed.), *The Collected Papers of F. W. Maitland* (Cambridge, 1911), vol. 2, p. 252).

bury. As Professor Calvin Woodard has shown, the late Victorians and their successors either ignored Maine or fastened on an increasingly narrow vision of what he had said about legal history. Their attitude served to exclude 'a wealth of "human", "environmental" and other "extra-legal" factors from the corpus of Legal History . . .'[7]

From the point of view of Victorian ideas as a whole, it is the claims of the later writers such as Pollock and Maitland which stand out as being novel and distinct. The demarcation of the appropriate approach to legal history has about it an air of certainty which is quite alien to, say, the open interest in alternative methods of investigation which is apparent in *Ancient Law*. In attacking the ideas for which someone such as Maine – at least in his early life – had tried to stand, Pollock and Maitland were imposing severe limits on what would be acceptable in the future development of English legal research. Of course, this determination to specialise was of inestimable benefit for historical scholarship; it produced very substantial advances in historical studies – perhaps the greatest which have ever taken place in England. But this does nothing to change the fact that it did much to restrict the range of questions which were deemed appropriate for *legal* analysis. Maine's failure to provide a convincing synthesis of law, history and philosophy – even of philosophy in the form of the scientific analysis of history – had a very significant legacy for English legal thought. It encouraged a more restricted understanding of what made for legal study; and it limited the scope of such claims as could be made that the legal past contained 'lessons' which could be used directly to improve modern law and standards of legal practice.

It may be that Maine's works were more significant for the development of the study of constitutional law, and that this does something to explain the views of Holdsworth and Allen with their insistent claim that he did so much for English legal history. This is not the place for an attempt at a full analysis of the growing importance of constitutional law within the late-Victorian educational arrangements for prospective lawyers: there is no question of briefly coming to terms with the constitutional works of, say, Anson. But it is at least necessary to consider the possible influence of Maine's ideas upon Dicey's very important theories relating to the historical development of the constitution because, as we have seen, Dicey made

[7] C. Woodard, 'History, Legal History and Legal Education', *Virginia Law Review* (1967), vol. 53, no. 1, p. 102. This stimulating article contains some ideas at variance with what is written here. I am indebted to Professor Geoffrey Best for this reference.

significant references to Maine's works and happily admitted to the part they played in the formation of his own ideas. At the very best, the normative elements in constitutional law would surely have provided an excellent opportunity for the development of an analysis using the approach of Historical Jurisprudence. For example, conventions could be praised in accordance with the extent to which they enabled the constitution to adapt over time to changing social circumstances. Also, Dicey is particularly important in this context because in places he forcefully denigrated the value of purely historical analysis in explanations of the constitution: anyone who doubts this should read his lively views on the place of history in constitutional analysis in the Introduction to successive editions of *The Law of the Constitution*.[8]

We have already seen that Maine and Dicey shared certain similarities of approach when they wrote about the influence of ideas upon changes in the law; for example, Dicey was happy to write very much in the manner of Maine when he remarked:

> a student is puzzled whether most to admire or to condemn the sensible but, it may be, too easy acquiescence of Frenchmen in the actual authority of any *de facto* government, or the legalism carried to pedantic absurdity of Englishmen, who in matters of statesmanship placed technical legality above those rules of obvious expediency which are nearly equivalent to principles of justice.[9]

His search for generalisations associated with the impact of certain central ideas led him to just the sort of assertions which appealed to Maine. In the Preface to the first edition of his *Law of the Constitution* Dicey observed that 'it deals only with two or three guiding principles which pervade the modern constitution of England'. Also, despite Dicey's claims for Parliamentary sovereignty, there are clear echoes of Maine's desire to attack accepted notions of sovereign power: here some of Dicey's statements almost could have come from Maine's hand; 'even a despot', wrote Dicey, 'exercises his powers in accordance with his character, which is itself moulded by the circumstances under which he lives, including under that head the moral feelings of the time and society to which he belongs'. Maine would have enjoyed

[8] The first edition was published by Macmillan in London in 1885. Also, see Dicey's *Law and Public Opinion* (London, 1904), pp. 455–62. For a view that Maine had an adverse influence on Dicey see Cosgrove, *The Rule of Law: Albert Venn Dicey, Victorian Jurist*, pp. 28 and 79.

[9] Dicey, *An Introduction to the Study of the Law of the Constitution* (London, 1975), pp. 362–3.

it and understood precisely when Dicey mentioned 'the legal notions of the common law, i.e. of the "most legal system of law" (if the expression may be used) in the world'; and this may be contrasted with the statement: 'that a federal system can flourish only among communities imbued with a legal spirit and trained to reverence the law is as certain as can be any conclusion of political speculation'.[10] Throughout, law is understood to some extent in historical terms, and history itself is largely explained by references to pervasive ideas.

It is striking that in considering the historical development of tensions between law and social interests both Dicey and Maine became concerned with the analysis of how popular ideas and the law should be kept in harmony.[11] Certainly, later on in Dicey's life, the quest for harmony became a major theme in his study, *Law and Public Opinion*. In other words Dicey, like Maine, gave harmony, understood by a reference to historical events, a place in his writing on law. He was concerned with the relationship between law and society and used his observations on their relationship in the course of arguments about topics such as the rule of law.

However, if they agreed upon the importance of ideas and a very important place for harmony in legal analysis, their actual recommendations for future social change were radically contrasted. As we have seen, Maine was led from this position to a savage attack upon the ideas of common lawyers, which was in complete contrast to Dicey's well-known attempts to justify the traditions of English law. For many, Dicey's approach still has great attractions, but even in Dicey's time it produced problems. For Dicey himself it did something to produce the conflict between what he believed lawyers should learn (law rather than conventions) and what he said about the need for lawyers to know and observe conventions. If the common law was to be preserved, lawyers had to be taught that the law was what was enforced by the courts. It would never reside in, for example, some set of politically based understandings as to what was appropriate. At the same time the actual working of the law in its constitutional context could not be explained apart from conventions and political ideas. The result was a continual struggle in Dicey's analysis of law between an 'anti-Maine' approach, which stressed the need for an autonomous understanding of the common law, and a very 'pro-Maine' approach which stressed the political and historical context of the law both for

[10] *Ibid.*, p. 80 and pp. 179–80.

[11] Particularly for Maine in *Ancient Law*, chapter 2.

the purposes of understanding what law was and how it could be used to preserve social harmony. In short, Dicey seems to have been unable to bring himself totally to accept or totally to reject Maine's analysis of law and this introduced irreconcilable perspectives into his own writing about the constitution.

This can do something to explain the subsequent development of constitutional law as an academic subject. Dicey's references to the common law were to provide a tempting target for Jennings with his determination to relate 'merely' legal notions to political reality. Jennings wrote an article called 'In Praise of Dicey'[12] which, in fact, praises Dicey chiefly for his inconsistencies. For constitutional theorists, Maine's ideas as reflected in the historical thought of Dicey have provided a very awkward legacy. Unlike the pure legal historians, the constitutional lawyers cannot shut him out completely because Dicey has used Maine in such a powerful, if selective manner. In short, it looks as if Maine's influence upon the evolution of constitutional law survives in a strangely refracted form by reason of Dicey's popular books which, in the last analysis, often involved using instruments of historical jurisprudence such as the explanation of law by reference to its capacity to reflect, harmoniously or otherwise, changing social interests.

Perhaps we can now see why men such as Holdsworth and Allen could interpret Maine as the founder of a school of historical jurisprudence and describe him as the man who made English lawyers think more carefully of their past. In a very general manner Maine may be said to have directed various legal minds to a reinterpretation of the place of law – particularly the common law – in the English constitution. He introduced a critical element into the lawyers' interpretation of constitutional history. But plainly this is at most a possibility; it has not enabled us to discover a definition of historical jurisprudence; and of course Dicey's use of history in the course of constitutional arguments may be related to numerous other writers whom he expressly acknowledged such as Edmund Burke. Maine's role in the development of constitutional ideas has yet to be fully explored.

Fortunately, we are on much firmer ground when we attempt to consider the reception of Maine's thought in the works of Paul Vinogradoff. His books may unequivocally be described as a form of historical jurisprudence, not least because Vinogradoff himself saw them in such terms, as is indicated by the title of one of his works,

12 *Public Administration*, vol. 13, p. 123.

Outlines of Historical Jurisprudence.[13] Vinogradoff accepted Maitland's criticisms of Maine but sought to show that Maine's comparative historical method was still valid despite his errors of fact.[14] For Vinogradoff there should be careful attention to individual cases before inferences were made, but when this was achieved it would be possible to show the 'formation, development and decay' of particular institutions. Indeed, it would be possible to arrange the material of legal history 'in accordance with divisions and relations of ideas rather than with dates'. And this, in his view, was what Maine had done.

Using this approach Vinogradoff perceived six stages of legal evolution, but, as Professor Stein has shown, the six stages in fact reflected different criteria and it is difficult to relate them to some specific method of analysis.[15] The first three related to a type of society, either totemistic, or tribal or civic. The last three related to legal ideas and reflected the elements of medieval law, or individualistic law or socialistic jurisprudence. Despite the strange contrasts between the various categories, it was clear that Vinogradoff was deliberately following Maine in some respects: for example, there was (very obviously) an evolutionary approach and (less obviously, but with full acknowledgment on Vinogradoff's part) a similar treatment of detailed subjects such as those relating to law which was 'declared' rather than consciously created. Indeed, Vinogradoff always acknowledged his great debt to Maine and one may say that his works constitute the clearest proof that one leading scholar of historical jurisprudence followed in his footsteps.

Unfortunately, beyond this point it is impossible to reveal the influence of Maine on this sort of thinking about historical jurisprudence in early twentieth-century England. Vinogradoff did not leave behind him anything which could possibly be described as a school of thought. In his capacity as a follower of Maine he was very much aware of his own isolation many years before he himself died in 1925. For present purposes, this sense of isolation is very suggestive since Vinogradoff was not a man to hide his feelings and there was a certain anger in the way he spoke about the reception of Maine's ideas. In 1904 Vinogradoff became the Corpus Professor of Jurisprudence and, in part because everybody knew that Maine had been the first Corpus

[13] Sir Paul Vinogradoff, *Outlines of Historical Jurisprudence* (Oxford, 1920).

[14] Vinogradoff's historical jurisprudence is helpfully considered in Stein's *Legal Evolution*, pp. 115–21. There is a need for a full study of Vinogradoff's place in English legal thought; only a few of his works are quoted in the present study.

[15] *Ibid.*, pp. 116–21.

Professor, Vinogradoff immediately took the opportunity to speak bluntly of those who were now disrespectful of Maine's achievement.

> His was one of those minds which radiate far beyond their immediate surroundings: the whole of my generation of students of law and history have had to deal directly or indirectly with the ideas propagated by him or similar to his, and the secret of such a potent radiation is well worth attending to. It is not unusual nowadays to talk in a rather supercilious manner of the lack of erudition and accuracy, of the allusiveness and vagueness of Maine's writings. Those who indulge in such cheap criticisms should rather try to realise what accounts for his having been a force in European thought, a potentate in a realm where parochial patronage and a mere aptitude for vulgarisation are not recognised as titles to eminence.[16]

What were these 'cheap criticisms'? Perhaps they were verbal rather than published. Certainly, Vinogradoff was not writing about scholars such as Pollock who either had kept silent about Maine in this context, or else, when not writing about legal history, developed ideas which were different from those of Maine but which still enabled them to make incidental references to his work. Perhaps Vinogradoff was aiming his arguments at those who had control over the everyday teaching of law. There is evidence (considered below, pp. 187–8) to show that it had become fashionable among these men to denigrate Maine's works. Such an attitude would have accorded nicely with their desire to place more and more emphasis upon the virtues of the common law and the desirability of learning cases and statutes.

In a sense, therefore, Vinogradoff was probably talking – for he frequently expressed his ideas in lectures as well as on paper – about the ideals associated with higher education in England. It was these ideals which had largely determined the fate of Maine's thought about historical jurisprudence, and it seems that Vinogradoff saw them as having some notably bad qualities; in particular, he saw higher education as being designed to pass on a certain way of life, rather than as something which could be used as an instrument for the discovery of new truths. This had very important consequences for the teaching of law at the universities, and, as always, Vinogradoff was not afraid to state them in clear and forceful terms. In England, Vinogradoff observed,

> Liberal education, or rather its concomitants, gets to be so expensive that only few persons can afford to give it to their sons. Scholarships and exhibitions widen the privileged circle, but do not throw down the barriers. Even mere numbers show that academic education in England is more a kind of luxury

16 Vinogradoff, *The Collected Papers*, vol. 2, p. 174. Also in *Law Quarterly Review* (1904), vol. 20, pp. 119–20.

for the select few than the necessary starting-point for many, because what are the six or seven thousand undergraduates mustered by Oxford, Cambridge and the smaller institutions, compared with the tens of thousands which go through the French or German high schools? It may be said that most of those who would attend university lectures on the Continent will study at a hospital or in a barrister's chambers in England: but far from being an objection, this observation only supports my point. Practical training in a barrister's chambers has nothing to do with academic training. Liberal and professional education are indissolubly connected on the continent; they are separated in England.

A young man goes to Oxford, not to learn anything definitely bound up with his future work, but to get up a certain amount of general knowledge, to develop as far as possible his literary tastes and abilities, and, more than anything else, to try life on a larger scale than he has known it at the public school. Only the select few can afford to spend so much time in general preparation, and England, still aristocratic, provides first of all for them; while continental democracy throws open the doors of the universities to professional training, and ennobles professional training by treating it scientifically and philosophically.[17]

The final reference to science and philosophy – indeed the whole attempt to ennoble professional training – provides the clearest possible echo of Maine's ideas. Law was to be understood as a remarkable aspect of man's attempt to develop civilisation; and the history of law contained important scientific and philosophical thoughts which should be pursued by prospective lawyers irrespective of whether or not the search for knowledge served the needs of a 'gentlemanly' education. For Vinogradoff it seems that the unfashionable standing of Maine's attempt to reveal the possible links between history, law and legal practice in both ancient and modern times was the result of what he regarded as restrictive developments in higher education. Historical jurisprudence could only thrive where practice and theory were linked.

Statements such as Vinogradoff's show just how important was the tendency to relate Maine's interpretation of historical jurisprudence merely to the belief that it involved the study of English legal history rather than adventurous generalisations about, say, the relationship between law and political institutions in different societies. In such a context, Maine's standing was at best that of a man with controversial and stimulating ideas or, at worst, that of someone who did not live up to the demands he was alleged to have imposed upon himself. In considering the decades which followed his death it seems clear that

[17] Vinogradoff, *The Collected Papers*, vol. 1, p. 279.

the effort to link historical jurisprudence to various forms of English legal history had both turned Maine into a 'straw man' and isolated Vinogradoff in his attempt to concentrate on the more central concerns of Maine's writing.

Thankfully, a very recent revival of interest in Maine as an authority on historical jurisprudence has been based much more firmly on what Maine himself regarded as important. In part at least it is the product of a desire to understand Maine in his historical context and thereby to obtain a better awareness of his intentions; Professor Stein's book on *Legal Evolution* points clearly in this direction. But, in part, too, it is the product of an attempt to take seriously, and even to use, Maine's observations on the relationship between law and society with a view to developing new ideas in the tradition of historical jurisprudence.

For example, Professor MacCormack has argued that it was characteristic of Maine's approach to historical jurisprudence that there was an 'attempt to show, firstly, how law and legal institutions were caused by, or somehow related to, specific social conditions and hence varied with these conditions, and secondly, that social development and therefore legal development could be viewed as a progression divided into a sequence of stages occurring everywhere in a particular order'. Such an analysis was likely to be challenged and

> ultimately the very breadth of its inquiry, together with the method of investigation, discredited it. In particular it has generally come to be thought that it is not possible (a) to treat social and legal progression according to a series of fixed stages, or (b) to look for universal features of social and legal phenomena in the sense that they can be supposed to be present in all societies at some stage of their development.

But, in response to this, Professor MacCormack has sought to go on and show that these criticisms can be admitted without destroying the case for a modified form of historical jurisprudence. In specific terms he seeks to show that

> it is arguably possible and profitable to investigate comparatively either very wide-ranging questions such as, what is the relationship between certain kinds of society and certain kinds of law? or rather more narrow topics such as the history of contract or the history of standards of liability (including the relationship between social and legal phenomena) or the history of particular legal skills such as the drafting and interpretation of legal rules.[18]

[18] From a paper by Professor MacCormack of the University of Aberdeen. The paper was presented to the W. G. Hart Legal Workshop of July 1984, and is quoted with the permission of the author.

Professor MacCormack is not alone in exploring possibilities such as these. Geoffrey Samuel has considered numerous potential forms of inquiry for a new type of historical jurisprudence. In doing so he has used Maine (amongst many others) to argue that the whole practice of law is a practice of history in that, as Maine stressed so often, it is 'taken absolutely for granted that there is somewhere a rule of known law which will cover the facts of the dispute now litigated'. As this itself suggests, Samuel has taken steps to explore the extent to which historical analysis is, perhaps of necessity, an element of any complete explanation of law.[19]

It seems, then, that Samuel and MacCormack have drawn speculative maps for future work in this area. The problems involved are obvious. In particular, it will be difficult to discover, still more to agree upon, a method which responds to all the justified criticisms of the old school of historical jurisprudence without at the same time producing merely isolated historical studies with little capacity for yielding generalisations. To put it briefly: better history is perhaps just as likely to reveal diversity in the relationships between law and society as it is to point to any type of uniformity.

In any event, there is something very refreshing about this revival. It is particularly in accordance with Maine's early ideas of the 1850s when he was writing *Ancient Law*. There is a growing but, at the same time, flexible interest in the possible role of history and comparative analysis in any attempt (jurisprudential or otherwise) to explain law; and this is what was of primary concern to Maine when, in the 1850s, he was thinking about his best work of jurisprudence. The fact that a sustained attempt to use these methods can now be made is shown by the analysis of Katherine Newman in her study, *Law and Economic Organisation* which considers numerous historical and anthropological studies of law in about sixty pre-industrial societies with a view to explaining why certain types of legal institutions are found in certain kinds of societies.[20] The result is a study which is, in many ways, highly critical of Maine's work; for example, it is suggested that *Ancient Law* underrates the variation and complexity of legal systems which Maine would categorise as 'primitive' or 'patriarchal'.[21] But there is also praise for his capacity to bring together a wide variety of

[19] From a paper by Geoffrey Samuel of Bristol Polytechnic; this paper, too, was presented to the W. G. Hart Legal Workshop of July 1984 and is quoted with the permission of the author.

[20] K. S. Newman, *Law and Economic Organisation: A Comparative Study of Preindustrial Societies* (Cambridge, 1983).

[21] *Ibid.*, p. 212.

sources in *Ancient Law* and, more important, it is recognised that he created a framework for the interpretation of diverse materials. 'Maine's use of historical and literary documents, extant societies, survivals and transitional cases to substantiate his observation of the movement from status to contract stands as an exemplary application of evolutionary methodology.'[22] It seems reasonable to suggest that we are witnessing the early stages of a revival of interest in Maine's historical jurisprudence.

SOCIOLOGY

Sociologists have received Maine's works at a very high level of generality. Sometimes his relevance has been explicitly acknowledged, but it is often difficult to trace precise applications of his thought. It is almost as if sociologists have responded to his ideas with the vagueness for which Maine himself was so often criticised; and to suggest this is, of course, almost a compliment because it hints at the possibility of a response which is more in accordance with Maine's thought than that to be found in some other modern disciplines which seek to dissect his work into little self-contained compartments.

However, it is clear that most of the major sociologists of the late nineteenth and early twentieth centuries displayed little overt enthusiasm for *Ancient Law*. It is highly likely that Weber had a full knowledge of Maine's books since his early research was concentrated upon ancient legal history.[23] Also, at various points in his writing, Weber makes some fairly extensive references to Maine's ideas. For example, the latter may have been of help to him in writing about the relationship between professional structures and beliefs and the development of law. There was much in Maine's works on the evolutionary stages of legal change which Weber could put to use in his analysis of capitalism and its history. But, beyond these points, and a few others like them, it is very difficult to trace links between Maine's general theories and those of Weber.[24]

In his recent study of Max Weber, Anthony Kronman has shown very clearly the extent of Weber's erudition in legal history. In respect of most legal subjects, Weber probably knew a great deal more than

[22] *Ibid.*, p. 9.

[23] See, for example, A. T. Kronman, *Max Weber* (London, 1983), p. 1.

[24] See, for example, Max Rheinstein, *Max Weber on Law in Economy and Society* (Harvard, 1954), List of Books Cited; but it seems that three of Maine's books 'appear to have been extensively used by Max Weber' – see pp. xix and xxi.

any of Maine's books could ever tell him: in particular Weber did not need to be told about the previous achievements of the leading historical jurists. It seems, too, that Maine contributed very little to Weber's interpretative methods. Kronman explains the legal work of his subject without ever having to make an extensive reference to Maine's ideas, and so, to put it bluntly, it seems that Maine contributed almost nothing to Weber's analysis of law. At best he provided some useful historical examples which could be used in arguments which were very different from those which Maine himself would have employed.[25]

In respect of Durkheim, however, Maine's reception was different. Durkheim referred explicitly to Maine's ideas on a number of occasions, and it is obvious that he was familiar with his works.[26] In recent years it has been pointed out that Durkheim may have been influenced by, amongst other things, Maine's emphasis upon the close connection between the nature of a society and the nature of its law; the importance of religion and ritual in understanding the development of law in ancient societies; and the significance of understanding the true qualities of penal law in the early stages of legal change. It has been suggested that Durkheim made very serious errors in interpreting some of the things which Maine wrote, but it has also been argued that the suggestiveness of Maine's categories had, ultimately, a creative role.[27]

It is possible that Durkheim's analysis of the evolution of contractual forms in terms of a change from 'status to contract' to 'will to contract' points to the importance of Maine's thought. However, the precise link is controversial; for example, when Durkheim analysed contract as a 'social' rather than an 'individual' phenomenon the influence of Maine is hard to see. As Hunt has emphasised recently: Maine at times may have been a significant source of ideas for Durkheim but it is very difficult to be certain about his influence. The substance of the problem in this context is that Durkheim was primar-

[25] Even when he refers to Maine explicitly it is apparent that Maine was never an exclusive influence upon Weber. Kronman's references indicate that his ideas happened to coincide with those of other writers: consider Kronman, *Max Weber* at pp. 58–9, 96 and 99.

[26] For example, E. Durkheim, *The Divisions of Labour in Society* (trans. G. Simpson) (New York, 1933), pp. 95, 144, 146.

[27] The debate has not yet closed, see L. S. Sheleff, 'From Restitutive Law to Repressive Law', *Archives Européennes de Sociologie*, vol. 16 (1975), pp. 16–45.

ily concerned with rebutting Herbert Spencer's notion of contract and Maine's thoughts seem to be put to use in a rather incidental fashion.[28]

The same sort of conclusion appears to be inescapable when the American social theorists of the generation which followed Maine are considered. Despite a mutual interest in 'Social Darwinism' there was very little recognition of Maine's occasional thoughts on this topic. It is reasonable to expect that W. G. Sumner, the prolific writer on social change, would have referred to Maine's achievements. The latter's concern with informal types of social control, and his comparative lack of interest in the sort of external sanctions associated with law, would surely have led him to a sympathetic view of Maine's early attempts to emphasise the extent to which law could *not* be used for the purposes of social engineering. Also, Maine's political views, and his associated belief in individualism, would have been highly congenial to Sumner. Yet, in fact, Sumner barely mentions Maine in his chief book, *Folkways*,[29] and there are very few references to him in his other works. It is possible to write an account of Sumner's entire life and works without mentioning Maine whilst, at the same time, numerous points of possible mutual interest are explored.[30] Perhaps the explanation is to be found in Vinogradoff's observation on the generally unfashionable standing of Maine's books in the decades which followed his death. Certainly, Maine's strange and incompetent references to American topics during the last years of his life could have done nothing for his transatlantic reputation.

In the context of English sociology itself the reception was equally disappointing. Hobhouse is often regarded as a founding father and in his capacity as the country's first Professor of Sociology, and a writer on evolutionary themes in social change, one could expect him to refer to Maine, if only to distinguish the latter's very conservative conclusions from his own more optimistic ideas. Yet Hobhouse made few references to him, and Collini has written an analysis of Hobhouse's work which reveals very clearly that Maine had little influence in this

[28] A. Hunt, *The Sociological Movement in Law* (London, 1978); p. 85, fn. 98 (Durkheim's familiarity with Maine); pp. 85–8 (the response). See also, S. Lukes and A. Scull (eds.), *Durkheim and the Law* (London, 1983), p. 11.

[29] W. G. Sumner, *Folkways* (New York, 1906): the only reference to Maine seems to be made almost in passing at p. 261.

[30] For proof that this is so see H. E. Starr, *William Graham Sumner*, (New York, 1925). It would have been easy to refer to Maine at, say, p. 448.

quarter.[31] One may add that after the First World War the evolutionary approach which Hobhouse had brought to English sociology was all but totally eclipsed and, obviously, this would do nothing to revive what little interest there had been in Maine. For the earlier sociologists an enthusiastic response to his ideas would have required commitment to a particular type of evolutionary analysis which they found unacceptable: for the later English sociologists all evolutionary analysis was suspect and Maine's name was inescapably linked to the latter.

Yet, eventually, a revival did take place. During the last twenty years there has been a much greater readiness to acknowledge not so much that Maine had a great influence as that he himself achieved something of value for sociological thought. For example, Nisbet and Bock have linked his name to a conservative tradition of social analysis which has a concern for regulated change, social cohesion and social continuity. As a result, Maine is seen as a man who stressed the defects of almost any sort of social observation which is divorced from historical awareness; and his name is now linked to those such as Burke who sought to find a place for history in what we would now call social analysis.[32]

This approach of Nisbet and others constitutes a stimulating reassessment, but for the moment at least it has been purchased at the cost of certain inaccuracies. For example, Nisbet has written in one of his sociological works that Maine claimed that 'all societies . . . tend to move from status to contract in their emphasis'.[33] But, as we have seen, this is not in fact what Maine said. His writings show that he thought that many societies never moved from an initial emphasis upon status. Nisbet has also written that 'Fustel de Coulanges endows religion with exactly the same causal primacy that in Marx went to property; in Maine law, and in Buckle, physical environment'.[34]

[31] S. Collini, *Liberalism and Sociology: L. T. Hobhouse and Political Argument in England, 1800–1914* (Cambridge, 1979), p. 27 and fn. 50 and 51. Note the comparative lack of interest in Maine in P. Abrams, *The Origins of British Sociology 1834–1914* (Chicago, 1968) and J. H. Abraham, *Origins and Growth of Sociology* (Harmondsworth, 1977).

[32] For instances see R. A. Nisbet, *The Sociological Tradition* (London, 1976) at p. 53; 'Conservatism', in T. Bottomore and R. Nisbet (eds.), *A History of Sociological Analysis* (London, 1978), pp. 80–118; n.b. pp. 81, 83, 104, 105. Compare this with Bock's treatment in 'Theories of Progress, Development, Evolution', *Ibid.*, pp. 39–80: n.b. pp. 68, 70, 72.

[33] Nisbet, *The Sociological Tradition*, p. 72.

[34] *Ibid.*, p. 239.

These may be accurate statements about Fustel, Marx and Buckle but, again, they constitute an incorrect assessment of Maine's ideas. For him, law did not have causal primacy; indeed law itself was usually the product of a variety of distinctively non-legal and wholly social forces. As far as Maine was concerned, for great stretches of history law caused nothing.

However, these errors do not destroy the value of this new approach to Maine; they simply point to the complexity of his possible role in the development of certain social scientific themes in modern thought. For example, T. B. Bottomore has done something to reveal Maine's significance in the attempt of social scientists to develop distinctions between different types of social union. He points out that there have been a variety of efforts to identify the major types of social bond. Hobhouse, for example, distinguished between three broad types of social union based respectively upon kinship, authority and citizenship. Durkheim distinguished two principle types of social solidarity, mechanical and organic. And Sir Henry Maine, Bottomore adds, made a distinction between societies based upon status and those based upon contract.[35]

These observations of Bottomore serve to bring together the two aspects of Maine's reception into sociology. They unite the attempt to find a place for him in the history of the subject and the attempt, also, to show that some of his perceptions are of value today. We shall see (pp. 169–80, below) that the distinction between status and contract is still very much alive in the current analysis of social change and often, both now and in the past, has been expressly linked to Maine's name. This is particularly clear in the response to Maine's thought on the part of Ferdinand Tonnies. However, before this can be understood it is necessary to consider briefly how Maine's ideas have been received into anthropological writing.

ANTHROPOLOGY

There are numerous clear instances of anthropologists responding, favourably or otherwise, to Maine's thought. It is well known that during his own lifetime he was involved in vigorous disputes with

[35] T. B. Bottomore, *Sociology: A Guide to Problems and Literature* (London, 1975), p. 39. But it has been suggested that such divisions hindered rather than assisted the development of sociology: see F. Parkin, 'Social Stratification', in Bottomore and Nisbet, *A History of Sociological Analysis*, p. 600.

some other writers, such as Morgan, who also were interested in ancient societies.[36] Maine's inability to come to terms with a number of well-grounded attacks on his own patriarchal theories revealed him at his most dogmatic and did not reflect well upon his work in general. It is, therefore, hardly surprising that in the years which followed Maine's death in 1888 his reputation stood as low amongst anthropologists as it did amongst most lawyers. Disrespect for Maine's ideas culminated in what amounted to emotional attacks on the part of Malinowski. So destructive and hostile were the latter's remarks about Maine that they may even have served, by a process of reaction, to shape Malinowski's own thoughts.[37]

However, by the late 1920s, some people were more moderate in their response. R. S. Rattray was prepared to mention Maine with restrained and cautious approval.[38] This hesitant endorsement later gave way to something like enthusiasm in the books of Robert Redfield who was impressed by, for example, Maine's analysis of status and contract.[39] A sharper, more contrasted response was to be found in the works of Adamson Hoebel who praised Maine in some respects but who also believed that he had committed serious errors in, for instance, his writing on primitive law.[40] Clearest of all, however, were the responses of Diamond (largely hostile) and Max Gluckman who, from the mid-1950s was prepared to denounce Malinowski's interpre-

[36] These disputes are explored in Feaver, *From Status to Contract*, particularly at pp. 161–7.

[37] Malinowski dogmatically asserted that Maine had claimed that crime was the only legal problem to be studied in primitive societies (B. Malinowski, *Crime and Custom in Savage Society* (London, 1926), p. 56); and of Maine's patriarchal ideas he wrote more than once of the fact, as he saw it, that they were 'based on authority rather than observations, on reticences rather than frank discussion of facts, on belief and moral prejudice rather than a dispassionate desire for truth' (*Sex, Culture, and Myth* (London, 1963), p. 92 where Malinowski's previous repetition of this statement is reprinted). Note the almost total and odd irrelevance of Maine in many studies associated with Malinowski's views, e.g. R. Firth (ed.), *Man and Culture: An Evaluation of the Work of Bronislaw Malinowski* (London, 1957); and H. I. Hogbin, *Law and Order in Polynesia: a Study of Primitive Legal Institutions* (Connecticut, 1961).

[38] R. S. Rattray, *Ashanti Law and Custom* (Oxford, 1929) at, for example, pp. 76, 345, fn. 1.

[39] Numerous references could be given: see for example R. Redfield, *Human Nature and the Study of Society: The Papers of Robert Redfield* (Chicago, 1962) at pp. 39, 233. Note, too, the enthusiastic use of Maine in 'Maine's *Ancient Law* in the Light of Primitive Societies', *Western Political Quarterly*, 1950, vol. 3, pp. 571–89.

[40] E. A. Hoebel, *The Law of Primitive Man* (Harvard, 1954), p. 283.

tation as a 'travesty' and sought to put Maine's ideas to explicit and wide-ranging use.[41]

Explaining these changes is not a simple matter. A lawyer has to be especially cautious in considering the reaction of anthropologists to Maine's ideas. A glance at the development of modern anthropology shows very clearly that historical analysis has been treated in radically contrasting ways by different anthropologists. Some have ignored it; others have attacked it; and others still have put it to a variety of mutually incompatible uses. Since, in this context, Maine has usually been associated with history, his reputation has been at the mercy of wide-ranging debates between anthropologists about the very nature of their discipline; and it follows that outsiders such as the present writer draw conclusions at their peril.

A good illustration of the difficulties involved can be found in a lecture specifically devoted to Maine by Sir Edward Evans-Pritchard. In places the lecture now reads like an attempt at compromise; it appears, indirectly, to reflect a belief that history played too large a role in late nineteenth-century anthropological writing and far too small a role after about 1920. However, to the present writer, the conclusion which results is both strange and, in places, curiously intricate. We are told that Maine

> gave us several sociological hypotheses of great value and displayed in doing so a clear understanding of sociological method, giving explanations in terms of relations between social phenomena and showing how one set of ideas or institutions affect others. This is a wide departure from eighteenth-century writers and their themes, dominated as they were by conjectural history and the notion of societies as natural phenomena with discoverable laws and stages of development.[42]

[41] For reference to the 'travesty' see M. Gluckman, *Politics, Law and Ritual in Tribal Society* (Oxford, 1965) p. 29: for some of Gluckman's discussions of Maine see, generally, *The Judicial Process among the Barotse of Northern Rhodesia* (Manchester, 1967) and *Ideas in Barotse Jurisprudence* (Yale, 1965). The references are considered in more detail below, pp. 170–1. For Diamond's views, see, in particular, *Primitive Law, Past and Present* (London, 1971) where he is often savagely critical of Maine: for good examples see pp. 45, 47 and 61. The preface (at p. 7) could hardly be more insulting in explaining why Diamond had modified his book of 1935: 'Less space is devoted to the examination and criticism (hardly necessary in these days) of the hypothesis, made famous by Sir Henry Maine, that "law is derived from pre-existing rules of conduct which are at the same time legal, moral and religious in nature", and that "the severance of law from morality and religion from law belong only to the later stages of mental progress".'

[42] Sir Edward Evans-Pritchard, *A History of Anthropological Thought* (London, 1981), essay on Maine, pp. 89–90.

It is difficult to explain this view other than in terms of a sort of retrospective myopia. Maine did not write deliberately about sociological hypotheses, still less about sociological method; when he did discuss the relations between social phenomena these discussions can only be understood in the context of his more extensive references to what Pollock called the natural history of law. As we have seen, Maine believed the latter to be discoverable by the scientific study of societies as natural phenomena with specific laws and stages of development. In short, Evans-Pritchard's attempt to praise Maine relies upon the elevation of a small and uncharacteristic part of Maine's analysis. It is as if the value of an *historical* approach such as Maine's is shown by the fact that Maine could use and develop worthwhile *non-historical* methods concerned with the interrelationship of social facts. In general, one has an impression of acute concern about the justification of historical elements in anthropological writing and an associated difficulty in explaining Maine's significance.

In fact the secondary literature on the development of anthropological thought has yet to achieve anything like the sort of balanced guide to Maine's reception which would assist an outsider. It has recently been suggested (by Jarvie) that there has yet to be anything like a satisfactory history of anthropological thought in general.[43] As far as Maine himself is concerned some historians (for example, T. K. Penniman) have regarded his work as being, at most, only narrowly relevant to later anthropological thought and even then it is vigorously criticised for being, for the most part, wrong in its conclusions.[44] He has been accorded only moderate praise and significance in some fairly detailed studies (for example those of M. Harris and A. Kuper);[45] and he has even been totally ignored in a collection of essays (edited by I. M. Lewis)[46] specifically concerned with the place of history in social anthropology.

However, in recent years there has been a change in perspective on the part of those writing about the history of anthropological thought. The outlook is, perhaps, more tolerant – certainly history seems to be

[43] I. C. Jarvie, *Rationality and Relativism* (London, 1984), p. 8.

[44] T. K. Penniman, *A Hundred Years of Anthropology* (London, 1935; revised and reprinted 1970), consider pp. 115 (fn), 118.

[45] M. Harris, *The Rise of Anthropological Theory* (London, 1968), e.g. p. 191; and A. Kuper, *Anthropologists and Anthropology: the British School 1922–1972* (Allen Lane, 1973), e.g. pp. 110–22.

[46] I. M. Lewis (ed.), *History and Social Anthropology* (London, 1968). Consider the reference to the decline of an interest in history in English anthropology at Introduction, p. xiii.

less of an issue – and Maine is considered in a more favourable and less contentious manner. For example, one writer (M. J. Leaf)[47] has stressed, amongst other things, the links between Maine's ideas and the nineteenth-century studies of language, and this leads him to accord Maine a fairly secure and valued place in early anthropological studies.

Another work has emphasised Maine's thought about kinship and, as such, is refreshing for its attempt to return to what Maine actually wrote on a specific topic. In his study, *The Building of British Social Anthropology*, Ian Langham has explicitly referred to Maine's claim that the force which bound the ancient family together was the *patria potestas*, the authority of the father. Langham sees that for Maine this gave early societies stability and cohesion and ensured that the relationships within any society were always traced through male links, i.e., in Maine's terminology, agnatically. In historical terms, Maine was concerned with showing that the *patria potestas* provided the mechanism for a change in the law governing women. There was a change from a woman's subordination to her blood relations to subordination to her husband; and the change could be seen in the new forms of marriage developed in ancient Rome. Under these the husband acquired rights over the person and property of his wife; and he did so not by virtue of his role as husband but by assuming the legal status of father. She was technically regarded as the daughter of her husband.

Langham links this to Maine's more general writing on the development of culture but he adds, disarmingly enough: 'It must be doubted, however, that Maine succeeded in making his study of *Ancient Law* sufficiently revelatory of the nature of non-literate tribal societies to render his book a contribution to anthropology in the modern sense'.[48] It is as if the modern interpretations of Maine's ideas are now at a stage where his importance in his own time is recognised but his place in anthropological thought as a whole is still unclear: is it part of it, or not?

Fortunately, in respect of legal anthropology itself some commentators have been more forthright. Simon Roberts, in his book *Order and Dispute*, has explored the 'Main Themes and Interests in

[47] *Man, Mind and Sciences* (New York, 1979), pp. 80, 106, 108–14, 117, 148. This is one of the very few studies which links Maine's thought to developments in the study of languages (p. 80).

[48] I. Langham, *The Building of British Social Anthropology* (London, 1981), p. 11.

the Literature' concerned with legal anthropology and stressed the fact that Maine argued that all societies passed through three stages.

In the first of these stages, the largest grouping was made up of a few kinsmen, presided over by the senior male agnate. This man settled disputes and handed out punishments in the group but he did so on an *ad hoc* basis; no firm rules underpinned or connected the various decisions he took. At this stage law had yet to emerge. In the form of society which followed, numbers of these small groups of agnates became clustered together under chiefs, but the (sometimes fictional) assumption of shared kinship remained the basic organising principle. Then came the territorial society, indicated by its identification with a particular tract of land. It was in the later part of the second stage and the early part of the third stage that 'law' began to develop, as the rulers started to pronounce the same judgements in similar situations, thus providing their decision-making with an underlying set of rules.

Roberts continued with the observation that:

A normative basis for decision-making was the key attribute of law for Maine. Later in the development of territorial societies, the handling of disputes fell into the hands of a specialised elite, who alone had access to the principles to be followed in their resolution . . . Later still, to ensure accurate knowledge of the rules, and to avoid the distrust resulting from them being the exclusive property of legal specialists, they were written down into codes. During this 'era of codes' a final development began. As societies changed, the demand came that the laws should change with them. Some societies developed devices for altering the rigid codes as this became necessary; others failed to do so. Thus, the territorial society could take on alternative forms, the 'stationary' or the 'progressive'. Within and alongside this overall evolutionary framework for the legal system, Maine also postulated evolutionary sequences through which different area of the substantive law, such as contract and the criminal law, would develop.[49]

In other words, Roberts has followed the jurists and focused attention upon Maine's interest in the evolutionary development of law; and it is these elements in Maine's work which enable Roberts to explain why the former is generally credited with having founded the area of study which has since become known as legal anthropology. Unfortunately, this claim raises problems. Obviously the present book seeks to show that there is a selective aspect to any suggestion, explicit or implicit, that the particular area of subject matter raised by Roberts was wholly typical of Maine's concerns or even that it was central to his analysis of law. The preceding chapters and sections have aimed to reveal the great breadth of Maine's interests and methods of approach

[49] S. Roberts, *Order and Dispute: An Introduction to Legal Anthropology* (Harmondsworth, 1979), pp. 187–8.

and, in doing so, I have tried to direct attention away from an emphasis upon his writing about, say, the specific stages of legal and social change or the emergence of law. For example, Maine's concern with the harmony of social and legal forces is clearly related to the aspects of his work which Roberts writes about but, at the same time, his concern for harmony transcends such observations and can, in fact, only be understood in relation to Maine's many other ideas concerning, for instance, the proper role of lawyers in Victorian society and the contrast between English and continental modes of legal thought. In other words, I am arguing here that Maine was far too diverse in his thoughts about the legal past for him to be typified in the manner adopted by Roberts.

Of course, Roberts could respond to this by saying that the value of Maine's contribution to legal anthropology does not depend upon Maine's intentions or even upon the proper understanding of his works as a whole in their historical context. Instead, Maine could be taken as having stimulated the growth of legal anthropology by providing forceful, if rather incidental, remarks about the possible correlation of social and legal phenomena in the course of advancing his broader commitments. Unintended fruitfulness is still a type of fruitfulness. Maine could unintentionally have created legal anthropology.

But to say this is to raise questions of which Roberts himself is very much aware. I have already said enough above to show that the relationship between Maine's statements and the works of later legal anthropologists is debatable, and it is significant that Roberts talks of Maine founding an 'area of study',[50] rather than a school of thought. Indeed, Roberts, following the tone of remarks expressed by others, stresses that the 'most cursory survey' of the modern literature concerned with legal anthropology 'reveals major differences of opinion about what should be studied, the methods to be followed in research, and the ways in which findings should be presented'.[51] Accordingly, it is to be expected that even within this one area of specialised study, Maine's ideas have been received in contrasting ways and it is all the more difficult to trace his role as an unintentionally creative legal anthropologist.

It is easy to illustrate these problems. In his *Anthropology of Law*, Leopold Pospisil makes claims on Maine's behalf which many people would find astounding. Pospisil, in the course of discussing legal

[50] *Ibid.*, p. 187. [51] *Ibid.*, p. 184.

anthropology, says that Maine's 'famous work *Ancient Law*, published in 1861, made an impact on English and on world jurisprudence that is comparable to the effect of Einstein on physics, Freud on psychology, or Durkheim on sociology'.[52] In this context Pospisil goes on to reason that: 'Maine's everlasting contribution to the field of jurisprudence and anthropology of law lies not so much in his specific conclusions as in the empirical, systematic, and historical methods he employed to arrive at his conclusions, and in his striving for generalisations firmly based on the empirical evidence at his disposal'.[53] In other words, Maine is praised for his methods and he is praised for just those empirical, systematic and philosophical characteristics which so many of his subsequent commentators (such as Pollock and Holmes) thought were singularly lacking in his work. Also, the present writer at least finds it difficult to see how Pospisil specifically relates these claims on Maine's behalf to the development of later legal anthropology. Perhaps it is fair to say that the reader is given an impression of Maine as a genius who, for all his possible influence, has been almost wildly misunderstood and who produced in legal anthropology just those qualities which many have thought Maine himself lacked.

A less lively but, at the same time, a careful and considered response to Maine's thought is to be found in the work of Sally Falk Moore. For example, in *Law as Process: an Anthropological Approach*, she praises Maine because, amongst other things, he 'never abstracted legal principles altogether from the social context in which they occurred', and she goes on to explore his more debatable ideas such as the distinction 'between kin-based and territorially-based organisations'.[54] Throughout, Maine is treated as a major figure in the development of anthropological inquiry (although, again, his precise significance is not explored) and there is incidental approval for some of his specific ideas.

Finally, a more qualified response, but one which also points to the extent to which Maine is now seen as relevant to modern anthropological debate in general, is to be found in his role in arguments concerning the respective merits of 'rule-centred' and 'processal' paradigms. For example, in *Rules and Processes*, Comaroff and Roberts state that 'scholarly research in the tradition of the rule-centred paradigm can be traced back at least as far as Maine's *Ancient Law*'. Maine,

[52] L. Pospisil, *Anthropology of Law: a Comparative Theory* (New York, 1971), p. 143.
[53] *Ibid.*, p. 150.
[54] S. F. Moore, *Law as Process: an Anthropological Approach* (London, 1978), p. 216.

they point out, was a lawyer and, much more controversially, Comaroff and Roberts argue that his major interest was in the origins of the English legal system, about which a considerable body of theory had already emerged. For this, and other reasons, 'His intellectual predilections were thus unequivocally "law centred", and they were addressed specifically to understanding the legal institutions of his own society.'[55] As such they argue that Maine's approach may be contrasted with that of Malinowski, who placed stress on the need to look beyond Western legal concepts for the purposes of comparative explanation, and who also emphasised the associated need to treat the problem of law and order (analytically as well as definitionally) firmly in the broader context of the study of social control.[56]

Again, the preceding chapters have tried to show that categorising Maine in this way is not entirely satisfactory. It is true, for example, that he looked at Indian law very much through Western spectacles. But it is certainly inappropriate to regard him as a man with an overriding interest in the origins of the English legal system. In other words, his preconceptions were western, but at the same time they were of the broadest kind and can hardly be called 'law centred'. He often attempted to argue against just those aspects of Western thought which were 'law centred'.

It may be that these views will not generally be welcomed by anthropologists. If this is so, they are asked to bear in mind that Maine's reputation in this area has usually been a compound of (a) a belief that he was in some sense a founding father and, at the same time, (b) a belief that he was a man whose work could be closely related to present debates. The above paragraphs have at least attempted to keep separate these issues, and when they are divided it becomes apparent that his significance in regard to either is not as great as has often been suggested by, say, those who have concentrated upon his alleged influence in later years and have justified their arguments by reference to his role as a founding father. Maine himself, incidentally, never claimed to be an anthropologist; even in his later works he never claimed to be writing anthropology. He was a Victorian writing about issues which happen to overlap with modern anthropological concerns.

This brief excursion may also have done little to satisfy some of

[55] J. L. Camaroff and S. Roberts, *Rules and Processes: the Cultural Logic of Dispute in an African Context* (Chicago and London, 1981), pp. 5–6.

[56] *Ibid.*, p. 11.

those lawyers who seek to reveal the modern importance of historical and anthropological jurisprudence. It is quite common to encounter a helpful analysis of Maine's ideas in a textbook of jurisprudence, and then to find it linked (sometimes only implicitly) to later developments in sociological or anthropological inquiry.[57] In part this is a product of the inevitable and justifiable need to categorise writers into what, at any time, are regarded as relevant schools of thought. But of course it tempts the reader into a belief in non-existent causal links between an earlier thinker and a later one. It also encourages a debate about the modern significance of ancient views which can almost parody the latter through abstracting them from their context. Perhaps the best question to ask is not, say, what was Maine's significance for legal anthropology, but rather, why has Maine, along with a few other Victorians, been singled out for such attention by some modern legal anthropologists? Again, if we accept the ideas of historians (such as Langham) that Maine did not intend to write anthropology, and we also accept with numerous anthropologists that most of his ideas are untenable (and have been seen to be so since before his death), it is the latter question which presses home. Why has Maine been useful for modern writers? Why have so many anthropologists and lawyers given so little attention in this context to the work of, say, earlier Jesuit writers responding to the discovery of the American Indians, or to the writing on early law to be found in the works of jurists such as Vico, or to the analysis of the social context of law in Montesquieu?

We should recognise that categories such as 'anthropological jurisprudence' now reflect the needs of modern jurisprudence and not necessarily the intentions and works of the major names associated with the schools concerned. If, today, history and anthropology are seen as being relevant to law, the modern jurist is perfectly entitled to use the works of a past writer in such a way as to develop modern debates and arrive thereby at a finer perception of the truth about law.[58] The observations of past jurists can obviously be used as legitimate and helpful sources of information in the course of de-

[57] See for example, W. Friedmann, *Legal Theory* (London, 1967, Fifth Edition), pp. 214–21 and then, for an unjustified 'link', p. 247.

[58] Dias, *Jurisprudence*, pp. 388–93 explores Maine's works in the context of the 'anthropological approach' and avoids historical pit-falls by stressing the 'pioneer character of Maine's comparative investigations' and, more generally, by clearly integrating the historical information into a modern sociological approach. The useful distinction between history as history and history as an instrument of jurisprudential analysis is considered below in Conclusion, pp. 211–15.

veloping modern jurisprudential arguments. But in such a context the modern jurist must at once concede that it is almost certain that he is not writing good legal history. He is not explaining how the subject has developed; he is not attempting to show that Montesquieu produced one idea and Maine another; and he is sometimes using the ideas of past thinkers in ways which would surely have struck those thinkers as being odd. In anthropology Maine's influence has been fruitful, but it has had only tenuous links with his own intentions.

SOCIOLOGY, ANTHROPOLOGY AND 'STATUS TO CONTRACT'

The nineteenth-century German theorist, Ferdinand Tonnies, wrote that

> the books by Sir Henry Maine, originally lectures given to illuminate the comparative study of early Roman institutions with Germanic and Indian ones, and later extended to the Irish clan system, did not by-pass the various contrasts between primitive communisms and modern social and political institutions and ideologies. The writer of this report became intimately acquainted with these . . .[59]

Maine's importance in this context is seen with particular force in Tonnies' development of the distinction between *Gemeinschaft* and *Gesellschaft* and it is these terms which have, as it were, served to carry forward into many modern debates Maine's distinction between status and contract. For example, the distinction is remarked upon in a way which is readily comprehensible to modern lawyers by Stein and Shand in their study *Legal Values in Western Society*. 'Tonnies', they write,

> distinguished two basic types of social grouping. The first, *Gemeinschaft*, is a community or fellowship of those sharing in some degrees a way of life. Its members consider the relationship an end in itself, rather than a means to obtain some particular end. The element which unites them is their 'natural will', which is the will to associate with others based on affection, sympathy, memory or habit. The groups they form may be based on blood relationship or friendship or neighbourliness or intellectual kinship. The other type of grouping, *Gesellschaft*, is a limited relationship based on the 'rational will', a conscious planning to achieve some specific end. Those involved in this type share a desire to obtain that end, and are willing to cooperate for that purpose, even though in other respects they may be indifferent, or even hostile, to each

[59] See, for example, E. G. Jacoby's translation of F. Tonnies, *On Social Ideas and Ideologies* (New York, 1974), p. 166. The translator's critical note on p. 166 does not relate to the present point.

other. These are ideal types, and are not found in any actual societies, but it is possible to characterise many social relationships as approximating more to one type than the other. Thus a family, college, religious community, or trade guild, has more of the characteristics of *Gemeinschaft* than has a limited company. The Middle Ages had more '*Gemeinschaft-like*' relationships than have modern times.[60]

It was this type of distinction between status and contract which was of the greatest use to the anthropologist, Max Gluckman. In the 1950s and 1960s he reacted very strongly against those who, as he saw it, had sought to exclude the historical insights of late nineteenth-century writers from modern anthropological analysis. In particular, as we have seen, he attacked Malinowski for having produced a 'travesty' of Maine's ideas and having thereby ignored the value of the latter's bold attempt to understand the major tendencies in the development of historic societies. At one point Gluckman even makes the remarkable claim that, when reading *Ancient Law* it was 'as if I was conversing with a modern anthropologist'.[61]

In part, Gluckman's enthusiasm arose out of Maine's specific observations on certain topics such as the relationship between law and religion. But even these points are related to what he saw as being Maine's chief insight, his analysis of status and contract. For example (and it is only an example) in his study, *The Ideas in Barotse Jurisprudence,* his use of Maine's concepts was almost embarrassingly dramatic. He wrote that

the Barotse is a society dominated by status and hence covered by Sir Henry Maine's most sweeping generalisation: 'If then we employ status, agreeably with the usage of the best writers (to designate the powers and privileges anciently residing in the Family), and avoid applying the term to such conditions as are the immediate or remote result of agreement, we may say that the movement of the progressive societies has hitherto been a movement from Status to Contract.'

Having quoted Maine, Gluckman continues:

The Barotse, in fact, in terms of technology and commerce stand, so to speak, further back on the scale by which Maine measured the movement of progressive societies than do most of the peoples whose law he analysed. Observations on their life therefore enable us to test some of his pregnant generalisations, as to whether in the early stages of law the law of Persons and the law of Things are inextricably intertwined (and I would add to this tangle the law of Obligations), whether the individual is submerged in the *Familia*, whether contracts are incomplete conveyances so that executory contracts do not

[60] P. Stein and J. Shand, *Legal Values in Western Society* (Edinburgh, 1974), p. 18.

[61] Gluckman, *Politics, Law and Ritual in Tribal Society*, p. 17; for reference to the 'travesty' see p. 29.

found obligations, whether substantive law is secreted in the interstices of procedure, to what extent religion, magic, and ritual dominate the law, and whether fictions are important in the development of the law. Since Maine had to work from remnants of Roman, Germanic, and Celtic Law, as these survived in a few documents, and from relatively poor records on the practice of Hindu Law, my detailed records of cases may help correct judgments on the way jurisprudential ideas and ideals operated in practice. Particularly, I may state at once, I believe that my cases, like other records of tribal law, dispose of theories that early legal procedures were highly formal. Otherwise, modern anthropological research, in my opinion, validates the chief outlines of Maine's analysis, once we recognise that he was in fact analysing relatively advanced types of legal systems. I am not sure but that 'Footnotes to Sir Henry Maine's *Ancient Law*' would be a more accurate title for this book than '*The Ideas in Barotse Jurisprudence*'.[62]

These apparently incidental references to the ideas of men as far apart in time and place as Tonnies and Gluckman demand justification. It would be much tidier to place them respectively in, say, the categories of 'sociology' and 'anthropology' or 'the nineteenth century' and the 'twentieth century'. But the neatness which this produced would have been purchased at the price of making Maine appear to use later academic categories which were not in fact in his mind. It would have ignored the wide appeal of generalisations such as those concerned with status and contract. It would have served to conceal the range of his writing, and the lack of concern on his part for full coherence of argument. Obviously, such an approach by Maine was likely to provide a reception which was random, sometimes associated only in an incidental way with many modern disciplines, and often united around nothing more than a very elegant, suggestive and clear-sounding generalisation. At the same time, however, it would be of the greatest value to other thinkers such as Gluckman.

Predictably, this varied response to the ideas of status and contract may be seen in studies of English law. Stein and Shand point out that it can be applied to, say, the study of cruelty associated with the various forms of female labour in industrial societies where the worker has lost all claim to legal status and associated forms of dignity. On a more theoretical level, Kamenka and Tay have stressed the links between categories such as status and contract and certain themes in later Marxist analysis. 'These contrasts', they thought,

entered quickly into the new sociology of the later nineteenth century through the work of Herbert Spencer and Sir Henry Maine; they were elevated into

[62] Gluckman, *The Ideas in Barotse Jurisprudence*, p. xvi. (Maine's chief statements about status and contract in *Ancient Law* differ in some respects from Gluckman's quotation.)

the fundamental concepts of 'pure sociology' by the German sociologist, Ferdinand Tonnies (1855–1936) in his classic *Gemeinschaft und Gesellschaft* (*Community and Society*, first published in 1877) and (much later) reinforced, in one way or another, by more than fifty years of empirical studies of differences between kinds of group cohesion, bases of legitimacy and exercise of authority.

As a result,

much of the contemporary use of the concept of alienation, even by a radical Western or 'critical' Marxist . . . reflects nearly a hundred years of sociological thinking and may be seen to have derived some of its strength from ideas which were developed and popularised in *Ancient Law*.[63]

Yet Maine himself, of course, would have been distressed by such a development. Enough has been said throughout this book to show that his political convictions were in no way revolutionary. We have also seen something of his antagonism towards those theories which postulated a 'pure' form of human nature which could then be used as a criterion for assessing the inadequacies of human institutions. The simple fact was that Maine was enthusiastic about relationships based upon contract, and he would have had no sympathy with any subsequent use of his ideas which sought to favour status or to use his terms to develop a very strong attack upon what he regarded as progressive social change. However, it seems to be just as indisputable a fact that Maine's distinction between status and contract was a source of inspiration to those who developed ideas which, subsequently, have been put to radical use. In other words, the categories created by Maine have proved to be of great value to the very type of interpretations Maine most ardently disliked. He opposed both their content and the sort of understanding of human nature upon which they were based.

In certain respects, this development is illustrated with even more force in the modern English debate about the relationship between the elements of status and contract in twentieth-century law. In its simplest form, it is at times suggested that Maine has been proved wrong because contract has not triumphed in progressive societies; instead, it is argued, there has been a reversion to status.[64] Such a line of

[63] Kamenka and Erh-Soon Tay, *Law and Social Control* (London, 1980), Chapter 1, 'Social Traditions, Legal Traditions', pp. 7–8. Note the anthropological references to Maine in chapter 2, 'Anthropological Approaches', e.g. at p. 51.

[64] For a bad example of this see *Encyclopaedia Britannica*, 14th ed. (1929), entry for Maine. (This appears to have distorted an earlier, more sophisticated entry by Pollock.)

argument is ill-founded because Maine never denied the possibility of such a development. He feared it, spoke out against it, and did all he could to thwart such a regressive change.[65] But, at the same time, he was fully aware that his own efforts, and those of like-minded men, might be in vain. The critics who attacked Maine on these grounds have ignored the fact that he stated that the development of progressive societies had *hitherto* been marked by a change from status to contract.[66]

An associated but much more valuable form of criticism is to be found in the works of those such as Friedmann and Kahn-Freund who have concentrated upon the problem of understanding what actually may have happened in British society.[67] Here Maine is seen as an analyst rather than a prophet. Friedmann, for example, considers at some length the twentieth-century battle (not too strong a word) between status and contractual elements in Western societies and concludes that there has been a significant return to the former. For example, the very idea of 'welfare' carries with it the notion that individuals have rights by reason simply of existing as citizens in society, rather than by reason of exercising their respective wills in such a way as to obtain contractual benefits. Even more obvious is the increasing preparedness of legislatures to pass laws restricting the rights of individuals and companies to contract in any way they wish. For instance, as is well known, it sometimes is impossible for a party to exclude liability in respect of defective products even if both parties to the contract, for whatever reasons, would accept such an arrangement. The primacy of individual decision-making has given way to regulated conduct reflecting values imposed by government; and Maine's distinction between status and contract is a convenient form of shorthand for describing these social developments.

However, the brief way in which the distinction is expressed may be misleading. It surely can be said that the twentieth century has witnessed persistent and intricate attacks upon the 'free will' theory.

[65] His ideas on India constituted an exception to this – presumably because sometimes he had doubts as to its capacity for progress: see A. C. Lyall, *Law Quarterly Review*, vol. 4 (1888), p. 135; 'no one would have been less disposed than Sir Henry Maine to hurry on this process in India'.

[66] *Ancient Law*, p. 170.

[67] For O. Kahn-Freund, see, e.g., 'A Note on Status and Contract in British Labour Law', *Modern Law Review*, vol. 30 (1967), p. 635. The topics revealed in the list of his published works indicate that the distinction formed a theme to a considerable part of his writing. See O. Kahn-Freund, *Selected Writings* (London, 1978), pp. 374–81. For Friedmann, see his *Legal Theory*, pp. 217–21.

There have been innumerable attempts to show that in fact the 'individualistic' or 'free will' theory is simply a mask; it is argued that it conceals economic realities, usually in the form of capital, and provides opportunities for those with economic power to manipulate those without such power. The individual who buys a railway ticket from British Rail, or an international airline ticket from any airline, has little if any scope for negotiating his own contract. When this sort of development is placed in a full historical perspective the issues are very complicated. Professor Atiyah's work, *The Rise and Fall of Freedom of Contract* shows just how intricate was the nineteenth-century development of 'individualistic' law, and there is no reason to suppose that the twentieth-century story will be any more simple. In Friedmann's words,

> only if we understand that, at least in contemporary industrialised society, status is a many sided thing, that the interrelations of private freedom and public regulation are infinite and complex, that no individual or group in modern society is either 'free' or 'status bound', can we begin to reevaluate the validity of Maine's doctrine for our own time.[68]

But, for some, the distinction between status and contract may be put to even more detailed uses particularly when the contrast is to be found in certain modern studies of the substantive law itself. For example, this is apparent in the work by Gray and Symes, *Real Property and Real People*.[69] Their interest in the distinction between *Gemeinschaft* and *Gesellschaft* – which they themselves see as being linked to Maine's analysis[70] – stems from their beliefs about how today's substantive law should be learned and used. They argue that it is essential to acquire both the capacity to cope with 'the mill of rigorous argument of the traditional kind' and the ability to see that 'law does not exist in a moral or social vacuum but is profoundly affected by the predominant values of the society in which [the student] lives'. It follows from the second requirement that 'the ultimate objective of a university education in law is not the learning of rules but the critical perception of value'.[71] As a result we may infer that if such a perception is to be achieved the lawyer will have to learn,

68 Friedmann, *Legal Theory*, p. 220.

69 K. J. Gray and P. D. Symes, *Real Property and Real People: Principles of Land Law* (London, 1981).

70 *Ibid.*, p. 16. They also point out that Lord Simon of Glaisdale refers to Maine's analysis of status and contract in *Johnson* v. *Moreton* [1980] AC 37 p. 65 (fn.).

71 Gray and Symes, *Real Property and Real People*, Preface.

amongst other things, that the social ideas associated with property are in a state of change and that notions such as *Gemeinschaft* provide the best hope of revealing the nature of such a change.

Considering the matter in more detail, Gray and Symes argue that it may be possible to point to three major phases in the attempt to justify the law of property: in other words there are three eras in the English conceptual approach to proprietary institutions. They begin with the age of 'feudal solidarity' and seek to explain its leading characteristics through a discussion of Tonnies' analysis of *Gemeinschaft*. In an argument which certainly has not found universal acceptance, they admit that it constitutes an idealised picture of human association but also assert that 'the abstraction is useful because it symbolises certain ideological features which clearly were more deeply rooted in communities of the past than perhaps in the society of the present day'. *Gemeinschaft* society was founded in 'a family-oriented, status-dependent form of association which elevated the importance of the values of affection, loyalty, voluntarily assumed obligation and community-based solidarity'.[72]

From this, the familiar argument follows. The breakdown of feudal society was replaced by an age of commercialism which became particularly powerful during the eighteenth and nineteenth centuries. As a result the world of *Gemeinschaft* was replaced by the world of *Gesellschaft*, and the latter brought with it the atomistic, self-determining individual locked into remorseless competition with his fellows. The social ethic was the maximisation of private profit and the legal consequences were, of course, of the sort described above: it was, in short, the age of freedom of contract.

However, all of this has, in its turn, been challenged by a reassertion of the *Gemeinschaft* society in 'the age of social welfare' which has been associated with measures which display 'a quite remarkable return to the idea of "status"'.[73] For property lawyers this is of significance because, as Gray and Symes seek to emphasise in a further controversial argument, 'the law of property is founded upon principles which are the entire antithesis of the values of the *Gemeinschaft*'.[74] In other words, it might be argued that the whole distinction

[72] *Ibid.*, p. 15. For a critical discussion as to their use of these distinctions see Bernard Rudden, *Oxford Journal of Legal Studies*, vol. 2 (1982), p. 238, and Stuart Anderson, 'Explaining Land Law', *Modern Law Review*, vol. 45 (1982), p. 346.

[73] Gray and Symes, *Real Property and Real People*, p. 18. Status is seen as being 'inherent' in the measures.

[74] *Ibid.*, p. 15.

between the two types of social union serves to reveal the extent to which the law of property as taught and used by today's lawyers is in conflict with many of the social conditions of modern Britain.

In some ways (as Gray and Symes themselves suggest) it is easy to attack the use of this method of analysis. *Gemeinschaft* and *Gesellschaft* may easily be used to typify certain societies but it has to be emphasised again and again that they remain abstractions only partly reflected in reality. Also, some of the modern legal writing concerned with the distinction seems to assume that the values to be found within the world of *Gemeinschaft* are in some way superior to those in the world of *Gesellschaft*. To put it very mildly indeed, this is a controversial notion.[75] Further, it has to be said that much of the language used in the debate is extremely vague; in the last analysis it really is very difficult to know what is meant by, say, a reference to 'community-based solidarity' and how this may be related to legal concepts.

However, it is possible to see how some future lawyers are likely to use the distinctions in ways which may clarify important issues. Plainly, there is a difference of some kind between, say, those of a wife's rights to the matrimonial house which arise by reason of her financial contributions to the house, and those rights which arise by reason of her being a spouse who lives in the home concerned. Within the categories as developed by Gray and Symes, the former is easily related to *Gesellschaft* and the latter to *Gemeinschaft*, and the fact that this is so should direct property lawyers to the additional fact that radical changes are taking place in the way property rights arise for the simple reason that we now have a system in which both types of law jostle uneasily side by side. If nothing else, by directing the mind to general social developments, the terminology involved alerts the lawyer to the possibility that real property law may continue to change rapidly in the coming years as it tries to accommodate itself to mutually inconsistent values. It might, for example, indicate that it is quite futile to seek one single coherent set of rules for this area of law.

However, even these qualified remarks go too far. It can be argued that elements of status and contract may be found in all societies. Certainly, it can be said that it is simply impossible to typify the complexities of, say, nineteenth-century land law with the word *Gesellschaft*. There were any number of contrasting elements within the system of real property, and as yet there is no proof that these were

[75] See remarks of Rudden, p. 241.

such as to produce a significant form of conflict within Victorian legal reasoning. It is even easier to attack the use of such distinctions by turning attention away from legal history and towards modern sociological thought. As Stuart Anderson has emphasised: in this context, why choose Tonnies?[76] The latter has been the subject of very extensive later criticism and his categories have been modified or even ridiculed.

However, all of the criticisms serve to highlight, once again, the extent to which Maine's ideas form what seems to be an indestructible element in modern debate: and they also, of course, contribute yet a further reminder that these ideas are now being put to uses which hardly accord with Maine's original intentions. Once again, we may sense how peculiar it is that Maine's interest in status and contract, and his enthusiasm for contract as the foundation of a progressive society, should be being used as an instrument for understanding and even applauding the possible retreat from contract and the return to status. Again and again we see that Maine developed ideas which were to prove very useful in attacking his own theories.

However, just as there is a limit to the value of providing a table of favourable and unfavourable remarks about Maine, so too there comes a point beyond which there is little to be gained from providing one example after another of the extent to which Maine's ideas may be pressed – sometimes admittedly with useful results – into the service of causes he himself would have opposed. Of more importance in an attempt to assess *his* jurisprudence is the related, but distinct, issue as to whether these varied forms of criticism have also done something to conceal the meaning and significance which Maine intended to attribute to the words and principles which have subsequently attracted so much attention.

For example, Sawer, in his book *Law in Society*,[77] has argued that Maine and his critics have not always been talking about the same things. Sawer accepts of course that some criticism has been both valid and relevant: after Diamond's research it is, for instance, necessary to be very cautious in accepting Maine's attempt to correlate distinct stages of social evolution with equally distinct forms of substantive law.[78] But, more generally, it is not appropriate for anthropol-

[76] Stuart Anderson, 'Explaining Land Law', p. 347.

[77] G. Sawer, *Law in Society* (Oxford, 1965).

[78] Sawer said of Maine that 'Both subsequent discoveries and reinterpretation have compelled reconsideration of most of his ideas': *Ibid.*, p. 62.

ogists and others to attack Maine by arguing that progressive societies of the twentieth century have displayed an increasing respect for laws which could only be explained in terms of status. For Sawer, this is unacceptable because he believes that to an overwhelming extent Maine was talking about the family structure in archaic societies when he discussed status. In progressive societies the longterm trend (hitherto) had been for the family to disappear as an independent unit of calculation: and, reasoning from this position, Maine 'could be taken to imply that in consequence of a regime of equal capacity, most social relations would now be established by contracts between individuals', but – and this is Sawer's point – 'this was not the aspect of the matter to which he paid most attention'.[79] In other words, in Sawer's view, Maine's concern with status and contract had been wrenched from its context in ancient history and given too wide an application. As a result it may be said that we have praised Maine too much for his daring generalisations and criticised him too much for his lack of concern with scholarly detail. He was less adventurous, but more thorough than has been thought, and the modern meaning attributed to one of his words (status) has done something to conceal the precise nature of his work.

Fortunately, Professor MacCormack has recently done much to explain the development of these different responses to Maine's use of the word 'status'.[80] The answer lies in the fact that Maine himself put the term to ambiguous use. MacCormack observes, firstly, that

> Maine himself was a lawyer and his use of the word status is much more cautious than that of those who in subsequent years have sought to apply his theory. In fact, he does not define status as such but from his general account of the family in archaic law two limiting factors in his use of the term can be discerned: (i) it applies only to 'forms of reciprocity in rights and duties which have their origin in the family'; it designates 'personal conditions only', that is powers and privileges derived from membership of a family and not to conditions resulting from agreement, (ii) it designates specifically the condition of subordinate members of the family (sons, and their children, unmarried daughters and slaves). All the actual examples of the effects or consequences of status given by Maine concern such subordinate members

[79] *Ibid.*, p. 66. Sawer argues that if Maine had given the matter primary attention he might have made more of the social stratification, immobility, inheritance of social position and attribution of specific law-clusters to specific classes found in some archaic societies. At p. 67 Sawer goes so far as to claim that 'nor did Maine assert . . . that the detailed incidents of all or most social relations could be established by individual contracts'.

[80] Geoffrey MacCormack, 'Status: Problems of Definition and Use', *Cambridge Law Journal*, vol. 43(2) (Nov. 1984), pp. 361–76.

and not the paterfamilias himself. Thus when he wrote of the movement of progressive societies being a movement from status to contract he meant that the subordinate members of the family ceased to be entirely subject to the paterfamilias and came to acquire an independent legal capacity of their own. Their rights and duties instead of being derived solely from their position in the family might be determined in accordance with their own will by contract.[81]

Secondly, however, MacCormack points out that Maine also used the word for a very different purpose when he sought to formulate a 'law of progress' and framed it in terms of status. Here he was doing more than describing a state of affairs; instead he was trying to provide an explanation for the existence of phenomena found in modern society 'by postulating a certain course of social evolution'. This can be seen in his famous statement that 'The word status may be usefully employed to construct a formula expressing the law of progress . . . we may say that the movement of the progressive societies has hitherto been a movement *from Status to Contract*.'[82] In brief, Maine sometimes uses the word to describe an ancient legal structure and he sometimes uses it to account for the transformation of those societies which have experienced progress.

Some of Maine's earlier critics touched upon these two themes in more general terms. For instance, Hoebel emphasised that Maine's 'polar types were designed not only to represent extremes in a range of variable social forms but also to describe development in the dimension of time'.[83] As Bottomore recognised, many early attempts at social classification implied evolutionary schemes.[84]

These observations do much to reveal the ambiguity of Maine's statements, and thereby explain the contrasted response to his use of status and contract; different critics have looked at different aspects of his work. However, any modern attempt to stress the imprecision of Maine's words and to divide their various uses into categories could draw attention away from his determined effort to provide a synthesis of numerous sources and arguments and, in doing so, both to record social events and explain social change. Professor MacCormack is correct and helpful in revealing ambiguities in various definitions and uses of the word status: for today's jurisprudence, assessing the

[81] *Ibid.*, pp. 362–3.

[82] *Ibid.*, p. 367 and fn. 25, quoting from p. 173 of the 1916 edition of *Ancient Law*.

[83] See his entry for Maine in the *International Encyclopaedia of the Social Sciences* (London, 1968), vol. 9, p. 530.

[84] T. B. Bottomore, *Sociology* (London, 1975), p. 119.

validity of Maine's distinctions is a necessary exercise. But this is distinct from an historical attempt to explore and account for Maine's motives in writing about status and contract as he did in *Ancient Law*. A modern analytical study cannot reveal the radical, questioning element in Maine's approach to legal study. He would have found it both strange and disappointing if he had been told that the lawyers of the twentieth century were to concentrate upon the problems of defining the qualities of particular laws rather than upon, say, the changing realities which produced new types of law. The modern critics could respond to such hypothetical disappointment with complete fairness by stating that the ambiguities remained whatever the general merits of his attempt to redirect the minds of lawyers.

But, to reemphasise the point which has just been made, Maine did not intend that his jurisprudence should amount to an invitation to debate problems of legal classification. After all, in his view, such detailed discussions had been responsible for Austin's failure to write the sort of jurisprudence which could be understood and enjoyed by informed laymen who could then bring their influence to bear upon the problems of legal change. Without the work of such men, legal analysis would become increasingly unrelated to social realities (as, at the same time, it became more and more dominated by jurists and practitioners rather than laymen) and political life would be controlled by an unprogressive, democratic sentiment which did not encourage careful thought about law reform. Maine's jurisprudence always contained an element of a 'social crusade'; as we have seen in considering *Ancient Law* in particular, he had something to tell citizens about their modern responsibilities. This introduced inconsistencies into his writing as attempts at description became linked with highly prescriptive assertions, but, in taking this approach, Maine did much to ensure the popularity of his work and thereby to give the phrase 'status to contract' an enduring role in legal debate.

AMERICAN LEGAL REALISM

In considering Sumner's lack of use of Maine's ideas we have already seen that it was possible for an American writer with theories which were in some ways very like those of Maine almost to ignore the latter's thought. In fact, similar things may also be said of the late nineteenth and early twentieth-century American thinkers who were more directly concerned with the law. For example, Oliver Wendell Holmes found much to dispute in regard to Maine's particular theories of legal change. Like many others, he was content to describe Maine as a genius and, almost in the same breath, to criticise him in strong terms. Holmes himself hinted at the immense difficulty of tracing Maine's thoughts in any part of the world when he said of the latter: 'he seems to have been impatient of investigation himself and I do not think will leave much mark on the actual structure of jurisprudence, although he helped many others to do so'.[85] Certainly, it would be difficult to argue that Maine determined the chief concerns of any particular thinker in America. John Chipman Gray made very respectful remarks about some of Maine's ideas in *The Nature and Sources of the Law* (1909); but throughout his study he confined his references to Maine's works to matters of detail rather than general theory.[86] Roscoe Pound might have been expected to have been influenced by Maine as a process of reaction against his chief ideas about individualism. It has recently been pointed out that Maine's ideas on the latter topic may well have assisted Pound in his attempt to create contrasting theories of law whilst, at the same time, Pound explained existing laws in terms of some of Maine's categories.[87] It seems in the case of Pound that we are presented with the same story of Maine's books being of very vague and questionable significance and, insofar as they had any influence, they were of at least as much use to a man who wished to oppose him as a man who wished to support him.

It is reasonable to expect a contrast to this in the history of the American realist movement. In the course of its development this many-sided school of thought was to become associated with certain ideas which look as if they could have been taken from the pages of Maine's works. A regard for the social context and social purposes of law was common to both. So, too, was a distrust of what might loosely be called abstract analysis in academic life and enthusiasm for tradition in the legal profession. Also, in some of its aspirations at least,

[85] Mark De Wolfe Howe (ed.), *The Pollock-Holmes Letters* (Cambridge, 1942), vol. 1, p. 31. The comment is to be found in a letter written shortly after Maine's death, so perhaps Holmes was even trying to be merciful. But Holmes praises Maine in 'Law in Science and Science in Law', *Harvard Law Review* (1889), vol. 12, p. 447. There is room for a more detailed study of Holmes' response to Maine: there are suggestive references in, e.g., M. de Wolfe Howe's *Justice Oliver Wendell Holmes* (Harvard, 1957 and 1963).

[86] Republished by Beacon Press in 1963.

[87] See Alan Hunt, *The Sociological Movement in Law* (London, 1978), p. 32. But the present, brief observation does scant justice to Hunt's analysis of Pound. See also Moore, *Law as Process*, pp. 84 and 133.

the realist movement might be said to have attempted to continue Maine's search for more 'scientific' ways of understanding law; and this was in turn associated with certain ideas about the desirability of codification.

Yet the realist movement acknowledged no general form of indebtedness to Maine's ideas. It seems that the clearest indication – and it is a slender one – of a link between his theories and later American thought is to be found in the work of those anthropologists who developed an interest in legal realism. If we may say that primitive law was the henchman of legal realism, we may also say that Maine influenced Hoebel's ideas about primitive law and thereby had some sort of indirect consequences for American realist analysis of law. However, although Hoebel referred to Maine, he could be extremely critical of the latter's view of primitive man and his institutions.

Having looked in particular at chapters two and four of *Ancient Law* Hoebel wrote that

> if ever Sir Henry Maine fixed an erroneous notion on modern legal historians, it was the idea that primitive law, once formulated, is stiff and ritualistic (and by implication weak in juristic method) . . . In most primitive trouble cases the situation is surprisingly fluid, but flowing within channels that are built by the pre-existing law and moving to a reasonably predictable settlement. The channels, however, shift and bend like the course of a meandering river across the bed of a flat flood plain, though flowing ever in a given direction. Men are at work on the law.[88]

In other words, Maine simply failed to recognise how it was that primitive law actually worked and this, of necessity, required modification to many of the ideas in *Ancient Law* where he spoke of stiff and ritualistic behaviour in the context of status. Indeed, in another place, Hoebel attacks one of Maine's dearest ideas in the form of the notion that kinship groupings were the dominant, in fact almost the exclusive, bond in primitive societies. In the words of Hoebel's contribution to the *International Encyclopedia of the Social Sciences* (where he related Maine's ideas to the work done by other scholars such as Diamond): 'Anthropologists have thoroughly established that Maine was wrong in his dogmatic assumption that the kin bond was the sole initial basis of political union and that its later subversion by the establishment of local contiquity on the basis of political action was an antipathetic reaction.'[89] Further criticism is reserved for

[88] Hoebel, *The Law of Primitive Man*, p. 283.
[89] *International Encyclopedia of the Social Sciences*, p. 530.

Maine's assumption as to the initial universality of patrilineal, patriarchal social organisation, characterised by absolute submergence of the individual within the whole. Quite simply, a great deal of what Maine wrote about primitive man has been shown by anthropologists to have been incorrect.

It is because of views such as these that Maine is not even mentioned in some works where one would otherwise expect references to his books. For example there seems to be no reference to him even in such interdisciplinary books as *The Cheyenne Way*.[90] Even more striking in this context is the work of William Twining. In his study, *Karl Llewellyn and the Realist Movement*, there is not a single mention of Maine and his works.[91] Of all the modern schools of jurisprudence, the American realists are perhaps the most closely associated with Maine's ideas and yet, clearly, it is possible to explain the growth of realist thought without a mention of Maine. In briefly considering Maine's influence on American legal realism one is driven to that place of last resort for those who try to explain the reception of a man's thought. With a few exceptions it seems that one has simply to say that there is an affinity between much of what Maine wrote and much of what subsequently was written. But, clearly, nobody was very enthusiastic about his books. If Maine did in fact have any significant influence on American realist legal thought it has yet to be discovered.

ENGLISH JURISPRUDENCE

Even before Maine died, there was an interest in whether or not he had done something to change the way English lawyers thought about their law. In 1880, Professor Holland wrote that:

> There have been of late years signs of a change in the mental habit of English lawyers. Distaste for comprehensive views, and indifference to foreign modes of thought, can no longer be said to be national characteristics. The change is due partly to the revival of the study of Roman law, partly to a growing

90 K. N. Llewellyn and E. A. Hoebel, *The Cheyenne Way: Conflict and Case Law in Primitive Jurisprudence* (Oklahoma, 1941). Note the fleeting references to Vinogradoff at p. 26 and (with a lack of enthusiasm) at p. 331. We may agree that the intensive analysis of 'trouble cases' in *The Cheyenne Way* was 'law's principle gift to anthropology (so far)' (see W. L. Twining, 'Law and Anthropology: a Case Study in Interdisciplinary Collaboration', *Law and Society Review*, vol. 7 (1973), p. 579), but it seems that Maine did not prompt the donor.

91 W. L. Twining, *Karl Llewellyn and the Realist Movement* (London, 1973). The same may be said of Wilfred E. Rumble's *American Legal Realism* (Cornell and New York, 1968).

familiarity with continental life and literature, partly to such investigations as those of Sir H. Maine into the origin of legal ideas . . .[92]

Unfortunately, this enthusiasm for Maine's liberalising influence upon the 'mental habits' of lawyers was soon qualified in Holland's analysis by the opinion that the chief source of new ideas had been the writings of Bentham and Austin. In other words, as far as Holland was concerned, Maine could never possibly be regarded as a jurist of the standing of the major utilitarian theorists; and the structure of the book which followed Holland's preface was in accordance with this view.[93] The references to Maine – and there are quite a number – consist for the most part of incidental remarks about isolated points of scholarship; the grand generalisations are given comparatively little attention.[94] Pollock found the right words for describing Holland's place in jurisprudence – and by inference the right words for Maine's declining significance – when he said:

Professor Holland of Oxford is to be congratulated on having done a piece of work that was much called for. Though several years have passed since the Universities and the Inns of Court proclaimed the importance of jurisprudence as a part of legal education, nobody has taken up Austin's unfinished work in a serious or satisfactory manner, or succeeded in making it very clear what jurisprudence really is.[95]

We have seen that Maine was remarkably honest about his own failure to develop a new jurisprudence; he never claimed that he had developed such a thing. But he can scarcely have derived much pleasure from reading Pollock's words when they were put into print a few years before the former's death. They made it look as if he had done nothing. In particular, they made it look as if he had not even attempted to take further the ideas of Austin; by implication, he had not responded to Austin in a serious or satisfactory manner. As if to

[92] T. E. Holland, *The Elements of Jurisprudence* (Oxford, 1880), p. vi.

[93] This is not to suggest that Holland was an uncritical admirer of the utilitarians. But he did wish to redress the balance of criticism somewhat in their favour. When speaking of the *Province of Jurisprudence Determined* he observed that 'the defects of the work were even more widely recognised than its merits'. *Ibid.*, p. vii. For useful remarks about the weaknesses of Holland's work and the peculiarities of other late Victorian jurists see Morison, *John Austin*, particularly at pp. 151–8.

[94] *Ibid.* The best exception to this rule is at p. 40 where Holland writes of 'that fertility of illustration and that cogency of argument for which his writings are so conspicuous'. But this respectfulness is hardly found elsewhere, and there are places where one would expect a reference to Maine but none is given (e.g. p. 281). N.b. the index to Holland's book is radically defective.

[95] F. Pollock, *Essays in Jurisprudence and Ethics* (London, 1882), p. 1.

confirm this, Pollock barely mentioned Maine in the rest of his analysis of what was happening to English jurisprudence. There are even indications that he indirectly criticised Maine's approach by attacking the less analytical, more philosophical, elements in Austin's work; in other words he had a certain disregard for broader forms of legal understanding. 'If there is one thing more than another', wrote Pollock, 'for which we ought fervently to thank Austin's labours, it is that at this time of day no rational being could or would occupy six lectures with the discussion of what positive law is not.'[96] It is less than wholly facetious to respond to this by saying that Maine, like Austin, devoted the greater part of his work to 'what positive law is not'; and, amongst other things, both Maine and Austin used this form of analysis to improve their understanding of what positive law is. Pollock seems to have forgotten how much importance Maine attributed to the refutation of theories based on natural law or natural rights and his vision of Maine's achievement was correspondingly narrow.

Pollock never relented in his attempt to restrict the relevance of Maine's work. He not only excluded Maine's theorising from legal history; he not only invited philosophers to, as it were, take over the domain of legal philosophy; he not only regarded Maine's ideas about utilitarian jurisprudence as irrelevant; a few years later he even went so far as to write a whole book on jurisprudence which began by considering the sort of issues which greatly interested Maine (such as the relevance of philology to the understanding of law) but which never attempted anything like a respectful or systematic analysis of Maine's ideas.[97] Pollock was always happy to correspond with Oliver Wendell Holmes and, in doing so, to praise Maine for his remarkable, almost intuitive, insights: but it is noticeable that his praise was concentrated upon Maine's analysis of very early legal ideas rather than upon his standing as a legal philosopher.[98] It was as if Pollock – for all his occasional words of praise – had done much to write Maine's ideas out of English legal thought even if, paradoxically, he frequently was involved in the publication of new editions of *Ancient Law*.

Salmond did nothing significant to break with this approach. After

[96] *Ibid.*, p. 2. Perhaps no other sentence better sums up the extent to which late Victorian jurisprudence became, as it were, inward-looking.

[97] F. Pollock, *A First Book of Jurisprudence* (London, 1896). There are no references to Maine in the index but see, for example, pp. 97 and 179.

[98] De Wolfe Howe, *The Pollock-Holmes Letters*, vol. 1, p. 121.

some pioneering works in the 1890s, he published his very influential work on *Jurisprudence* in 1902,[99] and his emphasis upon a rather limited understanding of what was required for 'practical purposes' did little to broaden the sort of interpretation which was characteristic of Holland and others. Admittedly, despite the emphasis upon 'practicality', Salmond did concern himself with some of the problems of ethical and political science; and his attempt to identify institutions in terms of their ends (civil justice, for example, has at its end the punishment of wrongs) was susceptible of enlarged 'non-legalistic' philosophical analysis. In other words there were elements within his works which could easily have been linked to the sort of jurisprudential ideas found in Maine's books. But, again, as far as Maine's legacy was concerned the result was very disappointing. For the most part even in respect of those places where his ideas were most clearly relevant, they were not analysed in any detail.[100]

Nevertheless, Salmond had some sort of respect for Maine. He roundly stated that 'Sir Henry Maine is a leading representative in England of the scientific treatment of legal conceptions in respect of their origin and historical development'.[101] But it was clear that Maine's thought was not closely linked to the important themes in Salmond's work and that the latter had some suspicion of the 'historical point of view'. For example, there was obvious emotion when Salmond insisted that

> There may have been a time in the far past, when a man was not distinguishable from an anthropoid ape, but that is no reason for now defining a man in such wise as to include an ape. To trace two different things to a common origin in the beginnings of their historical evolution is not to

[99] J. W. Salmond, *Jurisprudence* (London, 1902). The earlier work by John W. Salmond, *Essays in Jurisprudence and Legal History* (London, 1891), points to an acquaintance with Maine's ideas and, perhaps, a certain reluctance to acknowledge his influence. Maine's pleasure in claiming that the 'dry bones' of the Western past may be seen 'alive' in the East was surely echoed, in a hostile fashion, by Salmond when he wrote (without acknowledgment) in the Preface that 'The neglect of the study of legal history is doubtless due to the feeling that such a study is but the digging up of dry bones that cannot live.'

[100] Consider, for example, Salmond's attack on the imperative theory of law where he argues (at p. 56) that 'in *idea* law and justice are coincident. It is for the expression and realisation of justice that the law has been created, and like every other work of men's hands it must be defined by the reference to its end and purposes.' At a point such as this is would have been so easy to call in aid Maine's thought as, say, an antidote to the natural rights theorists from whom Salmond might wish to distinguish himself in the context of arguments about justice.

[101] Salmond, *Jurisprudence*, Appendix 4.

disprove the existence or the importance of an essential difference between them as they now stand. This is to confuse all boundary lines, to substitute the history of the past for the logic of the present, and to render all distinction and definition vain. The historical point of view is valuable as a supplement to the logical and analytical but not as a substitute for it. It must be borne in mind that in the beginning the whole earth was without form and void, and that science is concerned not with chaos but with cosmos.[102]

Maine's thought could hardly be expected to flourish in an atmosphere like this, and, given the approach of Salmond himself, it is perhaps no bad thing that the references to Maine fade somewhat from the later editions of his work.

Maine's reception into English jurisprudence reached its lowest ebb at the very place where, at one time, Maine himself had hoped to see so many imaginative reforms. In 1890, two years after Maine's death, Morgan Evans had been placed first in the examination in Jurisprudence and Roman law at the Council of Legal Education in London. Six years later he published a work for law students, *Theories and Criticisms of Sir Henry Maine*, and wrote revealingly of the fact that in Maine's chief books 'there is a great deal of writing that is absolutely useless to the student for examination purposes, and page after page has to be waded through in search of a theory'.[103] In response to this self-imposed problem Morgan set out to reproduce those elements of 'Maine' which were regarded as being relevant and, needless to say, the reader was informed about topics such as sovereignty and left in the dark in respect of, say, the comparative method. There is a certain sad humour to be gained from reading Morgan's proud claim to have located the ninety-three jurisprudential pages in the 2,000 pages of Maine's chief books. The jurist who had tried so hard to see the links between the law and the other forms of scholarship was now seen as a defective purist.

Of course, this makes it all the easier to understand the angry tone of Vinogradoff when he criticised English lawyers for their failure fully to grasp the nature of Maine's achievement. If Morgan's book is any guide to much of the fashionable thought of the day about legal education – and there is very good reason for believing that it was – Maine's ideas about the need to treat law as a form of intellectual adventure of the broadest kind had been almost forgotten. We have seen that in the context of, say, constitutional law, Dicey could do

[102] *Ibid.*, p. 54.

[103] M. Evans, *Theories and Criticisms of Sir Henry Maine* (London, 1896), Preface.

something to preserve Maine's ideas; and in respect of legal history Holdsworth might praise him, if in a somewhat convoluted manner. But in regard to jurisprudence Vinogradoff's enthusiasm for Maine seems to have existed in total isolation. In retrospect it can be seen that his attachment to public defences of his old friend and his works may have contributed to the failure of Vinogradoff to produce a younger generation of scholars which shared his own interest in historical jurisprudence. In this context, Maine and Vinogradoff had become linked and unacceptable.

When, after the First World War, there was something of a revival of interest in Maine the significance of this isolation was recognised by William Robson. In the course of a public lecture the latter considered many aspects of Maine's thought. He looked at his writing on the origin and development of law; he looked at his concern with the evolution of private law doctrines respecting property; he considered Maine's ideas about political institutions and political theories. In the course of doing this Robson did something to reveal the extent of Maine's erudition and the bias introduced into his analysis by his conservative (though not, as Robson saw it, reactionary) instincts: 'whatever the character of his political opinions or social views he was, as a teacher and writer, the most open-minded and progressive force of his day'.[104] But for the most part Robson was greatly saddened by what he saw as the English reception of Maine.

> Maine was, indeed, not only original, he was unique. That fact is to our grave discredit as lawyers. He blazed a great trail and opened up the heavens. He broke up the existing categories of thought and formed new and fruitful patterns of knowledge.
>
> But who, one may ask, has followed him? With the one great exception of Vinogradoff, we lawyers have remained cloistered in our narrow walls, treading complacently the old paths.[105]

At about the same time Sir Carleton Allen's response to Maine's ideas was both more moderate and more detailed. He identified Maine's historical jurisprudence with English legal history but he also wrote at length about custom and its jurisprudential significance, and this led him to quote Maine and to use the ideas of *Ancient Law*. He was often critical, as when he argued that Maine had 'certainly exaggerated the creative function of the codifier and law-giver'.[106] But, just as obvi-

[104] From the lecture 'Sir Henry Maine Today', p. 178.
[105] *Ibid*., pp. 178–9.
[106] Sir Carleton Allen, *Law in the Making* (Oxford, 1944), 7th ed., p. 227.

ously, he could combine this sort of criticism with a fascination for Maine's livelier ideas such as the argument in *Ancient Law* that the development of custom *follows* the giving of judgments rather than *vice versa*. Ultimately, however, Allen's respectful but cumulative qualifications to Maine's ideas point to a much greater regard on Allen's part for the ways of English lawyers and the capacity of the common law to cope with modern circumstances. Maine could never have written: 'On the whole, study of our age-old reports causes less surprise at the shortcomings of legal erudition than admiration for its range of resourcefulness both on the Bench and at the Bar.'[107] To put it bluntly, there is a certain complacency about Allen's view of the law and legal practice which Maine could never have accepted.

However, in places Allen could exhibit a sudden enthusiasm for the latter's thought. He refers to Maine's observations about the movement from status to contract as 'among the most famous in the whole of English juristic literature'.[108] At one time he even wrote of Maine's 'profound effect on the jurisprudence of this country'. Unfortunately, as with so many other critics of Maine, it is difficult to relate these favourable generalisations to further references to his specific achievements. For example, once again Allen did not seek to justify his remarks by exploring Maine's role as an historical jurist. As always, for Allen, it was doubtful 'whether any rigid line ever has been or ever can be drawn between historical jurisprudence and legal history';[109] and an emphasis upon this distinction did not lead Allen to praise Maine as either an historian or a jurist. Instead, once more, he followed Holdsworth's analysis and praised Maine in very general terms as the man who reminded English lawyers of their history.

However, one specific isolated observation of Allen's is of clear importance. He believed that Maine had introduced the word 'analytical' into English jurisprudence: it 'was apparently invented by Maine in his references to Austin in his lectures at the Inns of Court'.[110] For Allen, this was not a happy use of the word. Allen stressed that it had never been used by the so-called analytical jurists themselves (i.e. Bentham and Austin) and it was difficult to make sense out of this use of the word in a jurisprudential context. 'In itself, the term is misleading, for it suggests a type of jurisprudence which confines itself to pure

[107] *Ibid.*, p. 379.
[108] Allen, *Legal Duties*, p. 153.
[109] *Ibid.*, p. 13.
[110] *Ibid.*, p. 14.

analysis of legal rules. It is doubtful whether there has ever been, or even can be, a jurisprudence of this kind.'[111]

Whatever the merits of this conclusion, if Allen was correct and Maine did give the word analytical this use it certainly constitutes one of the curiosities of modern jurisprudence. Despite all his historical interests, a substantial part of Maine's significance for English legal thought must lie in the way he created a term for what is often regarded as a totally non-historical school of thought. It is as if Maine is not remembered for what he discovered but rather for the way he typified 'opposing' jurists.

Fortunately, some of Maine's more central concerns were soon to emerge again into English jurisprudence. In 1940, J. W. Jones' *Historical Introduction to the Theory of Law* provided a stimulating but all too brief account of Maine's criticism of the ideas associated with the common law. In this analysis, the hostility which Maine had so clearly felt towards the ways of English lawyers was seen as being typical of Maine's thought and not an irrelevant distraction. Jones' interpretation of Maine is both lively and convincing.[112] In a similar way, some historians of these years (such as J. W. Gough) were very much aware of Maine's writing and sought to use his ideas in books which looked far beyond the jurisprudence of the day.[113]

Since about the time of the Second World War, a number of textbooks have reflected and encouraged a gradual strengthening of interest in Maine. The various editions of Paton's *Textbook of Jurisprudence* referred students at numerous points to *Ancient Law*, and some of Maine's better known ideas (such as those concerning status and contract) were discussed in a balanced and helpful way.[114] In places, however, 'Paton' interprets Maine's thought as being colourful and relevant but seriously defective. For example, there is criticism grounded on modern evidence for Maine's statement that 'there is no

[111] *Ibid.*, p. 13.

[112] J. W. Jones, *Historical Introduction to the Theory of Law* (Connecticut, 1940). For example, at p. 58 Jones reminds us 'that sympathy with the historical approach did not necessarily imply hostility to codification as such, and still less an acquiescence in existing legal defects, was shown by Maine'.

[113] See J. W. Gough, *The Social Contract* (Oxford, 1936 and 1957). Of course, Maine would have regarded the use of his works in a study of 'the social contract' as potentially a backhanded compliment.

[114] See, for instance, G. W. Paton, *A Textbook of Jurisprudence* (Oxford, 1972), (Fourth Ed., ed. by G. W. Paton and D. P. Derham). Maine's name appears with some frequency in the recommended reading at the end of chapters. For balanced and judicious references to status and contract see fn. 4 at p. 46 and pp. 402–3.

system of recorded law, literally from China to Peru, which when it first emerges into notice, is not seen to be entangled with religious ritual and observance'.[115]

Elsewhere, a similar approach became more apparent as the years went by. Maine is the subject of forceful criticism but, at the same time, it is clear that he is regarded in an increasing variety of ways as being of relevance to modern debates. Lord Lloyd's *Introduction to Jurisprudence* places some stress not only on the debates about status and contract but also on the intrinsic interest of his methods and the need to see him in the context of the times in which he lived.[116] Dias makes the accurate observation that 'it is not easy to place Maine's contributions to the theory of law' and thereby reveals the difficulty in using his thought in a modern context; however, at the same time, he points out its clear value in coming to understand the 'anthropological approach' to law – in this respect at least Maine's thought may be given a constructive contemporary role.[117] Harris, too, has stressed the possible contemporary significance of Maine: we are reminded that Maine 'was no antiquarian, examining the past for its own sake'; and Maine was no romantic – 'legal forms and codes of thought of the past should be investigated, but not necessarily revered'. Harris even argues that Maine's ideas can be related to certain modern theories of justice. In terms of the amount of space allotted to Maine it seems that Harris provides the most extensive analysis to be found in any jurisprudential textbook to have been published since Maine's death in 1888.[118]

But to say these things is to reveal a marked divergence between the concerns of textbook writers and the content of specialist studies in modern jurisprudence. In regard to the latter, references to Maine are few and far between. His ideas are used by Unger, but it is noticeable that the observations which attract attention relate to specific problems (such as the capacity of custom and sacred law to compete with bureaucratic regulation in ancient empires)[119] rather than to any commitment to Maine's general theories. With the exception of

115 *Dissertations on Early Law and Custom*, p. 5.

116 Lord Lloyd and M. P. A. Freeman, *Introduction to Jurisprudence* (Fifth Ed., London, 1985). Of course this does not mean that Maine's historical judgments are accepted: see, for example, p. 872. There is an interesting discussion of status at p. 897, fn. 98.

117 Dias, *Jurisprudence*, pp. 338–93.

118 J. W. Harris, *Legal Philosophies* (London, 1980), particularly at pp. 221–5.

119 R. M. Unger, *Law in Modern Society: Toward a Criticism of Social Theory* (New York, 1976), chapter 2, fn. 6, p. 51.

Stein,[120] even those who have sought to explore the revival of interest in eighteenth-century Scottish thought and evolutionary theory have shown no interest in relating this school's ideas to those of Maine. Also, modern writers on Bentham and Austin have displayed little or no interest in Maine's reaction to the utilitarian jurists (although Morison's work is a welcome exception to this rule).[121]

However, the lack of interest in Maine is clearest and most significant in the writing of Hart and Dworkin. There was every reason for the historian of legal thought to have expected that Hart would refer to Maine's books. After all, in a well-known Preface to *The Concept of Law* Hart made the claim that he was, in part, attempting a sociology of law.[122] The extent to which he succeeded in doing so is controversial, but it was precisely the sort of objective which would have greatly interested Maine even if he would not have expressed himself in the same terms in 1861. Once again, law was being explained with reference to social observations, and there were ways in which such explanations varied sharply from that which might have been expected in the views of Austin or a professional lawyer. A jurist was looking beyond law in order to explain law, and he was doing so with more determination than could be found in the work of any English jurist since Maine himself. Yet, in the whole of *The Concept of Law* (both its text and its notes) there seems to be no mention of Maine.

By itself this is, of course, no criticism of Hart's analysis: obviously there is no argument for saying that a modern jurist must refer to all of his predecessors – after all, he may be trying, as it were, to escape from them. But, just as obviously, the failure to mention Maine suggests further discussion. In part his absence may have arisen out of the comparative lack of enthusiasm for his ideas in the books of someone such as Allen. As we have seen, Maine had never been forgotten but, of the lawyers, only Vinogradoff and Robson expressed a very favourable judgment on Maine's behalf.

In part, however, the explanation might be more interesting than this. For a modern jurist to take an interest in Maine a strong belief in the importance of historical explanation is almost a prerequisite: anthropologists apart, Maine has been typified so often as a legal historian or historical jurist that only an interest in these topics would be likely to lead a contemporary theorist to a reassessment of, say

120 Stein, *Legal Evolution*.

121 Morison, *John Austin*, particularly at pp. 148–52.

122 H. L. A. Hart, *The Concept of Law* (Oxford, 1961).

Ancient Law or *Village Communities*. It is fair to say that this interest in historical analysis is not apparent in *The Concept of Law*. For example, in his study of Hart and his work, Neil MacCormick observes that Hart's analysis of the transition out of a pre-legal social order is, in places, 'thematic and schematic rather than historical', and as such is open to the charge that it is based upon a form of constructive rationalism.[123] Elsewhere, MacCormick points out that Hart has nothing to say about Weber's attempt both to produce, on the one hand, a typology of different forms of legal domination and different modes of legal thought or rationality and, on the other hand, to relate these to historical developments and changes in society at large. Indeed, in this context it is arguable that Hart offers (in the words of another commentator) 'hostages to fortune' by appearing to talk of the necessary and sufficient conditions for the existence of a legal system without references to all (or at least more than a few) of the historical phenomena associated with the continuity of law.[124]

It is also clear in a forcefully argued section of his study that MacCormick is at pains both to refine and then to defend certain of Hart's ideas by means of historical analysis. This leads him to conclude that:

> the theory of law as a union of primary and secondary rules, unified by a rule of recognition, cannot be accepted exactly as Hart originally presented it to us. We have to allow for the possibility that there are other legal standards as well as rules strictly so-called. We have to consider the content and mutual interrelationship of rules of recognition, rules of adjudication, and rules of legislative change. We have to see at least in outline how such rules can develop in interaction with each other as an historical process.[125]

In order to justify this conclusion MacCormick engages in historical analysis which, at first sight, seems to be based upon the notion that certain historical facts, of themselves, require a modification of certain things said by Hart. But ultimately MacCormick is careful to avoid this sort of argument in favour of a more oblique but equally effective argument in which the historical discussion is used to provide an analytical model which 'shows that rules of recognition, change and adjudication are indeed necessarily interlocking and interacting, so that change in or redefinition of one must be mirrored by change in or redefinition of another'. Further, the great advantage of

[123] N. MacCormick. *H. L. A. Hart* (London, 1981), p. 109.
[124] *Ibid.*, p. 166, fn. 34, referring to Lloyd's *Introduction to Jurisprudence* pp. 196–7.
[125] MacCormick, *H. L. A. Hart*, p. 120.

using an historical content for this sort of model lies in the fact that arguments relating to it need not suffer from any form of vicious circularity.[126]

Surely, it is not too much to describe all of this as a useful type of historical jurisprudence. History is being used in the course of jurisprudential debate, and its role is not merely that of some supplement to non-historical reasoning. In this context history has the capacity to falsify a jurisprudential theory which could remain acceptable but for a reference to history.

It may be that a revival of interest in similar historical issues will also become apparent in the debates associated with the work of Ronald Dworkin. Any reader of Dworkin's essays who has an eye for historical analysis can rapidly become almost overwhelmed with the problems arising out of references to the legal past which are apparently integrated into jurisprudential arguments. A considerable number of these refer to the recent past – a period which has often produced more difficulty for historians than any other. For example, without exploring 'Salmond' or 'Paton' in detail Dworkin seeks to sustain 'a serious charge' and show that lawyers of the mid-twentieth century 'left the genuinely important issues of principle in the law untouched'.[127] Perhaps the present book has done something to show that works of jurisprudence may well serve as mirrors for the time in which they were written and that, as such, the works of jurists are likely to be addressed, more or less directly, to the major issues of the day. For the modern age to talk as it were, of its engagement with 'genuinely important principles' may do little more than point to an unexplored change in what were taken to be the 'genuinely important principles' of the past. It is particularly dangerous to hint at the possibility that past jurists were engaged in a trivial enterprise; and it is even more dangerous to elevate such an observation into a justification for alternative forms of jurisprudence. (The extreme condescension of the remarks which Victorian jurists often use in their discussions of natural law theorists now look very unimpressive when considered in the light of recent studies concerned with the strength and diversity of natural law theory.)

Also, anyone with a concern for legal history and its place in jurisprudence can only be somewhat startled by the following sort of statement in Dworkin's writing.

My immediate purpose, however, is to distinguish principles in the generic

[126] *Ibid*., p. 119.

[127] R. Dworkin, *Taking Rights Seriously* (London, 1977), p. 23.

sense from rules, and I shall start by collecting some examples from the former. The examples I offer are chosen haphazardly; almost any case in the law school casebook would provide examples that would serve as well. In 1889 a New York court . . . In 1960, a New Jersey court . . .[128]

To use cases at random like this presupposes quite exceptional bravery of historical judgment. In this context the cases are not, of course, being used to develop a conventional legal argument about whether, say, a particular decision is binding on a particular modern court considering particular facts: the cases are not being considered in regard to what modern lawyers have chosen to see as a proper, valid line of reasoning. Instead, the cases are used to illustrate historical truths, and their use in this jurisprudential context presupposes a very sophisticated capacity to relate today's ideas about principles and rules to previous ideas about such entities. To the present writer it seems that Dworkin regards the meaning of such terms as constant through time or else is confident of his capacity to recognise the modern meanings, as it were, amongst the old facts and the old law. If, even without rendering explicit the problems of anachronism, Dworkin has in fact succeeded in doing this, and has thereby integrated very sophisticated historical judgment into jurisprudential debate, he has done something most remarkable. But if his history is bad, and the above examples are typical, it would seem that significant parts of what he says are wrong.

[128] *Ibid.*, p. 2. This is not, of course, to deny a possible logical distinction between rules and principles; it is merely to question the application of the distinction to the world of particular men sitting in particular courts at particular times. At one point Dworkin makes the very interesting claim that: 'The story of principle supposes only that judges take the same general attitude towards the questions of fairness, and appeal to consequences, in ways and with emphases that differ from judge to judge and from period to period, just as these differ from person to person in ordinary life' (*Ibid.*, p. 309). This is surely a most daring assertion of relative continuity in legal history.

CONCLUSION

MAINE'S JURISPRUDENCE

Maine's books will always be read because they were so well written; they contain the finest prose in English jurisprudence, and the quality of their style gives them a capacity to create interest even when their content has been shown to be defective. They are proof that jurisprudence can be a form of literature.

However, any lawyer who reads Maine's works is confronted with the immediate problem of ascertaining precisely what he said about jurisprudence. In considering *Ancient Law* and its reception we saw that there is no such thing as a 'Mainian school' of legal thought with a commitment to specific and coordinated views on major issues; he produced no equivalent to the Benthamite or Austinian analysis of law. In fact, his ideas cannot be accommodated within the boundaries of any jurisprudential school. His thought is not fully explicable in terms of, say, German historical jurisprudence or legal anthropology. We have seen that his ideas have remained obstinately independent of the terms invented by others.

In the light of this, the common textbook description of Maine's jurisprudence may be defended as an appropriate starting-point for understanding his legal thought. The usual emphasis upon his rejection of unhistorical and utilitarian theories, and the positive attempt to explore 'the natural history of law' does much to reflect his enduring concerns. It also has an element of intellectual courage; writers of texts have had a formidable task in selecting aspects of Maine's thought about law because of the extent to which these aspects are closely linked to his other interests in politics, philology, the natural sciences, morality, social customs, literature, European culture, Irish social structures, the Comparative Method, the role of women, and so on. Anybody who tries to write about Maine's jurisprudence is confronted with the problem that the very act of isolating one element in his thought leads the mind away from the context in which he placed it, and thereby changes the impression of what he said about the element concerned. Maine often wrote more about the relationship between things than about the things themselves.

But it is just because of this that any complete description of his jurisprudence has to contain more than a mere description of evolutionary change in law. Nor is it sufficient to supplement the former by arguments about the failings of utilitarian legal theory and incidental observations on his commitment to reform. In this regard it is to be hoped that the claims made in the introduction of this book have been substantiated. For a complete account, the evolutionary information has to be integrated into a broader argument concerned with the responsibilities of lawyers and other citizens in matters relating to law reform and social change. It also is necessary to refer to the various uses which Maine made of history in the course of his analysis, however difficult it may be to achieve any precision in this respect. In other words, to repeat the view suggested in the introduction, we may say that Maine's lack of 'compendious' and 'logical' writing in jurisprudence makes a succinct description of his legal thought almost impossible, and requires that any brief account is expressed in a manner which is unrepresentative of his style. He was always more interested in revealing the inadequacies of preexisting categories than in developing his own. Categories conflicted with his desire to develop many themes based on numerous sources of information; and this was particularly apparent in his best work, *Ancient Law*.

However, even with all of these qualifications, we may repeat the final claim made in the introduction, and say that the content of Maine's jurisprudence may be briefly described by mentioning his evolutionary account of law and his related exploration of how good legal reforms could be achieved; these were very important and interrelated elements in his books. As for his approach, it consisted in presenting information about the past in such a way as to change how people thought about law. As we have seen, this was his most intense and almost emotional interest. An awareness of the facts of legal history ensured that lawyers and non-lawyers knew that there was nothing immutable in law, and at the same time it provided them with the best guide to the management of legal change. A critical interpretation of legal history was used to support both a description of evolutionary development and prescriptive views on social and legal improvement.

THE FAILINGS OF MAINE'S JURISPRUDENCE

In some respects the case against Maine's work is formidable. As we have seen throughout this study, one of his chief purposes was to ensure that law was not analysed in purely conceptual terms but was explained and criticised by reference to social and historical facts; one of the hallmarks of his jurisprudence was that frequently his arguments began with the observation of events rather than with statements of legal principle. Yet even his strongest supporters have to concede that Maine made errors in these references to the social realities of the past. Pollock, as always, tried to limit the damage inflicted by other commentators when he admitted that Maine was sometimes mistaken in matters of detail in *Ancient Law*, and that in his later writings he was either more careful 'or more ingenious in avoiding treacherous ground'.[1] But it was hardly a compliment to suggest that a man who was concerned with relating law to social circumstances made mistakes in his chief work and then, in subsequent years, sometimes employed mere ingenuity to avoid difficult subjects. Such defences only serve to support the direct attacks which have been mentioned in the course of this study and which so effectively questioned Maine's ideas about patriarchal society and other contentious topics. His standing as a jurist cannot rest upon the claim that he discovered the facts relating to the early history of law and its subsequent stages of development.

These shortcomings as an authority on legal history were well known by the end of the Victorian era, and since then his defenders have concentrated instead upon his analysis of topics such as the distinction between status and contract. The links between these terms and Tonnies' categories of *Gemeinschaft* and *Gesellschaft* have been explored at length, and numerous writers have used status and contract as instruments for explaining, respectively, the law of the Welfare State and *laissez-faire* economic policy. Unfortunately (as we saw in considering the reception of his thought) there is a severe problem in using these as proof of his insight as a jurist for the simple

[1] Sir F. Pollock, *For My Grandson* (London, 1933), p. 76. Pollock died in 1937 and these appear to be his final observations on Maine.

reason that he himself gave the terms a very limited scope. As we have seen, Geoffrey MacCormack has recently recognised that Maine's 'use of the word status is much more cautious than that of those who in subsequent years have sought to apply his theory'.[2] Whatever the explanation for the modern use of the terms, it is clearly difficult to praise Maine for a recent debate which does not reflect his own thought on status and contract. The great influence of his work in this context involved using his words for purposes which he never had in mind. If he is to be praised it has to be on the more general ground that he did much to engender a debate about the law and social progress, and this made it easier for later writers to transcend the limits of Maine's own use of the terms concerned. His writing contained elements which made it easier for others to develop their own distinctive thought in numerous directions. It is as if in this respect he achieved more as a publicist than as a jurist.

Neither the late Victorians nor modern writers have given attention to Maine's attempt to relate his jurisprudence to the problems of legal education and practice, and an analysis of this topic only produces another difficulty in advancing Maine's claims as a jurist. By the 1880s it was obvious that his thought on these subjects had become inflexible and unpersuasive and, as we saw above, most of his supporters chose to ignore it. At a time when Dicey and others were restoring the common law to a secure place in fashionable legal thought Maine remained a believer in codification. As Graveson has seen, 'his writings almost convey a feeling of remoteness from the Common Law'.[3] Nor, it seems, could he sympathise with the increasing emphasis on the study of cases and statutes in law degrees to the detriment of subjects such as legal history. Since he believed that it was the task of the jurist to write in a way which was comprehensible and appealing to both lawyers and laymen, it was clear that by reference to his own criteria he had not achieved what he had set out to do in this area. Of course, there is no question of in some way blaming Maine for failing

[2] MacCormack, 'Status: Problems of Definition and Use', pp. 361–76. But for an interesting example of modern confidence in the general applicability of his terms see R. Cotterrell, *The Sociology of Law: An Introduction* (London, 1984), pp. 125–6 and p. 138.

[3] R. H. Graveson, 'The Movement from Status to Contract', *Modern Law Review*, vol. 4 (1940), p. 261. In Graveson's *Status in the Common Law* (London, 1953) the statement is repeated with the suggestion that Maine may not have wished to create an impression of remoteness (see p. 34). Graveson added (at p. 50) that 'So far as the Common Law is concerned Maine's celebrated dictum was far from true in 1861 when he published *Ancient Law* . . .'

to prevent a change in legal thought; the relevant point is that he did not thoroughly develop and justify his highly critical views of the common law and legal education, and it follows that in an important respect he had not met his own requirements for a good jurist.

These shortcomings are important, but they are not as serious as the one observed by Fitzjames Stephen when he argued that: 'One of the very few unfavourable criticisms which Mr Maine's book suggests is that he appears to think, though he certainly never says, that when he has succeeded in giving the history of a system or theory, he had done with it.' Later, Stephen even added that 'he puts forward no philosophical theories at all, but leaves to others the question how far the truth of the theories which come before him is affected by the account which he gives of their origin'.[4] Stephen was surely correct in suggesting that a jurist cannot, as it were, merely contemplate the historical explanation of law; he also should evaluate it by reference to, say, the extent to which it can be stated in plain and systematic form, or justified in terms of some test such as utility, or, to use later ideas, explained in terms of rules. There is an important place for history in jurisprudence but jurisprudential analysis cannot be purely historical.

Defenders of Maine may respond to this by saying that he did pay regard to the merits of laws and legal systems. He did not merely observe their development. The present book has tried to show that all of his work was set within a critical framework concerned with the best methods for obtaining legal reforms; and even if this is not accepted, a normative approach is clear in his treatment of certain specific subjects. For example, his own limited use of the terms 'status' and 'contract' at least constituted part of an attempt both to describe and to estimate the merits of laws. Some enactments, such as those supporting slavery in the southern parts of the United States of America were to be criticised whilst others, such as those which supported freedom of contract, were to be praised. However, although these responses meet part of Stephen's argument, they do not respond to the full concern he felt for Maine's lack of interest in method. Stephen's concern was partly justified because Maine never carefully considered whether the fact that law was totally different in different places at different times made it wholly impossible to discuss the nature of law independently of place and time. To adopt the sort of

[4] *Edinburgh Review* (October, 1861), vol. 114, pp. 482 and 484. Also, see Feaver, *From Status to Contract*, p. 136.

language which he himself used, Maine failed to consider whether a scientific analysis of law presupposed an actual (or perhaps even hypothetical) entity called law which could be described in terms which were independent of the great variety of forms it took in different societies. In places Maine suggests that there is no such thing (or idea) as law apart from a social context. Such thoughts may be found in his writing on caste systems where he at least attempted to avoid the indiscriminate application of external, Western notions of law to the analysis of regulations. In doing this he seems to reject any idea of law which is equally applicable to all societies. In other places however he takes a different approach. His strange-sounding imposition of limits to the boundaries of legal change (through pointing out that there were limits to extremes of temperature on the earth's surface) seems to suggest a belief in some distinct thing called law which was susceptible of empirical testing by itself and could take only a finite number of forms in human arrangements.[5] Given these uncertainties it is easy to understand why Maine never gave an answer to the question: what is law? Nor did he put forward arguments that jurists were best advised to ignore the question. He avoided sustained discussion of the whole issue.

Nor was there any evidence of a systematic attempt to develop some method when Maine sought to use history to achieve advances in jurisprudence. It is impossible to suggest (as some critics still do) that he was original in using history for the purposes of jurisprudential argument. Maine himself knew that this had already been done in many different ways by Vico and Montesquieu.

Admittedly, there have been suggestions that his interest in the Comparative Method constituted an exception to his general failure to explore the theoretical relationship between law and history. For example, soon after *Ancient Law* was published, an article in the *Saturday Review* stressed very firmly that the comparative form of analysis was the most significant and striking element in Maine's interpretation of the past. It was of course a notable fact that Maine had looked to the past at all: 'In theology, in philology, in metaphysics, we are setting ourselves to apply the historical method. In every department of thought where a comprehension of the past is necessary for a comprehension of the present, we are endeavouring to rid ourselves of the errors which the intrusion of later ideas into the conceptions of earlier thought has so profusely introduced.' But

[5] *Popular Government*, pp. 157–8.

Maine's achievement lay in the fact that he went beyond mere enthusiasm for the past and recognised how information about India in particular could be given a new role in legal writing. It provided a form of comparative jurisprudence which gave a full explanation of legal change in places as far apart as England, Italy and the Indian subcontinent. Again, in the words of the *Saturday Review*:

> An inquiry into the history of jurisprudence has long been possible . . . The source that has given us comparative philology has also given us comparative jurisprudence. In India we find reproduced the elements of society which lie at the bottom of the Roman legal system. There we see crystallised in law, but moving and living, the corporate patriarchal family which has stamped on the legal system of early Rome almost all its main peculiarities. The comparison of the Roman and Hindu families has been to jurisprudence what the discovery of the common origin of Greek and Latin in Sanskrit has been to philology.[6]

To many Victorians this approach was capable of producing ever broader and more revealing analyses of social change. A recent study of nineteenth-century intellectual history has pointed out that to recapture the importance for contemporaries of the Comparative Method 'requires the cultivation of a mood of vicarious euphoria. In the 1860s and 1870s the map of learning seemed, to many members of the educated class in England, about to be redrawn in an exhilaratingly comprehensive and coherent way.'[7] For Maine it allowed the use of colourful generalisations which might otherwise have seemed absurd; legal ideas could be related in a lively way to the best scholarship of his day. The theory had the great advantage of being able to satisfy at once the sort of promptings which induced him to write for the *Saturday Review* as well as his ambition to reach the highest standards of legal writing. Perhaps, too, it satisfied a desire of a more aesthetic nature. Maine would have sympathised with a friend who believed that 'no poet can be fairly judged of by fragments, least of all, a poet like Mr Tennyson, whose mind conceives nothing isolated, nothing abrupt, but every part with reference to some other part, and in subservience to the idea of the whole'.[8] In every possible way, the Comparative Method was of assistance to Maine; like his ideas about progress – to which it was obviously related – it served as an instrument of synthesis which enabled him to bring together diverse

6 The *Saturday Review*, 16 February, 1861, p. 677.
7 Collini, Winch and Burrow, *That Noble Science of Politics*, p. 209.
8 A. H. Hallam, *Remains in Verse and Prose*, with a Memoir of H. F. Hallam by H. S. Maine and F. Luckington (London, 1862), p. 305.

topics and present them in an interesting manner which was at once colourful and scholarly.

His capacity to communicate enthusiasm for comparative studies helps to account for the popularity of *Ancient Law*, but it poses problems for anyone seeking to understand and assess his jurisprudential thought. As we have seen, the Comparative Method is *not* discussed at any length in *Ancient Law*. Maine never paused to consider all its implications; he never gave the method a thorough examination independently of the other issues which attracted his attention. There is no sustained elaboration of all its possible links with science, philology, legal practice, legal education, Roman law, Indian customs and the other topics to which he devoted substantial space. In *Ancient Law* elements such as these are integrated into debates about legal change which relate more than anything else to Maine's vision of the proper role for the educated, cultured layman or lawyer engaged in legal and social reform. By itself, his interest in the Comparative Method would never have induced Maine to write *Ancient Law*.

The lack of importance generally attached to the Comparative Method as an instrument for the explanation of law at this time is revealed by the fact that Fitzjames Stephen did not even mention it when, in 1861, he published his long review in which he compared *Ancient Law* with an edition of Austin's *Lectures on Jurisprudence*.[9] For Stephen and others with an interest specifically in jurisprudence what was of primary importance in Maine's analysis was his use of history as a means for correcting the errors of jurists who analysed law exclusively in terms of the present. The Comparative Method was merely one aspect of Maine's interest in the jurisprudential relevance of history, and it deserved no special attention.

It was only in later years that Maine himself made many references to the 'Method'. He used it to a substantial extent in his public lecture of 1875 when he explored 'The Effects of the Observation of India on Modern European Thought'.[10] But the closest Maine came to clarifying the issue was in the more restrained and less publicised *Village Communities in the East and West*, published in 1871. In cautious terms, he remarked that his work 'can only be said to belong to Comparative Jurisprudence, if the word "Comparative" be used as it

9 *Edinburgh Review* (October, 1861), p. 456. Stephen's references to the 'Historical Method' are irrelevant in this context.

10 Published in *Village Communities in the East and West* (London, 1876), p. 210.

is used in such expressions as "Comparative Philology" and "Comparative Mythology"'; and it seems that what he meant by this was that he would 'examine a number of parallel phenomena with the view of establishing, if possible, that some of them are related to one another in the order of historical succession'. Unfortunately he went on to add that 'I think I may venture to affirm that the Comparative Method, which has already been fruitful of such wonderful results, is not distinguishable in some of its applications from the Historical Method'.

He failed to provide an analysis of what he now associated with the latter approach. At most, he observed that when using these methods,

> we take a number of contemporary facts, ideas, and customs, and we infer the past form of those facts, ideas and customs not only from historical records of that past form, but from examples of it which have not yet died out in the world, and are still to be found in it . . . Sometimes the Past *is* the Present; much more often it is removed from it by varying distances, which, however, cannot be estimated or expressed chronologically. Direct observation comes thus to the aid of historical inquiry, and historical inquiry to the help of direct observation.

However, Maine soon surprised the reader with caution: he claimed he would

> be making a very idle pretension if [he] held out a prospect of obtaining, by the application of the Comparative Method to jurisprudence, any results which, in point of interest or trustworthiness, are to be placed on a level with those which, for example, have been accomplished in Comparative Philology. To give only one reason, the phenomena of human society, laws and legal ideas, opinions and usages, are vastly more affected by external circumstances than language. They are much more at the mercy of individual volition, and consequently much more subject to change effected deliberately from without.[11]

The modern social scientist would find this conclusion congenial. It seems to be influenced by a concern with finding a place in social analysis for the role of individual purposive behaviour. It looks almost as if Maine had anticipated later interest in the place of such behaviour in social explanation. However, his earlier reference to the problem of explaining the role of 'external circumstances' suggests that his concern here was, at last, to produce generalisations about the relevance of the Comparative Method for law: and at this point it is clear that he was adopting a notably modest set of claims for his use of the method

[11] *Ibid*., pp. 6–7 and 8. (The other lectures concerning India were added in certain later editions and it is convenient to use the third edition here.)

in a jurisprudential context. For example, in considering the sources of legal change he went on to observe that

> the sense of expediency or convenience is not, assuredly, as some great writers contended, the only source of modification in law and usage, but still it undoubtedly is a cause of change, and an effective and powerful cause. The conditions of the convenient and expedient are, however, practically infinite, and nobody can reduce them to rule.[12]

An historian seeking to account for Maine's thought can explain these hesitations by reference to the overriding nature of his other themes. Given his numerous sources it would have been very difficult for Maine systematically to relate all his ideas to any one method of analysis. In so far as he had a method it consisted in attempting to interpret a great many historical facts in a scientific manner, but his notion of science was such that he could avoid discussions about problems of methodology. He could simply use one historical 'fact' after another to attack one jurisprudential theory after another. In *Ancient Law* itself this was not of great consequence. It was wholly reasonable for him to suggest that English jurisprudence would benefit greatly from a consideration of the facts and ideas which he put forward. But for his future work his failure to develop and justify some particular method of inquiry was likely to lead to incoherence, in the sense that he would find it increasingly difficult to sustain the type of synthesis which he had achieved in *Ancient Law*. The relationship between his analysis of legal issues and his analysis of other phenomena was likely to become less clear and less convincing.

The importance of Maine's reluctance to develop a theory which could explain the precise relationship between historical facts and law may be appreciated by a comparison of his ideas with those of an earlier theorist whose chief work he had himself read. In the early 1850s Maine recommended his students to study the thought of the great Italian jurist, Gianbattista Vico (1668–1744). The latter had produced works specifically concerned with problems in jurisprudence but Maine probably had in mind Vico's general study: *The Principles of the New Science of Gianbattista Vico Concerning the Common Nature of the Nations*.[13]

In some respects there was much to attract Maine in Vico's work.

[12] *Ibid.*, p. 8.

[13] The commonly used modern translation is *The New Science of Gianbattista Vico*, a revised translation of the third edition (1744), by T. G. Bergin and M. H. Fisch (Cornell and New York, 1968) with a new introduction by M. H. Fisch. Also, see the recent compilation by L. Pompa, *Vico, Selected Writings* (Cambridge, 1982).

As Isaiah Berlin has pointed out, Vico's achievements were extraordinary: amongst many other things he was 'a bold innovator in the realms of natural law and jurisprudence' and he 'virtually invented an entirely new category of social sciences, which embraces social anthropology, the comparative and historical studies of philology, ethnology, jurisprudence, literature, and mythology, the history of civilisation and cognate studies'.[14] Vico could produce generalisations of great colour and force; just as Maine might say 'Except the blind forces of nature, nothing moves in this world which is not Greek in its origin',[15] so Vico, at the end of a long argument full of references to classical sources, would state something such as:

> From all the above we conclude that these principles of metaphysics, logic, and morals issued from the market place of Athens. From Solon's advice to the Athenians, 'Know thyself', came forth the popular commonwealth; from the popular commonwealths the laws; and from the laws emerged philosophy . . .[16]

For both men, grand generalisations about the past – often the classical past – are the finest way of reaching the truths of jurisprudence and these truths are, in turn, inseparable from so much more than purely legal analysis.

But there was much in Vico about which Maine must have been equivocal. It is easy to imagine him giving a mixed response to a passage such as:

> The most sublime labour of poetry is to give sense and passion to insensate things; and it is characteristic of children to take inanimate things in their hands and talk to them in play as if they were living persons. This philologico-philosophical axiom proves to us that in the world's childhood men were by nature sublime poets.[17]

Maine would have been delighted by the vivid phrases. He would have treated with total seriousness the reference to philology and the belief that in conjunction with philosophy it could reveal that at one time the nature of man was poetic. Indeed there are express references

[14] Sir Isaiah Berlin, 'The Philosophical Ideas of Gianbattista Vico', in *Art and Ideas in Eighteenth Century Italy* (Rome, 1960), pp. 156–7. He also remarks that Vico 'thought of himself primarily as a jurist . . .' (p. 217). Berlin has revised and expanded this study in *Vico and Herder: Two Studies in the History of Ideas* (London, 1976). The range of the modern response to Vico is striking: see, for example, G. Tagliacozzo and D. P. Verence (eds.), *Gianbattista Vico's Science of Humanity* (New York, 1976). The lack of English jurisprudential interest in Vico looks parochial.

[15] See *Village Communities*, p. 238.

[16] Vico, *The New Science*, s. 1043.

[17] *Ibid.*, ss. 186–7.

to this possibility scattered about in Maine's work, and, in places, he is particularly interested in exploring the relationship between poetry and early law.[18]

Yet, obviously, there would have been limits to Maine's enthusiasm. His commitment to the 'sober' pursuit of facts, and careful scientific reasoning in a fashion which would satisfy his fellow mid-Victorians, inevitably forced Maine away from anything hinting of mere charm. He himself would have been exasperated at the suggestion that philosophy could, by itself, be an adequate guide to an understanding of the past. In so far as Vico had moderated his philosophical speculations with philological observations he was to be commended; but it was obvious that even his philological judgment was not, in this particular example, properly historical in the sense that it was based upon an observation of modern behaviour rather than an analysis of the past use of words. To make matters worse, Maine would have known that Vico was using words such as 'poetry' in a technical manner and with meanings which were not always reflected in everyday speech. This would have offended against Maine's strong commitment to destroying 'professional' interpretations of words known only to a few 'practitioners'. It was this sort of consideration which must have held Maine back from endorsing Vico's sweeping views such as, say, that 'ancient jurisprudence is a severe kind of poetry'.[19]

It would be possible to compile long lists of ways in which Maine might have tried to solve his problems with 'method' by using Vico's ideas. Maine must have been impressed by someone who explored the classical world and (to quote Berlin again) was convinced that 'the validity of all true knowledge, even that of mathematics or logic, rests on its genetic or historical character'.[20] But Maine believed for most of his life that historical judgments were compatible with what he (Maine) took to be conventional science and it seems, to say it again, that Maine was not troubled by the major philosophical and historiographical issues which Vico was prepared to confront. Ultimately, a comparison with Vico shows very clearly just how uninterested Maine was in developing a method for jurisprudential analysis. He had no method.

But at least it is reasonable to refine historical claims made on his

[18] For example, in his analysis of the brehon laws of Ireland: see *Early History of Institutions*, pp. 32–3.

[19] Vico, *The New Science*, s. 1037: considered by Berlin in his early study (p. 188) and his later analysis (p. 50) referred to in fn. 14.

[20] See Berlin's early study (p. 162) and his later study (p. 10) referred to in fn. 14.

behalf, and point out that Maine was successful in his efforts to use history as an instrument for an attack on the utilitarian jurisprudence of Bentham and Austin. It is undeniable that he was successful in using information about the past as a method of invalidating utilitarian generalisations about the nature of law. He was correct when he showed that it was wrong to suggest that law could always be explained in terms such as 'command' and 'sovereign' because such terms were only likely to be relevant in considering modern examples of 'progressive' law. If there was something called 'law', which was in some sense independent of the societies in which it was found, then the utilitarians had not discovered it.

However, typically enough, Maine never provided a thorough exploration of the relationship between his thought and that of the utilitarian jurists. Instead he used them whenever it suited him to do so (as when he quoted Bentham in support of his arguments for not extending the common law to India) or else he manipulated their ideas to serve the critical purposes of his lectures. Manipulation is not too strong a word in this context. We have seen (in chapter 5, pp. 119–25) that in his study, *The Early History of Institutions*,[21] Maine at last gave Austin attention in some detail and in doing so he represented the latter's *Lectures on Jurisprudence* to be other than what they are. Also, on the few occasions when Maine attempted to reconcile his ideas with the thoughts of the utilitarians his reasoning came near to being circular. The utilitarians were irrelevant to ancient societies because utilitarianism was modern: the utilitarians were relevant to modern societies because their ideas were discussed in modern societies. He only rescued his arguments from this condition by saying that the chief value of utilitarian jurisprudence lay in its capacity to make explicit and clear the qualities of modern law which would otherwise remain concealed in the confused circumstances of rapidly changing, progressive societies.

For Maine's jurisprudence the consequences of all this were in some respects destructive. The fact that he had no general theory of how history related to jurisprudence made it potentially easy for his historical observations to become divorced from his thought about law. At least in *Ancient Law* his attempt constantly to relate history to law in the course of arguments designed to expose the weaknesses of those who ignored the past (such as the utilitarians and natural law theorists) ensured that this lack of a full analysis of the links between

[21] *The Early History of Institutions*, chapters 12 and 13.

law and history was barely apparent. But in his later works the problem became much more serious. The relevance of what he said about non-legal subjects to his ideas about law became progressively more obscure in *Village Communities, The Early History of Institutions, Dissertations on Law and Custom,* and *Popular Government*. There was much in these books which was simply legal history, or a form of anthropology, or political commentary. If Maine had developed a method of theorising about law this could hardly have happened; he would have had constantly to justify what he was doing in jurisprudential terms or, alternatively, he would have had to say expressly that he was no longer writing jurisprudence. Admittedly, on a few occasions he did exactly this (as when, for example, he was writing about very early custom) but these references are not always easy to understand and they do not provide any consistent guide to what he was doing. As a result Maine's lack of concern with method produced inconsistencies in his work which were observed by the Victorians and are just as apparent to modern lawyers who might be interested in the problems of interdisciplinary study.

THE ACHIEVEMENTS OF MAINE'S JURISPRUDENCE

However, there are virtues in inconsistency, and it is possible to say more of Maine than that he introduced some useful qualifications to utilitarian ideas. A lack of concern with rigorous juristic argument left him free to consider any historical subject, and to relate it in any way he chose to jurisprudential issues. If he had been greatly concerned with coherence of approach in the way that Stephen wished him to be his books would probably have been much less attractive to read, and, more important, his readers would not have been given such a variety of arguments and illustrations in which legal and non-legal topics were juxtaposed with a view to clarifying the nature of both in specific areas rather than by reference to a general theory.

Also, inconsistency in method does not necessarily produce inconsistency in theme. Maine used his numerous ways of writing about law to present certain observations which constituted a valuable contribution to jurisprudential debate. Even if he made factual mistakes he used many of his most vivid illustrations to show that law had to be explained by reference to its social context if it was to be fully understood. Much of what he said appears odd, even naive, to modern eyes. Many of his later thoughts in particular are indefensible. But it is suggested that Maine had achieved something of permanent value for jurisprudence. Positively, he had presented a forceful analysis of law in social terms and had also argued that this required a critical study of practitioners' legal thought and the obligations of jurists. Negatively, he had revealed the inadequacies of practitioners who pursued merely professional interests and jurists who described law without reference to social facts. He had developed a jurisprudence which was independent of both the professional tradition associated with Blackstone and the analytical approach of the utilitarians. In the context of English legal thought, his achievement was unique.

What, then, is the precise value of Maine's ideas for modern jurisprudence?

Firstly, he is still useful as a source of correction to arguments that any particular concepts are useful in the analysis of all legal arrangements in all places at all times. The modern commentators on the work of Bentham and Austin have revealed again and again that their ideas were often misinterpreted by those (including Maine) who said that they ignored the social context of law; but even if these views are correct they do nothing to diminish the value of Maine's criticism of *any* jurisprudential theories which at least implicitly claimed to be of universal application but which could only be related to the circumstances of a few societies. For Maine, the jurist should begin by looking to social arrangements and the methods of preserving harmony; only then should he consider possible explanations for the existence and nature of law. The cumulative impression of numerous social observations relating to law is such as to make it difficult for the reader of Maine's works to believe that any other starting point could be appropriate. Social observation should precede legal reasoning. His work challenges anybody who would take a different approach to provide reasons for doing so.

Secondly, Maine's work provides a very forceful reminder that jurisprudence involves much more than legal philosophy with or without reference to social facts. He may have failed to provide wholly convincing ideas about legal education in the sense that he never explored all his ideas on the subject systematically, or, in the end, persuasively, but his work in this area is proof that it is possible to view jurisprudence as 'the theoretical aspect of law-as-a-discipline (i.e. academic law)'.[22] Again and again, his thought reminds us that, in the

[22] W. L. Twining, 'Academic Law and Legal Philosophy: The Significance of Herbert Hart', *Law Quarterly Review*, vol. 95 (1979), p. 574.

words of a modern writer, 'The nature and scope of academic law is itself a central question of jurisprudence and a controversial one at that.'[23] For him there was nothing self-evident about the best form of legal education. It was something which had to be discovered and constantly justified in jurisprudential terms. It was an integral part of his analysis of how laws were created and how they functioned in society.

Thirdly, Maine also reminds us that jurisprudence may fruitfully be applied to problems in professional legal thought. One might say that he was concerned with the theoretical aspect of law as a practice by experts. He persistently related his thought about law to the practical work of lawyers. His work contains many suggestions that a jurisprudence which failed to explore the professional life and beliefs of lawyers also failed to respond to information which was essential to any understanding of how laws changed. In this respect Maine's thought is in accordance with modern interest in the significance of the attitude of legal 'officials' towards the laws which they administer and, even more directly, with the attempts to relate debates about 'professionalisation' to jurisprudential issues. For example, a concern with the image of law and lawyers even if it is integrated into, say, a general analysis of legal systems, makes a similar assumption about the need to explain law by reference to professional facts. Admittedly these professional studies could hardly be said to be (as yet!) in the mainstream of English jurisprudence, but like Maine's thought about legal education the belief in the importance of professional ideas for jurisprudence provides a valuable contrast to modern assumptions. It provides an alternative to the modern capacity 'either to treat legal philosophy as being co-extensive with jurisprudence or at least to suggest by implication that legal philosophy is the only part of jurisprudence which is both intellectually respectable or educationally worthwhile'.[24]

Fourthly, Maine's persistent use of history in the course of developing his ideas about the responsibilities of those involved in legal change is relevant to modern jurisprudence in a number of ways. For the late twentieth-century reader there is a provocative aspect to his lack of interest in method. His insistent demand that jurists ask historical questions requires a full theoretical justification which, very clearly, he does not provide. But later English jurists have done no

[23] *Ibid.* [24] *Ibid.*

better in this respect. Twentieth-century jurisprudence has produced no analysis of history which is in any way comparable to, say, Collingwood's philosophical attempt to develop a science of historical analysis in which there is an explanation of the precise relevance of the past to certain aspects of modern thought.[25] Maine's work, more than that of any other English jurist, at least requires that this task is undertaken by some successor. It is as if the presence of his books makes the issue ultimately inescapable.

A concern with the topic is so alien to modern English jurisprudence that it is helpful to illustrate its significance by a comparison with theology. Law, like theology, requires an understanding of both norms and facts. Legal norms, like theological norms, may be used to decide upon the legal or theological relevance of past facts. A theologian may, say, avoid a factual analysis in the course of a certain argument by saying that a certain possible event (for example, the Resurrection) can only be understood in terms of faith rather than by reference to any form of historical proof. Equally a lawyer may say that the fact that certain courts decided an issue in the past which is now apparently of relevance to a modern legal argument is not, in fact, relevant because the decisions have been rendered irrelevant by developments in the modern doctrine of precedent. Both lawyers and theologians may argue in ways which are entirely legitimate that parts of the past are relevant to modern argument and parts are not.[26]

But to state this is to raise precisely the sort of issue which, in an unsystematic way, was of interest to Maine. It is reasonable to respond to such a view by saying that the lawyer is not entirely free to rearrange his past in accordance with modern notions of validity because he very rarely thinks he is. It seems instead that he attributes importance to being, as it were, in communication with the past, and in having a capacity to apply information from the past (in the form of precedents, statutes and professional customs) to modern law. The argument can be taken further because of modern observations which are very like those made by Maine over a century ago. For example, it

[25] See, for example, R. G. Collingwood, *The Idea of History* (Oxford, 1946). The issues are touched upon in D. Beyleveld and R. Brownswood, *Law as a Moral Judgment* (London, 1986), pp. 95 (note), 271 (note).

[26] Admittedly, some lawyers are increasingly interested in the distinction. For a Scottish example see H. MacQueen, *Legal Studies* (March 1986), vol. 6, no. 1, p. 111; in this book review the reviewer distinguishes between the lawyer interested in a work only as a 'formal source' and the historian who wishes to know how it came to be written.

may be that legal historians will reveal that modern lawyers are not in communication with their past but rather are using an entirely modern non-historical reconstruction of their past. Lawyers are ill equipped to respond to this possible problem. Law students and practitioners and judges use libraries which are full of primary sources of legal history, in the form of law reports and statutes, but very few of them are taught the techniques of historical interpretation. Instead they develop the techniques of relating the words in these sources to what are acceptable modern legal arguments. Modern lawyers would surely be faced with a problem if legal historians were to discover, say, that the law reports between the mid-eighteenth century and the mid-nineteenth century were explicable only in terms of procedures (involving, for instance, the relationship between judge and jury) which are so different from today's procedures that isolated sentences or paragraphs or whole judgments from these reports are invariably misleading to the modern lawyer with no training in the use of the records of this era. Are the reports to be ignored? Or is the historical truth to be ignored so that words which happen to have been written in the past may play an anachronistic role in totally modern arguments?

How much of the past may be taken out of modern legal reasoning without the latter being totally transformed? Maine's thought serves as a continuous reminder that a conception of the past may become an essential component in a system of legal thought and that this conception may be at variance with the facts of legal history. His thought therefore suggests that a detailed analysis of professional and academic conceptions of the past might require us to change our understanding of modern law.

Also, today there appears to be an increasing interest in using accounts of the legal past as instruments of synthesis which enable the insights of separate disciplines to be combined. It is a matter of common knowledge that there have been numerous sociological studies of legal topics during the last twenty years. Equally, as we have seen, there has been a rapid increase in the number of studies concerned with legal history. Most of these appeared later than the first phase of sociological works, but it is now common to find studies of modern legal history, particularly in certain areas such as labour relations and criminal law, and it is also apparent that the frontiers of the sociological and historical areas of work show an increasing propensity to overlap. The early achievements of Abel-Smith and

Stevens in *Lawyers and the Courts: a Sociological Study of the English Legal System, 1750–1965*[27] have been followed by numerous later studies such as Larson's *The Rise of Professionalism: a Sociological Analysis*.[28]

In a slightly more oblique way it is possible to see similar issues being addressed in the work of E. P. Thompson. For example, his book, *Whigs and Hunters: the Origin of the Black Act*,[29] is not a directly sociological work but, like many of the sociological inquiries, it raises issues concerned with the nature of law and the extent to which certain concepts and phenomena may be said to relate exclusively to certain social conditions or, alternatively, to transcend time and to be perhaps a necessary part of Western law. For instance, it raises as an issue the extent to which one can talk of the same notion of the rule of law being present in both the eighteenth and twentieth centuries.[30] In a way which is strikingly similar to Maine's, it is clear that Thompson is often concerned with the role which law plays as a means of producing or destroying social harmony. Throughout, legal history is seen as being something which may be related, sometimes very closely, to the philosophical, social and political views of both the past and the present, and there is acute concern for the place of law in the creation or destruction of social continuity and the preservation of human rights.

It was as if, in Maine's view, it was better for the jurist to travel than to arrive. In *Ancient Law* in particular his thought has an open-ended quality; he attacks well-established assumptions and suggests new lines of inquiry without seeking to impose a complete explanation upon all the facts of law and legal history. The general criticisms of Victorian contemporaries, such as Maitland, Pollock and Stephen, and the modern criticisms with their detailed qualifications to his ideas about status and contract, have all revealed serious shortcomings in aspects of Maine's thought: they have revealed a lack of rigour in his analysis. But these criticisms leave intact the merits of *Ancient Law* as an experimental work which seeks constantly to test legal ideas in the light of historical information. When the work is reread today it

[27] B. Abel-Smith and R. B. Stevens, *Lawyers and the Courts: A Sociological Study of the English Legal System* (London, 1967).

[28] M. S. Larson, *The Rise of Professionalism: A Sociological Analysis* (California, 1977).

[29] E. P. Thompson, *Whigs and Hunters: The Origin of the Black Act* (Harmondsworth, 1977).

[30] *Ibid.*, pp. 258–69.

instantly provokes new questions about the relationship between modern assumptions and the past realities of law. Is Hart's analysis of law compatible with what we know of legal history? What are the implicit historical assumptions in Dworkin's writing, and can they be justified? Is the modern interest in Marxist explanations of law founded upon an unacknowledged revival of belief in a form of evolutionary legal history which has yet to be articulated and adequately defended? Can a lawyer of the late twentieth century explain the place of the past in legal reasoning with the sophistication which Collingwood achieved in respect of non-legal thought? The role of history in modern jurisprudence is almost totally unexplored; and the significance of this is made apparent when the reader of today turns back to Maine's works and finds that they can be used to destroy orthodox views and replace them with an awareness of great diversity in the history of law.

INDEX

CAMBRIDGE STUDIES IN ENGLISH LEGAL HISTORY

The Law of Treason in England in the Later Middle Ages
J. G. BELLAMY

The Equity Side of the Exchequer
W. H. BRYSON

The High Court Delegates
G. I. O. DUNCAN

Marriage Litigation in Medieval England
R. H. HELMHOLZ

The Ancient State, Authoritie, and Proceedings of the Court of Requests by Sir Julius Caesar
EDITED BY L. M. HILL

Law and Politics in Jacobean England: The Tracts of Lord Chancellor Ellesmere
LOUIS A. KNAFLA

The Legal Framework of English Feudalism
S. F. C. MILSON

The Judicial Committee of the Privy Council 1833–1876
P. A. HOWELL

The Common Lawyers of Pre-Reformation England Thomas Kebell: A Case Study
E. W. IVES

Marriage Settlements, 1601–1740: The Adoption of the Strict Settlement
LLOYD BONFIELD

William Sheppard, Cromwell's Law Reformer
NANCY L. MATTHEWS

The English Judiciary in the Age of Glanvill and Bracton, c.1176–1239
RALPH V. TURNER

Pettyfoggers and Vipers of the Commonwealth, The 'Lower Branch' of the Legal Profession in Early Modern England
C. W. BROOKS

Sir William Scott, Lord Stowell
HENRY J. BOURGUIGNON

For EU product safety concerns, contact us at Calle de José Abascal, 56–1°,
28003 Madrid, Spain or eugpsr@cambridge.org.

www.ingramcontent.com/pod-product-compliance
Ingram Content Group UK Ltd.
Pitfield, Milton Keynes, MK11 3LW, UK
UKHW010336140625
459647UK00010B/640

* 9 7 8 0 5 2 1 5 2 4 9 6 4 *